TREASURES
OF THE DEEP

TREASURES
OF THE DEEP

THE EXTRAORDINARY LIFE AND TIMES OF
CAPTAIN MIKE HATCHER

HUGH EDWARDS

HarperCollins*Publishers*

HarperCollins*Publishers*

First published in Australia in 2000
Reprinted in 2000
by HarperCollins*Publishers* Pty Limited
ABN 36 009 913 517
A member of HarperCollins*Publishers* (Australia) Pty Limited Group
http://www.harpercollins.com.au

HarperCollins*Publishers*
25 Ryde Road, Pymble, Sydney, NSW 2073, Australia
31 View Road, Glenfield, Auckland 10, New Zealand
77–85 Fulham Palace Road, London W6 8JB, United Kingdom
Hazelton Lanes, 55 Avenue Road, Suite 2900, Toronto, Ontario M5R 3L2
and 1995 Markham Road, Scarborough, Ontario M1B 5M8, Canada
10 East 53rd Street, New York NY 10022, USA

National Library of Australia Cataloguing-in-Publication data:

Edwards, Hugh 1933– .
   Treasures of the deep: the extraordinary life and times of
   Captain Mike Hatcher.
   ISBN 0 7322 5885 5.
   1. Hatcher, Michael. 2. Shipwrecks. 3. Underwater
   exploration – Biography. 4. Treasure-trove. I. Title.

910.452

Cover photograph of *Song Saigon*: Hugh Edwards
Printed in Australia by Griffin Press on 79gsm Bulky Paperback

7 6 5 4 3 2   00 01 02 03 04

CONTENTS

CHAPTER ONE
Ghost Ships of the Gaspar Strait   1

CHAPTER TWO
A Ship to Australia   14

CHAPTER THREE
Getting Wet   31

CHAPTER FOUR
Land Sharks Bite Harder   47

CHAPTER FIVE
Diving the Dead U-boats   70

CHAPTER SIX
Death Visits the Dive Team   86

CHAPTER SEVEN
The Rat Boat and the Refugees   97

CHAPTER EIGHT
A Cargo of Porcelain   117

CHAPTER NINE
The *Geldermalsen* Gold   130

CHAPTER TEN
A Twenty Million Dollar Sale   142

CHAPTER ELEVEN
Expect the Unexpected   161

CHAPTER TWELVE
The Thai Incident   179

CHAPTER THIRTEEN
The Killing Fields of Cambodia   207

CHAPTER FOURTEEN
The Secrets of Condor Reef   228

CHAPTER FIFTEEN
The Great Junk   257

APPENDIX   279

'The credit belongs to the man who is actually in the arena, whose face is marred by dust and sweat and blood, who knows the great enthusiasms, the great devotions and spends himself in a worthy cause. And, who at best, if he wins, knows the thrill of high achievement, and if he fails at least fails daring greatly, so that his place shall never be with those cold and timid souls in the outer who know neither victory nor defeat.'

John F Kennedy, 1917–63

CHAPTER ONE

Ghost Ships of the Gaspar Strait

The sun came up red and angry over the South China Sea on the morning of June 5, 1999, reflecting pinkly off the white upper works of *Restless M* as she rolled her blue hull at anchor on the light swell behind the reef. It would be a fateful day as it turned out. But it began like any other.

The cook was already bustling about, busy with his aluminium pots in the galley. The meal, as always in south-east Asian waters, was rice and fish.

To the south, the green jungle peak of Gaspar Island rose through the morning mist to split the Gaspar Strait. It was too far distant to see the single house beneath the coconut palms on the beach. No other people lived up on the hill or on the shore. By Malay tradition it was a troubled strand, a place of bad spirits. *Han tu*.

In a past century the beach had been thick with shipwreck bodies, washed up there like layers of intertwined driftwood dark along the tidemark. That was the reason for the island's reputation as an evil place. The crew of *Restless M*, though they did not realise it at breakfast that morning, was about to become a part of that old and terrible story. A story in which more people were drowned on a black monsoon day in 1822 than were lost in the infinitely more famous *Titanic* disaster of 1912.

1

Soon *Restless M* was underway, a bubbling wake behind her, the Avon 'rubber duck' diving dinghy jerking at its tow line astern. By the time she reached her area of operations the south-east trade wind was flicking spiteful white-caps off the wave tops. It was the time of the south-east monsoon, the summer pattern of prevailing winds which affect every activity in the South China Sea.

Restless M's crew, some still munching bits of breakfast, settled into their long-familiar work patterns. Their eyes were watching the gauges and screens, looking for a blip on the magnetometer (the torpedo-shaped device towed astern and used to indicate the presence of iron), a hump on the level bottom shown on the echo-sounder, an unusual pattern revealed by the side-scan sonar. Always hoping for a strike. Though by now their hopes and expectations, eroded by months of false alarms and failures, were truly at their lowest ebb.

However the job still had to be done. The 80-footer covered ground in the slow methodical progression which the crew called 'lawnmowing'. Named, of course, from its supposed similarity to that other shore-going occupation. It was just about electronically as unexciting, they said. Up and down, to and fro, in measured lanes, eliminating hundreds of kilometres of 'dead' sea bottom from the search. There was one important difference however. So far as is known no-one has ever found treasure with a lawnmower.

Aboard *Restless M* there was always the possibility that the next search lane steered, the next nautical mile, might be the one. That the next hour, next day, might see 'The Big One'. That hope never entirely died, though by now the pulse was weak.

The steersmen in the local Indonesian and Malaysian fishing boats – low-hulled craft with sharply raked bows – had ceased wondering what she was up to. *Restless M* had become as much a part of the scenery as the soaring frigate birds and the occasional line squalls hissing over the waves north of the Gaspar Strait.

Her position was a little over two degrees of south latitude below the imaginary 'line' of the equator – a position north of Java, east of Sumatra and south of Singapore. Borneo, now named Kalimantan and the home of the orang-outang ape, the hairy 'red man of the trees', lay huge and brooding beneath its dense jungle foliage under the clouds on the eastern sea rim.

It was a very historic piece of ocean.

For centuries square-ended Chinese junks, bluff-bowed Dutch and British East Indiamen, lateen-rigged Arabian dhows, Malay praus with bamboo sails and tall Makassar schooners plied the Trade Winds routes. Sailing craft of all shapes and sizes and nations furrowing the Gelasar or Gaspar Strait with their keels. The designs and sail plans differed radically, but they had one other thing in common besides the ocean. All of them depended on wind to make their voyages. In this part of the world, which Europeans called the 'Far East' from their own geographical position, the seasons were so regular and possible to predict that they became known as the Trade Winds. The name taken from the cargoes moved between countries and continents by wind power.

In the monsoon of the northern winter the north-east trades blew the junks and dhows and laden East Indiamen down out of China and the Malacca Straits to Batavia (modern-day Jakarta, Indonesia). Some went directly to the Sunda Strait which was the gateway to the rolling blue vastness of the Indian Ocean. The opposite summer wind, the south-east trades, in their season, blew the other way, bringing the incoming ships from Europe up through Sunda and on to Malacca and Canton and Macao.

All the ships with their precious cargoes of silver, spices, tea, porcelain, silks, and sometimes gold, passed through the waters where *Restless M,* a blue-hulled bloodhound, was now searching. She was probing and sniffing the seabed with her electronic devices, seeking among the coral and sand flats for the scent of something manmade ... an undelivered cargo.

It was a likely area for a shipwreck. All of those ships of past years had to sail between the islands of Bangkha and Beliton passing either side of Gaspar Island. They had to go through a perilous pass of wide-flung coral reefs to complete their passage through the straits. At the lower end of the South China Sea they had to circumvent the series of reefs which included the Belvidere and Warren Hastings Shoals. These were hard-to-sight hazards reaching up hungrily for passing keels.

Restless M's measured tracking on this particular day was in the region of the notorious Belvidere Rock – stained granite boulders rounded and eroded like human skulls, symbolic of the many shipwrecks in the area. There were no lighthouses, buoys or warning signs to mark the danger in those days, and there are still none today. On dark nights or when the north-east monsoon whips the tropic sea into a wilderness of white-running wave tops, the reefs become invisible below the surface. The corals rise sharply in submarine slopes and cliff faces from the seabed. Too steep for the lead lines of the sailing ships to give adequate warning. For many of them the lookout's desperate cry 'Surf ahead!' came too late.

Ships of all sizes and all nations have struck and perished here, the choking cries of their drowning people extinguished in the night. They became the ghost fleet of the Gaspar Strait, taking the secrets of their violent ends and their lost cargoes to the bottom with them. Sunk 16 fathoms (96 feet or 29 metres) down they lay with their cannon, the bones of their lost people, and their memories. Grown over by gardens of coral and bright orange gorgonia fans, watched over by sharks and fish until one day, perhaps, the shadow of *Restless M* would pass overhead.

❀

Restless M's task as a salvage vessel was searching for lost cargoes. The big silver Dutch ducatons, Rix dollars, and pieces of eight of the 17th and 18th centuries would delight any discoverer.

And the thought of gold always increased the heart rate. But the exquisite porcelains created by Chinese potters in past centuries were as valuable proportionately as silver or gold. Provided the sea had been kind to them. Over the years *Restless M* had sniffed out millions of dollars worth. But on June 5, 1999, by the Belvidere Rock, it had been a long time between drinks.

True, Captain Mike Hatcher, the most celebrated salvor of south-east Asian seas, had made a major strike with *Restless M* in 1983. With his partner Max de Rham he had discovered the 1752 Dutch East Indiaman *Geldermalsen* on the Admiral Stellingwerf Reef. The Zeeland vessel had carried the kind of cargo most would-be salvors only dreamt about. The 'G', as they called her affectionately, made Hatcher's reputation. An auction of the gold and porcelain from her salvaged cargo at Amsterdam in 1985 realised $US20 million. A fabulous reward.

Geldermalsen was the glamour side of salvage work, the aspect of salvage which attracted the newspapers, the television, and the filmmakers. The bread-and-butter of the business, barely noticed, came from tin and non-ferrous metals, copper, brass and bronze, from modern wrecks. These included German U-boats, sunken merchantmen and warships, the victims of World War II. They helped Hatcher become a self-made millionaire.

That was in the 1980s. In the 1990s Hatcher's legendary luck had metamorphosed into a losing streak. 'Hatch' was still using the same methods, but good wrecks had become harder and harder to find. 'It's there waiting,' he would say of a target, the glint of determination in his eyes never softening. 'It could be on the next survey line.'

When he did at last break through with a find of centuries-old jars and ceramics in the Gulf of Thailand, the Royal Thai Navy surrounded his salvage barge with gunboats. They put limpet mines on his anchor chains and robbed him of his prize, even though he was in international waters and 55 nautical miles from the nearest land.

'Power comes from the barrel of a gun,' the Chinese leader Mao Zedong once sagely observed. Hatcher may have had a moral case. But the Thais had the artillery loaded, primed, and pointed at Hatcher's barge. It was a hold-up in a nautical sense.

'It was worth between eight and ten million dollars,' he lamented later. The Australian government refused to intervene because of the perceived risk of upsetting trade relations with a close neighbour.

It was back to 'lawnmowing' for Hatcher and his crew. They spent another three fruitless seasons in war-ravaged Cambodia and Vietnam and another summer at Ternate in the Moluccas (the former Spice Islands), extending the search further and ever further from their base in Singapore. Finally the money ran out. In June 1999 *Restless M* was on her way back to Singapore via the Gaspar Strait. All aboard knew only too well their situation. Mike Hatcher's long-term band of investors had become tired of 'dry holes' like Cambodia, to use the oil-drilling parlance, and they were becoming frustrated at watching their money go down into big swirling holes in the ocean.

Hatcher had apparently run his race and the news of his discomfort spread quickly among the other off-shore operators in south-east Asia – in particular those with salvage, oil and mining interests. He had been the public face of ocean salvage for 20 years and most were sick of hearing his name and seeing his photograph in the newspapers and on television. There was little public mourning for Captain Mike Hatcher and some even gloated at his unhappy situation. 'He's gone from a rooster to a feather duster!' they crowed. 'Bitten off more than he can chew this time. Hatcher's finished. Gone. He just won't lie down.'

His jaded investors were proving increasingly difficult to convince. Even his renowned and usually indomitable enthusiasm and eagerness had begun to fall on deaf ears. 'If we keep going long enough,' Hatcher told them, over and over, 'we must ultimately succeed. It's logical when you look at it and think about it.'

'Keep going long enough' was his trademark phrase. Now it had worn thin. Logic was one thing, the voices of doom said dolefully, it cost nothing, but operational costs were quite another matter. Every day that *Restless M* trolled her instruments up and down cost hundreds of dollars. A week cost thousands. After months and years they added up to millions. Cambodia alone had seen three million sunk without a trace. A truck-load of US greenbacks, the modern 'gold' of south-east Asia, gone forever.

Aside from the cost of the boat and the fuel and the equipment, the crew had to be paid and fed. By mid 1999 those aboard *Restless M* hadn't seen a pay cheque in three months. Most of them privately did not hold out a high degree of hope of seeing a fully back-dated wage packet even when they reached Singapore. The cupboard, they knew, was bare.

Facts were facts. Underwater Sub Sea Services, Mike Hatcher's operating company, was technically broke. It was out of funds. Insolvent. Busted. The gamble – for wreck searches, like searches for gold ashore, were always gambles – had failed.

Or so it seemed.

Hatcher had gone ashore one last time. He had flown from Bangkha Island down to Jakarta for a final appeal to the investors by telephone. The response, which even he by now anticipated, was negative, to give it the kindest possible description. But back on board *Restless M* around 6 pm in the evening of June 5, the side-scan sonar picked up an unusual pattern on the seabed.

'It looks like something,' skipper Alistair Feast suggested hopefully. 'What do you think?'

Abdul W Rahim, Hatcher's most experienced diver and a man who had been with him since 1979, shook his head. 'Reef,' he said. 'Coral lumps and rock.'

'Anything on the magnetometer?' Alistair asked Arasan, the Indian-Singaporean operator.

'Sorry, Alistair,' was the reply. 'There's nothing I can see.'

'Reef,' said Rahim again.

❊

That night a piece of bad luck befell the crew of Restless M. It was the sort of thing which happens occasionally at sea, but at that moment it was exceptionally bad timing and it further depressed the already despondent crew. The Avon diving inflatable dinghy, Mike Hatcher's favourite toy and pride and joy, was no longer out astern on its line. Someone had tied a bum knot and the 'rubber duck' had broken free and disappeared.

'Oh God!' said Alistair Feast, dreading the satellite phone call he would have to make to Jakarta. 'The wrath of Captain Mike' at what he'd perceive as gross negligence would be as ferocious as a South China Sea thunderstorm, and almost as predictable ... 'Find it!' Hatch roared on receipt of the news. 'Find it, you incompetent bastards! Find it if it takes for-bloody-ever! Hear me? Do it or I'll have your guts for garters!'

'I don't think he actually needed the phone,' remarked Alistair later. 'I could have heard him from Jakarta without it.'

The crew of Restless M searched the surrounding waters all day and questioned local fisherman, but it was to no avail. The dinghy was gone and they (and Hatcher) would just have to face that unpalatable fact. Dejected, they returned to their last point on the survey to check out the swirls on the print-out of the side-scan sonar. Early on the morning of June 7 Rahim pulled on his gear to inspect the area. Though he remained sceptical about the identity of the target he went into the water cheerfully enough. A dive broke the monotony of the survey work and all anomalies had to be investigated thoroughly regardless of surface opinions.

When Arasan was about to signal for the anchor to go down on the 'anomaly' Alistair shook his head. 'You'll smash the porcelain!' he said jokingly. They gave him a derisive look, but just to be on the safe side anchored a little distance away. They could just imagine Hatcher's reaction if, on top of losing the rubber dinghy, they dropped a 60-kilogram iron anchor in the middle of a cargo of pottery. It was a million-to-one chance, but it was a risk they weren't prepared to take. A buoy was placed to mark the spot.

Now the divers were ready. Yoni was back-up for Rahim. The target was at a fair depth, the echo-sounder showed 31 metres, or about 100 feet. Down that far they would have to watch their bottom time because of the risk of the 'bends' (decompression sickness) if they stayed too long. But Rahim did not anticipate that their inspection would be lengthy and he was accustomed to the 'stops' on the ascent where divers rested to work the potentially dangerous nitrogen bubbles out of their bloodstreams.

They jumped from the side of *Restless M*, holding their masks to their faces with one hand, already ruing the loss of the diving dinghy which made access to the water much easier. The two divers sank below the surface in a white crystal cloud of bubbles, then turned over and headed down along the buoy line with strong beats of their fins. The water was a deep blue and they were down to 25 metres before the blur of the bottom became vaguely visible, the light decreasing as they reached the 30-metre mark.

The seabed was a level sandy floor, with little in the way of plant life or distinguishing features. Rahim attached his search line to the buoy line and then swam out progressively, circling until he reached its 35-metre limit. He marked the spot and began a new circle search, another 35 metres. This time he saw fish in the distance.

'Good!' he said. Fish usually meant a reef and as he swam towards them he saw, with satisfaction, a rise with a crowning cloud of fish of all shapes and sizes. It was exactly what he had expected. As he closed in on his objective in the slightly dirty water and dim light at a depth of 100 feet, the marine life increased. There were coral trout, snapper and several other varieties of colourful reef fish. Blue, green, red, some with all the colours of the rainbow. Demoiselles, angel fish, orange and white clown fish and blue-runners. This was great. The cook was a fanatical and skilful fisherman and would rather fish than eat or sleep. There would be coral trout for dinner!

Then something else caught Rahim's eye. It was blue and white and circular and was reflecting light right back at him. It was very familiar but very unexpected.

'It can't be!' he exclaimed to himself. Abdul Rahim was an extremely experienced diver. He had been with Mike Hatcher on the sunken German submarine, the U-IT, 170 feet down in the inky blackness of the Malacca Strait. Inside the submarine was a cargo of rubber and tin. There were also the mummified bodies of some of her crew – those unlucky ones who had been unable to escape when she was torpedoed in 1944 by the British submarine *Tally-Ho*.

He had also been a senior diver on the salvage of *Geldermalsen* in 1985, a memorable experience which had included the raising of gold bars. He had helped lift the huge bronze guns, broken by enemy cannon fire, which marked the site of the 17th century naval battle between the Dutch and the Portuguese off Malacca. He had seen three divers die on various salvages and knew all too well the fine line between triumph and disaster. He was not a diver who was likely to be excited by the unimportant or the trivial.

'Impossible!' he shouted in a cloud of bubbles. He closed his eyes. He must be dreaming, imagining, fantasising. 'Raptures of the deep' was a well-known effect of diving at depth, but usually the phenomenon only occurred in waters deeper than 150 feet. It could cause divers to hallucinate or do irrational things ... like offering their mouthpieces to a passing fish. But surely Rahim was not deep enough to be experiencing delusions. He had never had the problem to this degree before, and certainly not at 100 feet.

He opened his eyes again warily. The blue and white circular object was still there, still reflecting light, and now he saw other similar shapes out on the sand. In the reef ahead of him were regular forms, row upon row, just as he had seen them on *Geldermalsen*. Were they the edges of plates, bowls, saucers?

'Impossible!' he shouted again. But this time he knew that what he was looking at was real. It was what was described in salvage language as the 'spill' from a cargo. The 'reef' was, in fact, a solid mass of porcelain standing up from the seabed in imitation of a natural coral reef. A few plates and bowls had spilled out onto the sand beyond.

It was a cargo and a wreck of awesome size.

Most scuba divers know that it is not possible to articulate the spoken word clearly into a rubber mouthpiece at depth, but exceptionally boisterous shouting can sometimes be heard. When Yoni, the second diver, heard Rahim's exultations he reacted with alarm. Hearing distant, discordant sounds his first thought was that the normally calm Rahim had been attacked by some underwater creature and was calling for help. Or dying in agony. His alarm increased when a dark figure came fast towards him in the low visibility and half-light. But when he saw with his own eyes what Rahim had seen he understood the reason and he contributed some noises of his own. This was it. It was really the big one and the two divers shared the privilege and excitement of being the first to see it.

The dimensions of the wrecksite were astounding. The cargo mound covered more than 42 square metres and had formed an artificial 'reef' standing some four metres high on the seabed. The mound was a solid mass of porcelain and later excavation showed it to extend a further two metres down below seabed level to the hidden keel of the vessel. The timbers still remained, buried up to the waterline in the soft sand. The mound was overgrown by corals and sponges, but the rims and shapes of plates and bowls could clearly be seen along with jars and vases.

The divers had thought that the *Geldermalsen* cargo was big. So it was, in comparison with previously known shipwrecks. But this cargo appeared to dwarf all others. Where *Geldermalsen* had about 180,000 pieces of porcelain in her holds, this unknown vessel probably had many times that amount. She was an ocean-going road train, a bulk carrier of past centuries.

'Impossible!' Rahim had said earlier, but now the cry had changed to, 'We've got it! We've found the big one!' The bubbles of triumph burst on the surface far above. Inside the mound, as well as beside the porcelain and unseen on that first dive, was an extraordinary range of artefacts – the personal effects of the crew and passengers who had sailed with her on that fateful voyage.

Opium and quicksilver (mercury) would be revealed along with European wine bottles and glasses, a sextant and pocket watches – also a chronometer. The ink pads of the Chinese clerks and the stamps which made their seal or 'chop' on the lists of tea and silks, peppers, and fine porcelain would be found with the cargo. There were also iron and brass cannon to repel pirates and a long, ornate bronze gun of probable Chinese origin with a flared muzzle. An elaborate dolphin lifting handle was in perfect condition.

There were trade goods, boxes of needles, pocket knives, Chinese brass padlocks, incense burners, candlesticks and a hundred different items, intended no doubt for sale in the great market town of Batavia.

There were also the bones of some of the unlucky crew and passengers who went down with the vessel and had found themselves trapped below fallen beams. The divers could not have guessed at that moment of identification the quantity and quality of the cargo, or the frightful death toll which had accompanied the disaster. But the ghosts below the shiny surface of the Gaspar Strait were about to reveal their secrets.

❁

Later that day the telephones began ringing. The calls went first from the South China Sea, the Gaspar Strait and Belvidere Shoals to Jakarta, and from there all around the world – Singapore,

London, Amsterdam and to several states in Australia. As the news spread like ripples when a stone is thrown into a pond, I eventually received a call at home in Western Australia.

'We've found it,' Mike Hatcher said. 'We got the big one.' There was a pause, then, 'This is really it!' He allowed me a moment for the news to sink in. Then, in his usual style, didn't waste time coming to the point. 'Get your gear together and get yourself up here!'

There was a moment of hesitation and a sense of déjà vu – I had responded to a similar request once before and had found myself on a rolling wet junk deck off Cambodia in a line squall, surrounded by flashing lightning, thunder pounding like drums and wave caps peaking. A time when the pumps failed, there was no radio contact and I vowed 'never again'.

But somehow this sounded different.

'OK, Mike,' I said, 'I'll be there.'

'Good,' Hatcher replied and hung up to make his next call. There was a lot to organise, and the first task was to bring a large group of skilled people together from several different countries. A salvage of this size would require divers, technicians, photographers, seamen, winch drivers, boat crew, carpenters, cooks and crate handlers, like the 'butchers and bakers and candlestick makers' of the old rhyme. There were a thousand pieces of equipment to gather, including diving gear, a decompression chamber, air-lifts, a 180-foot three-storey salvage barge, a 130-foot tug and stand-by vessel, *Restless M*, a 50-ton crane plus a score of generators and air compressors, all fuelled and ready to go.

United Sub Sea Services, the supposedly defunct dragon, was far from dead. Awakened, like the dragon of legend, it was flicking its tail and breathing fire from both nostrils.

Captain Michael Hatcher was back in business.

CHAPTER TWO

A Ship to Australia

Mike Hatcher, as the reader will have already guessed, is a man who likes to buck the odds, a man who relishes a challenge and is often at his best when things are at their toughest. The prospect of glory pushes him forward, like a rugby player battered and bloodied, who breaks through the tackles, pounding with flying boots down the line, his eye on the corner flag and the try that will win the game.

In his work he has always been incredibly persistent but seldom patient. Hatch can hold onto a dream and keep doggedly after it, refusing to call it quits long after many others would have seen the sense in giving up. He is icy cool under the threat of danger, but can fly off the handle at the most trivial annoyance. Thankfully, once a tongue-lashing has been delivered, he holds no grudges. He has little time for bureaucracy, people who live by appearances or who promise more than they can deliver.

He is also fiercely loyal to anyone who has served him well, especially the group of men who had been with him since the Malacca Strait days of the 1970s and 80s. These included divers AW Rahim and Suliman and magnetometer and side-scan operators VJ and Arasan.

❁

14

After he attained fame following the recovery of the *Geldermalsen* cargo, most of the writers who set their pens to describing a very complex character over-simplified their pictures of him. That was understandable. Judging him by his deeds alone they regarded him as some sort of 20th century buccaneer, a contemporary Elizabethan more suited to the days of Drake and Raleigh than the computer age. Indeed he would have looked well on a quarter-deck with frock coat, a telescope and a three-cornered hat. 'Fire me a broadside Master Gunner and bring the scoundrels' main mast down!'

But there are other sides to the personality than the image of the flamboyant master salvor. Sometimes Hatch is introspective, lost in thought; he can be suspicious, surly at times if he thinks someone is trying to take advantage of him. One of the most surprising facets of his character, which the world rarely sees, emerges when he's at 'home' on his 10,000-acre property in the ranges out of Grafton in New South Wales. There, amongst his cattle in the paddocks between timbered hills filled with birdsong, he can truly relax. When his daughters Michelle and Naomi are with him, each one holding a hand, those close to him see a different man.

While the nature versus nurture polemic may never be fully understood, there are elements and cornerstones both hereditary and circumstantial that have shaped Mike Hatcher's personality. If there is one particular trait which he may have inherited it surely must be courage. Both his father and his grandfather were awarded medals for acts of bravery. On October 10, 1922, the *Barnsley Independent* newspaper in Yorkshire, England, ran a story on an incident in the Barnsley Main Colliery (coal mine). For his part in it Mike's grandfather, Arthur, was awarded both the Edward Medal and the *Daily Herald* Order of Industrial Heroism by King George V. A rare distinction for a working man.

The newspaper heading was BARNSLEY MAIN HERO and the story told how the 39-year-old coal miner with a wife and seven children had saved the lives of four other miners at the risk of his own. He had flung himself in front of a fully-loaded runaway skip which was careering out of control on a downward slope inside the mine. Trapped in the tunnel ahead, with no way of escape from the skip thundering down the rails towards them, were four of his horrified workmates. Hatcher threw himself in front of the skip and chocked it with his own body. He paid a heavy price – he suffered serious spinal injuries, was never able to work again and was awarded a life pension.

Interviewed in Beckett's Hospital after the event, Arthur Hatcher told a reporter from the *Barnsley Independent* that he had heard the roar of the skip coming down the rail line incline and had thrown himself across the rails because 'there was nothing else to throw'.

Mike Hatcher's father George Albert Hatcher joined the British Army at the age of 16. He was involved in fighting in various frontier locations of the British Empire and won the Military Medal in Palestine. This prestigious award is for conspicuous bravery under fire and is more often given to officers than enlisted men.

Unfortunately, good fortune did not follow for young Michael Hatcher, his elder brother David George Hatcher and younger sister Jessie Cynthia Rosetta Hatcher. The Hatcher children had a particularly hard start to life and what may be fairly described as a wretched childhood.

There is always an inclination to ascribe blame, and certainly the civic authorities of the time had strong opinions about the circumstances of the three Hatcher children in 1942. But the judgements may have been harsh given the upheavals of wartime England.

At that time Hitler's forces were assembled just across the English Channel. George Hatcher was enlisted as a soldier and was seldom home and his wife Elsie found his absences harder and harder to handle. They had been married while he was stationed at York, he was barely 20 and she only 19. The first child, David, was born in 1937 in the first year of their marriage, Michael in 1940 and Jessie in 1941. Aside from rare moments of leave Elsie barely saw her youthful husband.

Dealing with loneliness and the difficulties of bringing up three children, Elsie was a natural target for the attentions of other men. By 1942 George Hatcher had risen to the rank of instructor sergeant and was undergoing intensive training in preparation for the coming North African campaign. Hearing stories of his wife's alleged romantic liaisons he went AWOL (Absent Without Official Leave) and returned to England to confront her.

'Finding the allegations to be true,' a later report of the NSPCC (National Society for the Prevention of Cruelty to Children) said, 'he told her he was finished with her.' The trauma was such that George did not return to his regiment but ran away to Coventry, his world destroyed. It was not an uncommon story in wartime England where men were away on active service and wives were left lonely for long periods. There were music hall jokes about it, but it was anything but funny for those directly involved.

The Army posted George Hatcher as a deserter and stopped his pay from the time of his departure. They also stopped that portion of his wage regularly sent to Elsie Hatcher and the three children. Without money for the rent and food and without George she was unable to cope. She sought the advice of the NSPCC. The inspector reported the children were in good condition ... 'the mother stated that she was in possession of a letter written by another woman to the father and that she wished the children to be put in a home so that she could go to work. The PAC refused to take the children but granted the mother PAR [provisions and rent].'

Eventually George returned to his unit, where he was promptly court martialled and reduced in rank from a sergeant to a private soldier. Meantime Elsie wrote to his commanding officer 'stating that she was leaving the children and did not wish to see them or the father again'.

Faced with this new shock George was granted three days leave to sort out his family problems. Obviously his commanding officer thought highly of him, for the previous charge of desertion was one of the most serious military offences. In World War I deserters from the British Army in France were summarily executed by firing squad. But the Army's compassion could not prevent the disintegration of the Hatcher family. Elsie had appealed again to the NSPCC for help. This time there was a dramatic difference in the health of the Hatcher children. A NSPCC inspector visited and found a very sorry situation. David was five years old, Michael only two and Jessie was barely 10 months, and all were in a deplorable state.

The report read, 'Inspector found the three children in a dirty, neglected condition and suffering from impetigo. All the furniture had been returned to the suppliers and the mother intended leaving the children that day.'

Repair of the marriage, a reconciliation, was clearly out of the question. The mother was about to leave and as a serving soldier the father was destined for North Africa with the Eighth Army and was in no position to personally care for his children. There was no guarantee that he would come back alive. The only option was to put them into a home. On April 14, 1942 David, Michael and Jessie were admitted to Hollins House in Yorkshire, their childhood family home life brought abruptly to a close.

'Under the circumstances,' the NSPCC report stated, 'immediate shelter was granted. It was decided to offer admission for the duration of the war, but it was [also] suggested that the case be reconsidered in 12 months.' The Hatcher children went from one home to the next – Hollins Hall in Yorkshire was the first, followed by Cloan in Auchterader in Yorkshire and a succession of others around England.

The hopes that one day their father might be able to look after them again never eventuated. George Hatcher went to North Africa with the 3rd Paratroop Division in support of the campaign against Rommel. In 1943 he was badly wounded in the first paratroop landing in Africa and repatriated to the emergency ward in the Leatherhead Military Hospital, Surrey. That was the end of the war for George Hatcher, M.M. At the time of his injury he had taken the first step back up the ladder of promotion and had been listed as Lance Corporal. The notes of the orphanage through the years 1943 to 1944 contain various references to the relations between George, his wife Elsie and the children.

At different times it was noted that George was adamant there could be no reconciliation with his wife and no return to a domestic situation. He wanted a divorce and he was concerned that he should be awarded custody of the children once the war was over. He did not want his wife to ever see them again, he said. Elsie also wrote in 1944 saying that she too wanted the children. 'As she is now in a position to provide them with a good home. Acting as housekeeper to a man she hopes to marry ...'

In the stalemate that followed, the Hatcher children went to neither parent and grew up as wards of the State. Although the people running these institutions were no doubt kindly folk with their charges' best interests at heart, they could not give them love. Indeed for women such as Mrs Langridge, who supervised Mike Hatcher's first years, the instructions were clear cut. Staff were forbidden to 'get involved'. It invariably meant heartbreak on both sides.

The orphanage reports graphically detail the early life of Michael Hatcher from the time the three children were brought in with impetigo sores, their hair unkempt and in a 'verminous' condition. Aged two, the time when children are beginning to learn to talk and forming their association with adults, Michael was completely untrained in any aspect of life and traumatised by the family break-up. According to an initial report, he was 'covered with impetigo on admission. Still in a very septic condition. Fretful child. Swears and has had no training'.

In his early years he was described as disruptive and aggressive, a problem child in the schoolyard, but later his reports improved. In August 1943, aged only three, he was admitted to Bridge of Earn Hospital with a broken leg. Described in Cloan reports as 'a lively youngster' he had been climbing on a laundry basket and 'fell with his leg under him ... it was a clean break of the femur'. The femur, of course, is the long bone of the upper leg. A most painful injury. The accident had one beneficial result. It brought a visit from his father who had taken leave and spent the best part of two days with his son.

The young Michael was rarely out of the wars. On March 21, 1944, it was reported that he swallowed a part of an engine! He was admitted to hospital where an X-ray revealed he had ingested (but thankfully passed soon after) a nut.

A list of homes (orphanages) and schools shows that the three Hatcher children were separated and flung far and wide during these early years. In 1953, aged 13, Michael found himself at Dr Barnardo's Home in Crowborough, Sussex, attending the Beacon School. His sister Jessie meanwhile was at High Barn and brother David at Southborough. For a time Michael's lot seem on the up – in 1950 his school report stated he was growing into 'a very pleasant lad indeed, passionately fond of his [pet] rabbit'.

However in 1951 and '52 there was a downside. The homes had reported that both Michael and Jessie were subject to 'brain-storms' also described as 'fits of uncontrollable temper'. Temper? Or a combination of frustration, forlornness and despair.

More than 40 years on Hatcher is never far from those darker moments. Sipping a Bintang beer while sitting on the upper deck of his contracted salvage barge the *Swissco Marie II* in 1999, gently rocking on the South China Sea, a fortune in porcelain on the seabed below, he appeared to be far removed from those bad old days.

He shook his head, his expression momentarily bleak. 'It just doesn't go away,' he began, looking out to the horizon. 'Only someone who has grown up in an orphanage can understand it. The people looking after us did their best, but they could never replace a parent or a family.'

Michael had a choice, and instead of wallowing in the misery he turned it around and began to develop his formidable will to succeed. The superintendent of the Beacon School noted that the 12-year-old Michael was 'a very pleasant and charming boy in his normal times, but quite a lad when he is crossed in any way … I like the boy tremendously, but often want to kick him in the pants!' In June 1953, a year later, another report read 'Behaviour generally good. Has grown out of his "brain-storms" and is a fine lad now…' At that point Hatcher was at a crossroad. His future, his school reports indicated, probably lay in farming or manual work. He was described as 'robust'.

Dr Barnardo's Homes, founded by the social reformer Thomas John Barnardo in the 1850s, were committed to helping destitute children. Barnardo was an extraordinary man. As a doctor in London he was attending 16 deaths a day and was depressed by the endemic poverty, poor food and lack of medicine. London in the mid 19th century was overflowing with homeless people, many of them children with nowhere to sleep, forced to steal in order to survive. While many citizens proclaimed the hopelessness of the situation, Thomas John Barnardo resolved to tackle it himself.

He established a shelter for impoverished children in 1868 in a rented donkey stable, and in 1874 set up the first of his famous 'Ever Open Door' establishments at Stepney Causeway, one of the poorest parts of London. By the 50th birthday of Barnardo's Homes he had worked in the streets of London for 29 years. He had rescued 27,000 wholly destitute children, helped 60,781 others through his 'Ragged Schools' and migrated 6805 to Australia, South Africa and Canada.

From humble beginnings where the most he could offer a child was a cup of cocoa and a blanket, he progressed and expanded, setting up schools and Barnardo's Homes all over England. He proudly claimed that the children were 'Rescued from degradation ... washed, dressed in clean clothes, fed, drilled, educated and given a door to opportunity'. The aim was always to bring up a healthy and educated child, ready for a job and with a chance in life to compete with the more fortunate ones who had grown up with families.

In the 1950s Australia was encouraging immigration on a 'populate or perish' basis. Strong children of British stock were particularly welcome and the Barnardo's organisation in Australia offered a transitional point for child migrants coming from the United Kingdom. Michael, reported as being 'keen on adventure stories', was anxious to go. Jessie was less certain. She had heard Australia was 'a wild place' but wanted to be where Michael was. David was adamant that he wished to remain in England. He had friends there.

What of the Hatcher parents?

Barnardo's records show that George Hatcher had contributed his regular Army allowance to the costs of keeping the children for the duration of the war, but after the strong expressions of interest by both parents in 1944 the record showed blank spaces. The last known address of George Hatcher failed to provide a response to letters after October 1944. A pencilled note in the margin of the children's papers recorded that George Hatcher had migrated to Australia, 'S.S. *New Australia*, 13:12:52. Father and stepmother now in Australia. Last known address PO Coolangatta. No interest in children'.

Did this have any influence in the decision of Michael and Jessie to become 'Ten Pound Tourists' and migrate to Australia too? The records of Barnardo's Homes were confidential and it is unlikely that the comment relating to Hatcher senior would have been passed on to his children. Coincidentally, they would make their own voyage to Australia on the same ship that George Hatcher had travelled on two years before. Mike Hatcher is adamant that in later years he had no idea his father was in Australia.

Until he met him face to face.

Michael and Jessie set sail on the migrant ship *New Australia*, arriving at Circular Quay, Sydney, in November, 1954. 'After England Australia seemed such a huge place,' Michael recalls. 'Huge and lonely.' He was sent to Dr Barnardo's farm school at Picton and was once again assessed and his condition reported. This time it was compiled by the Youth Welfare Section, Vocational Guidance Bureau of New South Wales. Australia had its own bureaucracy too.

'The boy appears to be a manual and unskilled type,' the report stated. 'He prefers agriculture and does not like arithmetic and English. He says that he is no good at school and hopes to leave as soon as he is fifteen.' It was dated November 24, 1954, and signed by DE Rose, Director of Youth Welfare.

❋

Before he came to grips with the workplace, the young Hatcher had an even tougher assignment. The boys at Picton school were a hard bunch who regarded an orphanage newcomer as a 'foreigner' and fair game. They mocked Hatcher's 'Pommie accent' and saw him as a natural target for bullying. That proved to be a mistake. 'They could beat me but they couldn't break me,' he recalls. 'I wasn't big and I wasn't the best fighter, but there was no way I was going to give in. They got sick of me getting up and coming back at them.' He ultimately earned respect and a place in the playground pecking order.

When he was barely 15 years old Barnardo's sent him off to work on his first farm. He had learned the basics of agriculture at Picton and was now deemed fit and ready for the real world.

A lot of farmers applied for 'Barnardo boys' to work for them. Some were decent people, but there were others who simply saw the lads as cheap and exploitable labour.

If there was one thing that Barnardo's had drummed into the young Hatcher, it was the need for cleanliness. On his first night at the new job he came in dirty with muck from the cow yard. His tea was served in the kitchen and the farmer's wife haughtily refused his request to take a hot shower. He was expected to wash outside in an enamel basin of cold water.

'I left the next day,' he recalls. 'Back to Barnardo's for a new posting.' On the next job Hatcher was sitting on a stool milking a cow in the milking shed when the farmer came past and delivered a hefty clout to his ear.

'You filthy little bastard!' he shouted. 'You haven't washed your hands!'

'I would never, ever, milk without washing my hands,' Hatcher recalls angrily. The superintendent at the Beacon School might have predicted Hatcher's response.

'I just saw red. I jumped up, grabbed a piece of four-by-two timber and walloped him with it. The whack knocked him down and I kept on hitting him as he crawled out of the cow shed pleading for mercy. The farmer's wife drove me down to the train. She didn't seem too upset about it. In fact I had the distinct impression she thought it was funny.'

There were sighs as he returned to Picton. But there would be a few more of those before Mike Hatcher settled into a steady job. One bachelor farmer tried to sexually abuse him and got 'a right cross for his pains'. Another family were socialites. He got on well enough with the farmer but the wife insisted on treating him as a servant.

'Sweep the verandah!' she commanded, handing him a broom on the eve of a big dinner party.

'That's not my job,' Michael protested. 'I'm a farm worker.'

'Do it!' she said, 'or else!'

'Do it,' the farmer pleaded. 'Just to keep the peace. My life won't be worth living otherwise. I'll make it up to you.'

'The farmer wasn't a bad guy,' Hatcher remembers. 'But he wouldn't stand up for me when it counted and giving in then would only have been postponing the inevitable.'

So he left that job too.

Australia was starting to seem like an immense and lonely place and each new experience seemed to confirm the hopelessness of his position. In everyone's eyes, including his own, he was a misfit, incapable of settling in anywhere.

'I had no-one other than Barnardo's to turn to and they were becoming increasingly impatient with me. There was nowhere to go. That was the frightening thing. It had become a matter of sheer survival, both mental and physical. They weren't good years. I had a really negative view of the world. Everyone and everything seemed to be against me. At that point I could easily have become a criminal and ended up with a life in gaol.'

Sometimes in later years, working underwater deep down in the Malacca Strait, or off the east coast of Malaya, or on Admiral Stellingwerf Reef, the childhood images would return, unwanted and unwelcome. 'I always tried to put all that out of my mind. But occasionally there'd be a flash, a picture I didn't want to see. I can deal with it now, but I still don't like it.'

Then, when all seemed worst, the miracle occurred. He found a decent, caring family who treated him as a human being.

'On the first night they set a place for me at the family dinner table. On previous jobs I'd had to eat out in the kitchen or out in my room. Me and the dogs outside. I kept waiting to hear it was a mistake because I couldn't believe it.'

The Edmunds had a dairy property at Bundanoon in New South Wales called 'Corinda Grange'. For the first time, Michael, now aged 19, received award wages. 'A princely eleven pounds, twelve shillings and sixpence a week! It seemed a lot of money in 1959. The Edmunds were wonderful, wonderful people. They were

Seventh Day Adventists or Jehovah's Witnesses or something like that, but they never put any of that on me. I could do as I liked. But they were the most Christian people I have ever met.'

He soon had his introduction to the country town social scene.

'I was driving the utility down the road when the local sergeant of police pulled me over on the basis of some trivial offence,' he recalls. A huge man, he loomed beside the driver's window and solemnly recorded Hatcher's name and address in his notepad. The pencil moved with slow deliberation, aided by an occasional lick at the end.

'All right, son,' he said sternly when he had finished. 'You have two options. You can pay a fine now, or choose community service!'

Young Hatcher blinked uncertainly. 'Community service? What's that?' he asked.

'You can join the local rugby club, son. We train on Tuesdays and Thursdays, 5 pm. Don't be late!' The notebook snapped shut and the sergeant was gone, footsteps scrunching on the gravel.

When a slightly bemused Michael Hatcher arrived at Bundanoon Rugby League Club for his first training run, he found that the big sergeant was the Club President. He was also the recruiting officer.

That was to be the first true period of happiness. He loved the exertion, the challenge the camaraderie of rugby. Like most country football teams Bundanoon travelled every other weekend. Win or lose there was a keg of beer after the game, rousing renditions of old rugby songs and of course the girls, who came along to wave their rattles and scarves and cheer the heroics of the team.

Mike Hatcher now found he had a social life, a group of friends, an interest outside work and the confidence in himself which had previously been conspicuously absent. From being a surly, suspicious youth, too ready to take offence, expecting the worst of all situations, he became the cheerful extrovert of later years.

A happy ending to the sad childhood story?

'Call it a happy beginning,' he says. 'My life really began at Bundanoon.'

A Barnardo's report of October, 1959, reads 'A decent lad, starting to think of the future. Wants to spend a further 12 months with present employer [the Edmunds] and hopes to share farm on a dairy after this'.

❀

It was while visiting Sydney that a remarkable event occurred. Michael Hatcher had just acquired his first motor car, a Morris 10, for 270 pounds. He often saw his sister Jessie, and one day they were driving through the eastern suburbs when they saw a sign on a building site. It read:

G. Hatcher
Bricklayer

and gave an address and telephone number.

'I wonder?' said Jessie.

'It couldn't be,' said Michael. 'There must be Hatchers all over the place. Why would it be him?'

'I'm going to see, anyway.'

They called at the address but Michael refused to get out of the car. Jessie knocked on the door and sure enough, their father George Hatcher came out.

'What are you doing here?' he asked her in amazement.

She dragged him by the hand over to the car to meet his son. 'I hadn't seen him since I was three and had no memory of him,' Mike recalls. 'I was in hospital at the time. This was the first time I'd ever really seen him.'

A Hollywood scriptwriter would have relished the situation . . . had father and son and daughter embracing, vowing to let bygones be bygones, and starting a new life together in the antipodean sunshine.

'It didn't quite work out like that,' Mike remembers. 'Funnily enough I got on really well with Win, the lady with Dad, but he and I never really hit it off. Perhaps I had too much anger beneath the surface. Maybe he had some guilts. Together they didn't add up. Jessie did a lot better with him.'

Barnardo's also had some doubts. Though Michael was by now well-launched in the world, happy with the Edmunds at Bundanoon and with his rugby, they still kept a commendable eye on his welfare. In one of the last Barnardo's reports the tone might be regarded as somewhat prim by modern-day standards. 'I am never too happy about the tie Michael has with his father,' it read. 'For the situation is not a good one. In fact there is considerable doubt as to whether Mr Hatcher is actually married to the woman with whom he is living[!]. However it would be wrong to interfere at Michael's age and he obviously gains some contentment of mind from the association.' Barnardo's had done a wonderful job with the Hatcher children. Now it was time for Michael to stretch his wings and fly.

'I'd already worked out that I was never going to buy the farm as an employee,' he says. 'I had a natural aptitude with machinery – maybe it goes back to swallowing those nuts as a three year old!' He decided to do a course in civil engineering. The course had a practical aspect and would involve work on the Snowy River Hydro Electric Scheme, the biggest engineering project undertaken in Australian history and a mammoth operation even by world standards. There were 16 major dams with a storage capacity equivalent to more than 13 times the volume of Sydney Harbour and 100,000 workers from 30 countries around the world, often working in freezing conditions.

The 'Snowy' was a defining experience for the young Hatcher and aside from the personal gains, he acquired skills which would be useful to him in later life – blasting and the use of explosives, concreting, welding and cutting iron and steel with an oxy-acetylene torch.

At the age of 22 he headed for the bright lights of Sydney. 'I became a construction manager for Frank O'Neil swimming pools. Sydney has a rocky terrain and we had to do a lot of blasting. One day we were blowing out a hole for a pool near a block of flats. I had two Italian workmen with me, neither of whom spoke any English. I thought the job was going too slowly, so next time they drilled the rock I doubled the charge.

'It went up with a hell of a bang. Pieces of rock went everywhere. This guy out in the road with a brand new Holden was lovingly polishing it. He was just doing the final touches with a chamois, standing back to admire it, when a head-sized piece of sandstone came plummeting down out of the sky. It landed WHAM! in the middle of his roof and totally wrecked it. Boy, was he angry! He came storming over to the job ready to commit murder. He started by yelling at me. I shrugged my shoulders, pointed at the Italians and blamed them. They had no English, couldn't understand what was going on and yelled back at him. Which made him madder than ever of course.

'So there they were, shouting and gesticulating at each other. I figured it was a good time for me to be somewhere else and quietly left them to it!' He grins at the memory. 'I always had a natural inclination to hurry the job along a bit. To maybe whop too much of a charge in the hole. There were a couple of funny incidents in salvage.'

In Rabaul Harbour, after World War II, the rusting relics of the Japanese invasion were utilised wherever possible in the early days of the Peace.

'There was a Japanese ship bows on to the beach. The locals built a bitumen road along her deck and turned it into the wharf. It worked pretty well until I blew the propeller off the stern for scrap metal. The charge went up with an almighty WOOSH! Then there were other rumblings and crashes and a huge cloud of dust and rust flakes and pieces of ship rose up over Rabaul Harbour.

'Hello,' said Hatch innocently. 'What's happened here?'

As they nervously inspected the ship, it was apparent that the explosion had not only parted the propeller from the shaft, but had also collapsed the ship's deck! And not only that, the bitumen road had fallen inwards into the vessel's rusting internals.

Rabaul no longer had a wharf.

Oops!

CHAPTER THREE

Getting Wet

Mike Hatcher is always happy to talk about the practice and principles of salvage, those finite qualities which can make the difference between success and failure in recovering shipwreck cargoes.

'Balls,' he says with emphasis. 'Above all else a good salvage man has to have balls. By that I mean the courage to back yourself when no-one else believes in you.' The Spanish call the quality 'cajones', which means much the same thing.

'Self-belief is all important. On the other hand you don't make it a straight-out gamble. You should never ever put your life savings on one spin of the roulette wheel. That's stupid. My own personal rule is that I don't sell any of my real estate to go treasure hunting. I never gamble in the ordinary sense of the word. I don't play the pokies, go to the races or the casinos. I can't see the sense in it. The odds are too heavily stacked against you. The bookmaker and the casino both have to make their money. They take their 10 or 25 per cent or whatever, so it's never an even bet. You might win once, twice, or even more with a lucky break. But if you go on long enough the House must get your cash in the end. Simple.'

He is cynical about governments becoming deeply involved in gambling. 'On every packet of cigarettes the government insists on a notice stating that tobacco is a health risk. But do they put a notice on a lottery ticket stating that your chances of winning are millions to one against? Or on a poker machine? Do they print the odds over the entrance to a casino? Not on your life! They're too greedy for the money that comes in either directly or through taxes. Our odds are better. With wreck searches it is basically a matter of research, technique, and time. Given those three things and commensurate effort you must in the end succeed.'

Time, of course, is the major problem.

Time in salvage, as in so many areas of human endeavour, means money. In salvage it can be very big money. If the search or the recovery takes too long then the cost of the exercise exceeds the likely profit and a loss results.

'That's where the fine line of judgement comes in,' says Hatcher. 'Most salvors know of cargoes that are too deep, too dangerous, or in areas where it would take too long to find them.' Then he raises a finger and adds the important qualification. 'At present. Nevertheless, the science of wreck-hunting continually advances. The improvements in side-scan sonar, magnetometers, robot cameras, and global positioning by satellite have all made quantum leaps in recent years. What is impossible today may be very possible tomorrow. We'll be there when it happens.'

So how does he do it?

The principle on which he works is fairly simple. He puts the skill and experience gained from 30 years diving and salvaging in south-east Asian waters on the line as his part in a salvage. Investors, large and small, put up the money for the search and get dividends of 70 per cent return after costs when a strike is made. The equipment, the survey vessel, the salvage barge (when a hit is registered) and standby vessels, are contracted. Divers and crew are also contracted for the particular job, though he tends to retain the same operators year after year.

In the case of the vast cargo first sighted by AW Rahim in June, 1999, the costs were in proportion to the size of the project ... thousands of dollars a day. The salvage barge *Swissco Marie II* was literally an island in the sea – three storeys high, 180 feet long and 45 feet wide. Forty-two men, including divers, lived, worked, ate and slept aboard her while she spent three straight months at anchor above the wreck. In addition there was a standby tug, *Swissco 88*, 230 tons and 130 feet in length, and the ever-faithful *Restless M* and her crew. Every man involved in the operation was an expert in his own right.

In the late afternoon, with the peak of Gaspar Island low on the southern horizon, the sun setting over Sumatra to the west, Captain Michael Hatcher liked to sip a Bintang beer on the top deck of the *Swissco* barge and reflect on the day that was done. Trevor McInery was supervising the cleaning and packing and recording of artefacts, and would have already given his boss a list of cargo recovered for the day. Usually there were blue and white porcelain cups, saucers and bowls, candlesticks, incense burners, teapots large and small, parasol handles and various trade goods of the day. Sometimes there was a curiosity, such as the bright gleam of gold dust, a silver Spanish 'pillar' dollar, a Chinese coin with a square hole in the centre, or the liquid glint of mercury. Human bones were no longer brought on board. 'Bad luck,' the Malays said. 'Let them rest down there in peace.'

What were the circumstances of that fatal voyage? Who made the porcelain, who packed the cargo, and who sailed with the ship? More importantly who died and who survived the disaster whose evidence now lay in the burial mound of cargo 100 feet below *Swissco Marie II*?

The research, like most everything else, was contracted out. Faraway in England, working through libraries and colonial records, historian Nigel Pickford was poring over English and Dutch East India Company shipping lists. He was looking up old newspapers like *The Calcutta Times* and the *Java Gazette*, examining the sailing directions in pilot books such as Horsburgh's classic volumes, seeking any entry, however small, which might provide a lead towards revealing the identity of the ship and the names of the people who sailed on her final voyage. Already Pickford had turned up a paragraph from James Horsburgh's *Directions for Sailing to the East Indies*, Vol 2, 1827:

The South Westernmost end of Belvidere Shoals is in latitude 2 degrees 15 minutes South, and bears from Gaspar Island Peak North 27 degrees West, distant about 10 or 10 and one half miles; they extend from thence to the North Eastward about 4 miles, being composed of several patches with from 6 to 10 feet of water on them and a Black Rock above water at the North Eastern extremity. The sea breaks on them when there is much swell and they may be easily avoided in daylight, with a good lookout, particularly as some of the patches are dry at low water ...

An American ship, however, belonging to Mr Astor of New York, was wrecked on these shoals a few years ago, and not long after a large Chinese junk was wrecked there. Part of her people floated to Gaspar Island and some of them were found floating about on pieces of wood and other fragments of wreck, who were saved by the laudable exertions of a country ship belonging to Calcutta, that fell in with them at the time ...

The vessel below the *Swissco Marie II* appeared from her cargo and personal possessions to fit the description of 'a large Chinese junk.' The dates on the Spanish pillar dollars (1797 and 1804) were also compatible with the period. Pickford duly promised more information.

❀

So Hatcher sipped his beer and gazed out portside to the 'Black Rock' of Belvidere Shoal mentioned by Horsburgh. He watched the sun go down in crimson glory and pondered the immediate and forthcoming concerns. Interspersed with the thoughts of business came the occasional peaceful image – of paddocks of his cattle station at Grafton ... cattle belly-deep in grass or the smiling faces of his two little girls Naomi and Michelle. He was content, but the road to this point had by no means been easy.

He served a long apprenticeship in the salvage business before any significant dollars came his way. But besides the time and effort, it is curious how often a fortunate meeting or event helped him along. 'Hatcher's luck!' his competitors say sourly. Maybe so. But when Michael Hatcher set out on the adventure trail there was more than luck involved.

❀

Since the 1960s Hatcher has spent more time afloat than ashore. Living on a boat for long periods he seemed by nature destined for the sea. Yet until he was in his mid-twenties (apart from the migrant ship voyage to Australia in 1954) he had never set foot on a boat, let alone taken the tiller or steered to a distant destination.

But this was soon to change. On holiday in Coolangatta he met up with a bunch of lads from the Manly Surf Club in northern Sydney. They got on well, played some football, and upon his return to Sydney he decided to join. He quickly became involved in the social life of the club and eventually became social secretary. Over a period the club had built a lot of extensions and had accumulated a $10,000 debt with no way in sight to recover it. Hatcher decided to organise a series of 'themed' parties – Arabian nights, Roman nights, Greek nights and so on and recalls with much mirth that the South Sea night was going really well until he lost his grass skirt! Gradually the club began to peg back the debt, though there were those in the senior club committee who looked somewhat sourly at some of the more boisterous goings-on.

'The crunch came when we decided on a harbour cruise,' Hatcher recalls. 'We hired a Sydney Harbour ferry and when the big day came along we'd only sold about 200 tickets. We barely had the price of the ferry hire. Then someone had the bright idea of ringing Bob Rogers, a popular radio personality. His nightly show was the flavour of the day. Everyone listened to it.

'"What about putting a call out for us?" we asked him.

'"Manly Surf Club?" he asked. "Be delighted. I swim there sometimes."

'So he kept putting these calls out. "Hello there. Anyone cruising? Looking for a party? There's a great floating show on the water ... Manly Surf Club..." and so on.

'People flocked down. We ended up with so many on board that you couldn't move. We sold all our beer and raffle tickets and made a fortune with the roulette wheel. We ran out of prizes and began raffling cartons of beer until we ran out of them too. "Don't worry," said my ratbag mate Spaney, "I'll fix it." He tore off a few tickets and gave some to me and some for himself and some of the other committee guys. He drew the tickets out of the hat, and surprise surprise, the winners were guess who? We didn't have to give out any prizes. To cut a long story short we made a fortune and paid off every penny of the club's debt!'

Did he get a warm thank you, a pat on the shoulder and a 'Well done!' from the president?

Hatcher shakes his head sourly. 'They gave me the sack. I was hauled up before the senior committee. They were stern-faced and very concerned about the damage apparently done to the club's reputation by shonky raffles and underage kids playing the roulette wheel. Nobody mentioned the money we'd raised for the club!'

It was suggested that though the club couldn't further injure its respectability by keeping him on as social secretary he could be an 'advisor' since he obviously had good ideas for fund raising.

'Stick it!' said Hatcher, and stalked out.

One good thing that came from his association with the surf

club was meeting New Zealand girl Jan Carryer. He fell madly in love and followed her back to New Zealand when she went home. There he found her father making barbeques and incinerators. 'These would go just great in Sydney!' said Hatch. 'Give me some to try!'

They went so well that the whole family moved over and established a thriving business. They were bought by all the major stores including Grace Bros and David Jones. Hatcher was the salesman and one day while organising some brochures he found himself at the printing office of Harold Vourne, a well-known yachtsman and sailing author. Mike Hatcher looked at a picture of a yacht under full sail on Vourne's desk.

'Jeez – that looks like fun,' he said.

'It is. There's nothing quite like it,' said Vourne. 'What are you doing this afternoon?'

'Working, I guess,' Hatcher replied.

'No you're not.' Vourne pushed his chair back from his desk. 'You're coming sailing.' It was a Wednesday afternoon and Pittwater had regular twilight races. Hatch's first day on a boat.

He was instantly hooked, and soon became a regular and even started planning to buy his own boat and sail around the world! But first there were a couple of small issues to take care of – he had to save the money and he had to learn how to sail. He joined the Manly 16-foot Skiff Club and took lessons. The North Steyne Surf Club lifesaving instructor also taught sailing and scuba diving, Hatcher took both courses, and at the age of 27 was about to completely change the direction of his life.

The yacht *Islander III* was the most important purchase he had ever made. She was a carvel-built, plumb-stemmed 34 footer, made from Huon pine in Tasmania in 1917. She was not flash but she was sturdy and in the right hands quite capable of ocean sailing. Mike Hatcher had yet to develop navigational and handling skills, but he had a lot of determination and more than a little luck.

'My first voyage was from Sydney to Port Stephens,' he recalls, 'and I used a road map.' He intended to be away a fortnight, but enjoyed the sea-going life so much that it was five weeks before he returned. When he finally sailed back into Sydney waters, he had decided he would indeed sail around the world. Goodbye to taxes, goodbye to the frustrations and constraints of civilisation. The roving life for him!

By now the romance with Jan Carryer had faded and Hatcher was involved in a new and passionate affair with Jaquie, the daughter of an English squadron leader. When *Islander III* set off from Sydney there were bets at the yacht club that Hatcher would not get past Brisbane. In fact he nearly didn't get as far as that. He was still reading books on navigation when *Islander III* was caught in a gale off the east coast. 'I had her lying-to with sea anchors while I desperately read Hitchcock's book on the theory of sailing, trying to find out what to do! It was a case of self-taught self-help.'

The yacht survived the gale, but the romance with Jaquie did not. She had had enough of the dangers and discomforts of small boats by the time they reached Townsville. She didn't share Hatcher's unbridled optimism, the naivety of inexperience at the prospect of overcoming the hazards of the ocean on a circumnavigation of the world.

Undeterred, his personal faith unshaken, Hatcher pressed on, threading his way through the Torres Strait (which had proved such an obstacle for James Cook aboard *Endeavour* in 1776) to Thursday Island. He arrived broke. But fortunately there were construction jobs going on a dam in the middle of the island and his Snowy Mountains experience stood him in good stead. 'They called it T.I. or "Thirsty Island". And that was a good name for it,' Hatcher said of his time there. 'Jeez they drank a lot of booze! A party every night.' Thursday Island soon palled, but with cash saved from construction work he was on his way again on the Great Adventure, hoping to sail across the Pacific.

'I sailed for New Guinea, the sunset glinting on the empty bottles on the T.I. beach. Here goes for a tropical paradise! I thought. That was the last toast on leaving.'

Alas, Port Moresby in Papua New Guinea proved a let down. Dirty and disappointing, it fell far short of the tropical paradise Hatcher had imagined. 'Never mind,' said the locals cheerfully. 'You've got to realise that this is the arse-end of PNG. There's some lovely places further round. Try the Trobriand Islands.'

When Mike picked up his clearance papers at Port Moresby the harbour master asked him how long he thought he'd be away. Hatcher thought five weeks ... Five months later he was still in Bougainville with a boatload of carved island wooden artefacts. He had taken the advice given him by the locals in Port Moresby and spent all his money on tobacco and betel nut. With this bank of basic 'capital' he became 'Trader Mike'. In classic Joseph Conrad style he traded through the islands exchanging 'baccy' and betel nut for artefacts, cruising until there was no room for another carved walking stick or devil mask down below in *Islander III*.

'It was good timing,' he recalls. 'The biggest copper mine in the world was opening up on Bougainville and most of the technicians, engineers and truck drivers were Australians, all looking for a bit of local colour on their days off. I found that they'd built a yacht club, but there were no boats. When I rowed ashore from *Islander III* she was the only yacht in the bay. They welcomed me with open arms.'

The first drink offered by the manager and his wife was free. Hatch was able – just – to pay for the second one. But then the cupboard was bare. The Hatcher pockets empty.

'Any chance of credit?' he asked, expecting a polite but firm refusal.

'Sure,' they said. 'How much do you want?'

He was delighted to find that he had sailed into a land of plenty. The carved walking sticks, which he had expected would bring about $5, were in short supply and the price was $50.

'Struth,' he exclaimed. 'By the end of the week I had $450, and the miners were flocking to pay for charters with the boat to go fishing and diving.'

While at Bougainville he met a group of divers who were picking over the remains of a sunken World War II destroyer for copper and brass. Non-ferrous (non-iron) metals were fetching big prices in the reconstruction of the post-war world and there was a ready market. Hatcher joined the team in his spare moments and gained enough experience to consider going out on his own.

In the evenings the divers would sit down with a beer and talk about the great wrecks of history – the Dutch East Indiamen, the gold-laden clipper ships sailing from Australia, the World War II wrecks proliferating throughout the Indonesian Archipelago and the South Pacific, the submarines loaded with gold and mercury. Rabaul Harbour was frequently mentioned as being a graveyard of Japanese wartime shipping.

At the mention of Rabaul Hatcher pricked up his ears. He had a boat, New Britain wasn't too far away, and it fitted in with his plans. He left Bougainville $4,500 richer, and with a new diesel engine installed in *Islander III* to replace the unreliable petrol-powered relic whose hard-starting bad habits had so often been a cause of rage and frustration.

His luck continued. There were indeed wrecks in Rabaul and a beachcomber named Pat Roberts, married to a local Papuan girl, had the government concession to do the salvage work. But he was more than happy to sit on the beach taking a share as an 'armchair admiral' while Hatcher, young and keen as mustard, did the diving work.

One of Mike's first jobs was to blow the propeller off the beached freighter which formed the wharf, a tarmac road running on the top. The resultant BANG! as we have already seen, collapsed the rusted sides of the vessel and dropped the 'wharf' into the water.

'It took a while for the locals to forgive me for that,' he recalls. 'But eventually I was able to convince them that it really was an accident. I put it to them that I'd done them a favour. If the wharf was that unstable it was likely that sooner or later one of their trucks would have dropped into the rusted innards of the wreck and maybe killed a few people.'

There was no shortage of other wrecks along the beaches of Rabaul Harbour. But the problem was that the harbour was the crater of an extinct volcano and the underwater profile was shaped like a cone. The water deepened rapidly from the shore plummeting down to depths too deep for Hatcher's basic scuba gear.

One particular wreck almost cost him dearly.

'It was wooden and I thought that was pretty strange,' he remembers. 'Then I found that the winch on the foredeck was brass and the anchor and anchor chain were bronze! It really threw me. Why should a wooden vessel have all this expensive gear? Then I twigged. Of course! It was a minesweeper, constructed of wood and non-magnetic materials to avoid magnetic mines. It turned out to be a real bonanza!'

He found that not only were the fittings brass or bronze, but that the whole cabin section was constructed of brass panels. She yielded no less than 15 tons of brass.

However he almost paid a heavy price. Like many young divers he had become nonchalant about time spent at the bottom of the ocean. He had been warned of the risk of the bends but privately thought it couldn't happen to him. The stern of the mine-sweeper was quite deep. One afternoon Hatcher worked deeper and later and longer than usual. He came up, towelled off, refilled his scuba tanks and began to make his evening meal. Suddenly he paused, unable to believe for a moment what was happening to him.

'I began to get a tingling in my fingers. I tried to ignore it, thinking, imagination. It will just go away.' But the tingling persisted and now pain began to spread up his arms. Something was seriously wrong and he knew at once the likely cause.

Hatcher had read about decompression sickness and knew all too well it was the major occupational hazard of the deep sea diver. Over the years thousands of divers in all parts of the world had died from decompression sickness. Countless others had been paralysed. Some losing the use of limbs, others becoming paraplegics or even quadriplegics. Crippled for life. Helmet divers of the old copper 'hard hat' days were traditionally stooped and bent in retirement, racked with pain in their joints.

Between the years 1910 and 1917 a staggering 145 pearl divers died in north-western Australia. Casualty rates were equally high in the Torres Straits in Queensland, Darwin and other Australian pearl diving locations. At Broome in one year, 1914, in a fleet of 400 vessels, 33 men died from decompression sickness. There was no record of how many others were crippled.

Modern divers are equally vulnerable and the pain of the bends, causing cramps and muscle spasms, has been described by one pearl diver as, 'the worst form of pain you could ever suffer. Because as bad as it might be, at the time, you were always afraid it was going to get worse'. Sometimes the pain became uncontrollable. Screams in the night when the pearling fleet lay to at anchor could only mean one thing.

The public are generally aware that an attack of decompression sickness can be the penalty for diving too deep and too long. If properly trained, divers are aware of the actual physical reasons. The knowledge is necessary for their long-term survival and is compulsory today in all diving courses. Hatcher had learned as part of his scuba course that the air we breath is composed of various gases, most significantly oxygen and nitrogen. Oxygen absorbed through our lungs is the life-force that keeps us going while nitrogen does not play a significant part in our ordinary environmental pressure of 1 Atmosphere (33 pounds per square inch). But nitrogen becomes a concern for divers when atmospheric pressures are increased, because given sufficient pressure and sufficient time, nitrogen changes from a gas into a solution.

When diving, the weight of water on a diver's body at 10 metres is double the pressure at the surface. At 30 metres there is three times the surface atmospheric pressure. At that depth nitrogen can become a solution and the liquid can be absorbed into the bloodstream after a certain time below. This runs harmlessly enough in the veins and arteries until the time comes to ascend. Should the diver come up too quickly, the concentration of nitrogen increases, fizzing in the bloodstream like the bubbles in an uncorked bottle of champagne.

Nitrogen bubbles expanding too quickly in the bloodstream can block arteries feeding the joints and the spinal column, or in the brain. Pressing on nerves they can cause agonising cramps and pain. They can also cause a stroke, heart stoppage or paralysis. Scientists discovered the correlation between nitrogen absorption and deep sea diving early in the century, and they also found the cure. In Britain an eminent physiologist, Professor JS Haldane, drew up a series of tables for Royal Navy divers. If a diver stayed past a certain 'safe' time at depth, tables showed how he should slow his ascent to allow the nitrogen to work itself safely out of the bloodstream.

That knowledge, the use of diving tables, passed on to the pearling industry and the donation of a recompression chamber by the diving dress manufacturer Heinke Pty Ltd, of London, reduced the diver deaths in Broome from 33 in 1914 to an average of one per year. Today all diving, commercial and recreational, uses tables which are revised and updated periodically.

Modern commercial divers either work with a combination of gases called 'mixture' with helium replacing the nitrogen or they are placed in 'recompression' chambers upon reaching the surface. There they breathe oxygen under pressure while they are gradually brought back to the surface pressure of 1 Atmosphere.

Chambers attached to hospitals in most areas of the world where diving is carried out are also used for medical treatment of divers who have misjudged their time and suffered an onset of decompression sickness.

Mike Hatcher, shrouded in the darkness of *Islander III*, in Rabaul Harbour, knew that he was hundreds of miles from the nearest decompression chamber at Thursday Island. He also knew that he had perhaps only minutes to take decisive action. In either event he could die on the deck because it would be morning before anyone ashore was aware that there was anything seriously wrong.

'It was one of the worst moments of my life,' he recalls. 'I cursed myself a thousand times for my foolishness. I was very aware at that moment that I'd become increasingly casual about reading my tables and observing my bottom times. It didn't matter so much in the shallow water in which I had been working. But now I was at the deep end of the wreck. The danger is always that you're not initially aware that anything has gone wrong. After a time you dive with an attitude. She'll be right, mate. It might happen to other people but it doesn't happen to me. Then one day – bingo!

'Suddenly, you know you're in trouble. At that point it's too late to be sorry or for any vain regrets. (And, believe me, you have plenty of those.) If there's no medical help available there's only one remedial action you can take. You have to get back over the side. And if it's night time and the water is black as ink and you're scared shitless that's just too bad! You do it or die.'

The remedy was all too familiar in the pearling fleet days. But conditions were vastly different in Rabaul Harbour where Hatcher was on his own with *Islander III* anchored to a wreck, now invisible at night in the black water 20 metres below her keel. The 'cure' consisted of going down deep enough again to find sufficient depth and water pressure for the nitrogen bubbles to be re-absorbed, then to ascend slowly, very slowly, to the surface until the nitrogen was mercifully released from the bloodstream and breathed harmlessly out through the bubbles rising from the diver's mouthpiece. The more time and the slower the ascent, the better the chances of a complete recovery.

'I was terrified,' Hatcher admits. 'I had no light. I couldn't see my hand in front of my face. I couldn't even read my watch to tell the time. All I could do was go hand over hand by feeling down the anchor chain to the bottom. From there I had to work my way slowly upwards. I had a 70-cubic-foot tank and reckoned I could get an hour and ten minutes of air out of that. I calculated that I had to stage at 30, 20, and 10 feet. But in the dark I could only guess.

'My biggest worry was that my arms, where the pains started, could become paralysed or too weak and I'd let go of the anchor chain in the darkness. If that happened I wouldn't know where I was. I'd be lost in a void of blackness not knowing what was up and what was down. I was also concerned about the sharks. Rabaul Harbour is full of them and the tiger sharks grow up to five metres. They were OK in the daylight when I was working, but the popular theory was that they hunted at night. There I was diving blind, a sitting target for any of them, large or small, that liked to try a taste.'

(To the sharks night or day made little difference. They have delicate sensory receptors in their noses called the 'ampullae of lorenzini' to enable them to detect obstacles or other animal life in total darkness.)

Clinging to the anchor chain Hatcher saw phosphorescent shapes, some frighteningly large, whizzing by in streaks and flashes. Whether they were sharks, dolphins, big fish, or shoals of squid he never knew. By guesswork he gradually ascended the chain. In the final stage, three metres below the surface, he could see the comforting dark shape of the boat and the faint twinkle of the stars.

And he was deeply grateful to be alive.

'I had a lot of time to think, and a lot to think about,' he recalls. 'That particular experience has stayed in my mind throughout my diving career so strongly that I haven't made that mistake again.'

At long last the scuba tank was expended and the tingling and the pains were gone. Michael Hatcher dragged his weary body over the side of *Islander III*. His gear was dropped in a sodden heap on the deck, and he collapsed into his bunk, mentally and physically exhausted.

A lesson well and truly learned.

CHAPTER FOUR

Land Sharks Bite Harder

With the attack of the bends behind him, a wiser Mike Hatcher had become a fully-fledged salvage diver. He still had a lot to learn, but by now he knew the basics of the trade. And some of the dangers. He had also changed direction in a literal sense. Where previously he had intended to sail on and on into the rising sun in the traditional yachtsman's east-about-circumnavigation of the world, he had now decided instead to go west-about around the northern tip of New Guinea with the old colonial capital of Singapore as his ultimate goal.

Where he once had no particular career ambition other than travelling, Hatch now saw his future in salvage. Rabaul had been good to him, depositing thousands of dollars into his pockets. But the real riches, according to the other divers, were to be found in the Malacca Strait and the South China Sea. The waters there, they said, were littered with wartime wrecks. Most had bronze propellers, all had copper piping in their boiler condenser tubes and some carried valuable cargoes of rubber, tin and copper. Sunken German and Japanese submarines were reputed to have been carrying mercury and gold in the last desperate days of the war.

All were worth money. A lot of money. Millions, in fact.

But what most appealed to the young Michael Hatcher was not the money so much as the adventure. With his own boat, as master of his own fate, he now saw the waters of the Indonesian Archipelago and Malaysia as his great opportunity.

He did have some pangs about leaving Rabaul – he had cut his teeth there in salvage diving after all. He had also made a number of good friends including Pat Roberts, one of the great characters of the islands. But he was driven on chiefly by ambition ... though there were other reasons why it wouldn't be such a bad idea to be on the move again.

For instance, there was the matter of the girls' basketball team. 'There was a young missionary in Rabaul who used to come diving with me from time to time,' Hatcher recalls. 'One day he said, "We're looking for someone to coach the girls' basketball team. I'd like you to think about it."

'Who me?' Hatcher replied in surprise. 'I don't know anything about basketball.'

'That doesn't matter,' said the missionary. 'The girls are keen and they just need a little encouragement. You'll pick up the basics as you go along. Think of it as community service. Putting something back.'

'I'll give it a go,' said Hatcher doubtfully.

It became more interesting than he had anticipated. 'After practice the missionary used to keep one or two of the best-looking girls back for "extra coaching". The girls were lovely, all islanders with big happy smiles, white teeth flashing in dark faces. They didn't have a lot of skills, but they bounced about the court with great enthusiasm. You would have had to have been a saint not to notice that some of them were pretty well endowed.' Mike Hatcher did notice that some of the girls who were kept back for 'extra coaching' were still around the Manse in the morning. 'Little alarm bells began to ring,' he recalls.

Finally he confronted the missionary.

'Hey,' he said. 'I thought you were a man of God?'

'So I am, Mike, so I am.'

'But these girls ... this *extra* coaching? Does it take all night?'

The missionary winked at him. 'It's in the bible, mate. Look it up. The Lord said go forth and multiply!' There was a song, popular at the time, called *Multiplication*. The theme expressed was 'Multiplication is the name of the game!' The missionary may have had the pleasure in following the song's instructions, but there was pain, inevitably, to follow. Multiplication was indeed the result of his ministrations.

'Suddenly about half the basketball team was pregnant,' Hatcher recalls. 'All hell broke loose. The missionary got the sack, and everyone was looking for someone else to blame. As the former coach of the basketball team – a very ex-coach, I can tell you, by this time – my own position didn't look too good. It was time to be moving on.'

So Mike and his one crewmember – a nurse by the name of Ruth – readied *Islander III* and they left Rabaul Harbour and nosed their way up the New Guinea coast. On his way Hatcher picked up a United Nations charter carrying officials surveying coconut plantations in Irian Jaya, the former Dutch New Guinea.

'The people came out to greet us. They thought the Dutch were coming back. But European colonial rule was over. They got the Indonesians as their new masters, changing one for the other.'

There was an idyllic sojourn in Bali. 'It was before the real tourist boom. I was the only yacht in the harbour. That made me really popular. For a while we became part of the local scene. There was a band called The Prophecy with some of the president's [Sukarno's] kids playing in it. I remember we went out once for a night cruise with the band. After an evening of moonlight and soft music and quite a bit to drink the moon went down and I couldn't find the way back into the harbour ... We had to drift around until daylight.'

Hatcher was delayed in his bid to reach Singapore by a factor with which he would become very familiar in the future – the monsoon. At that time of year, trying to sail north, the north-east monsoon was right in his face. Like the sailing ships of yesteryear he found he would have to wait for a gap in the change of direction of the trade winds or for the south-east monsoon which would blow him up to Singapore and the Malacca Strait. He managed, with difficulty, to get as far as Jakarta but there he was stuck, at least for the time being.

He and Ruth went ashore to have dinner with the skipper of an oil company survey vessel. While they were being entertained, thieves broke into *Islander III* and stole all their money and clothes. It was a major setback. Generously, the skipper gave them money and fuel and an introduction to Don Gillies, the manager of a company called Petrosea. As the name indicated, the company was involved in oil exploration, construction work and various other marine enterprises. As a consequence of this fortuitous meeting, Mike Hatcher spent six months in Sumatra in 1971 building roads and bridges, his Snowy Mountains experience once again standing him in good stead.

Most of Sumatra was still jungle, and the road was going through thick forest and rough terrain. Three Indonesian surveyors worked ahead of the construction teams.

'One morning when I drove into work in my jeep there was a hell of a commotion down the track ahead of the work gangs,' Hatcher recalls. 'I went to see what the problem was and there was one of the Indonesian surveyors lying on the ground in a big pool of blood and the other two were up a tree.'

The labourers were all pointing to the jungle and rolling their eyes in fear till only the whites showed. Hatcher asked them what had happened.

'They just kept pointing. The bloke on the ground looked sort of strange. I couldn't work it out for a moment. Then I realised he had no head, apart from the fact that he had been eviscerated.'

'Tiger, tiger!' said the workers, finding their voices and jabbing their fingers towards the green wall of the jungle. The surveyors had been working ahead of the road gang and sleeping in a tent with the ends open. The previous evening they had been sitting in their tent when a tiger suddenly appeared out of the night, pounced on the unfortunate surveyor nearest the entrance and dragged him outside. The other two screamed and ran up a tree while the tiger began to eat their companion before their very eyes.

'I could tell from the expressions on the faces of the work gang that it was their opinion that the tiger hadn't gone any distance and was probably watching us from cover. The surveyors wouldn't come down from the tree, so we had to bring it down with a chainsaw. We sent them home because even after they'd recovered from their state of shock they were useless. We had to get replacements sent up. For a long time after that no-one wandered too far from camp.

'As for the surveyor, we buried him and notified head office. There was nothing more we could do for him. Sumatra was that kind of place in those days. There were a few more risks than on the ordinary construction job. You could add poisonous snakes, pythons, crocodiles and scorpions to the list.'

There were other risks as well. It was only five years since the major communist uprising had been savagely put down by President Sukarno's supporters. Deaths throughout Indonesia totalled many thousands in what became a civil war, a life-or-death struggle for power. There had been a Sumatran rebellion in 1958, and the northern island was traditionally fiercely independent and antagonistic to rule from Java. Under the Suharto government which followed Sukarno's fall from grace after the uprising, the police and army (with the approval of the western powers then engaged against communist insurgents in Borneo, Malaysia and Vietnam) actively suppressed any signs of a communist resurgence.

Hatcher hardly expected politics or banditry to intrude on his jungle roadworks, but there came the day when the local chief of police and his aides arrived in a jeep and a cloud of dust.

'They lined the workers up and began interrogating them,' Hatcher recalls. 'After a time they had about a dozen segregated and sent the others back to work.' The chief of police came over to Hatcher. 'He spoke good English and asked me if they could borrow one of our trucks. He was very polite about it. But there was the matter of the sub-machine gun slung from his shoulder.

'"You've got the machine gun," I replied. "You can do anything you like. Will I get the truck back?"

'"Oh, yes. We only need it for a little while."

'So they loaded the guys into the truck and went off down the road towards the river. Sometime later they brought the truck back. It was empty.

'"Will you be taking any more?" I asked the chief, wondering whether we would be left short of workers.

'He shook his head and smiled. "You won't have any more trouble," he said.

'"Trouble?"

'"Yes," he smiled again. "Those were bad men. Did you know they were going to murder you tonight?"'

❀

In Sumatra Hatcher was earning $US5000 dollars a month (providing he was alive to claim it) – a small fortune in the 1970s. But he was determined to succeed at ocean salvage, and convinced Petrosea to put up the funds for a salvage on the wreck of a vessel called *Loch Ranza*. She had sailed south from Singapore at the time of the Japanese invasion but had been caught by the Japanese amongst the islands in the Riou Strait and burst into flames when she was shelled. She was carrying aviation fuel on deck and the crew quickly and sensibly abandoned ship and went ashore in the boats. The ship carried on until she hit a reef and ended up lying with her bow and superstructure out of the water. The Japanese cut all the topsides off and salvaged the steel, but there was no record of any salvage of her cargo of tin.

Loch Ranza was believed to have been carrying 200 tons of tin, worth approximately $43,000 a ton, or a total of $8,600,000. There was no record of any salvage and Hatcher was certain it was still there. If he were right, his share was to be wages plus (he thought) a 17.5 per cent commission. The company paid expenses.

'I arrived in the area,' Hatcher recalls, 'not exactly in grand style. The survey "vessel" allocated was a local wooden boat with a 50-horsepower outboard motor. But we had to make a start somewhere and finding the wreck was the first step. I went to the nearest village and asked the head man if he knew of any shipwrecks in the area. He said he'd show me and beckoned me to follow. There hanging up in the village was the ship's bell with the name *Loch Ranza* written across it. It seemed almost too easy.'

The wreck was lying in fairly shallow water, bows on to the reef, the stern in deeper water. The superstructure was gone as Hatcher had been told. But the holds still seemed to be sealed. At first glance it looked like an easy job, but as things eventuated the salvage of *Loch Ranza* proved otherwise.

'The company brought a barge down to work the wreck,' Hatcher recalls. 'There was a 50-ton crane and a grab to pick up the tin in the holds. We figured it would be a breeze and I was itching to get started. But because Petrosea was doing a lot of work in Indonesia, including the main road in Sumatra, they had to be very careful about protocol with the Indonesian government. They were given a licence to work the wreck on a share basis. The government sent along an Indonesian lieutenant and some soldiers to make sure that everything was done properly.'

Loch Ranza was a big 7000-ton merchantman with nine holds. Her bow rose out of the water, the propeller lying at 75 feet. Hatcher salvaged that and it weighed in at some 27 tons of bronze. She was also carrying aero engines, solder, long lengths of bar brass, whisky, beer and general supplies for Singapore.

When she reached her destination there was widespread panic – the Japanese were bombarding and the city was only two days away from falling. *Loch Ranza's* main cargo was stowed deep within the ship, but the tin was loaded in a hold on top of it and the aeroplane fuel was loaded on deck. The million dollar question was which hold was the tin in?

They blew some exploratory holes in her side, but there was such a jumble of various cargo that they were none the wiser. The Indonesian lieutenant suggested they try the 'Bomo' – the witchdoctor. They had nothing to lose, Hatcher reasoned, and so the local witchdoctor was brought along. He performed an impressive ceremony with spells and incantations.

'The tin is in the Hold No 3,' he finally announced through an interpreter.

'Is that the third hold from the bow? Or is it counted from the stern?' Hatcher asked.

'Oh, my magic isn't that strong!' replied the witchdoctor.

Explosives were placed to blow the hatches off and open the decks so that the grab could probe the holds. It coincided with the arrival of some senior Indonesian officials anxious to see the work in progress. The lieutenant was equally anxious to impress them. 'Make sure it's a big bang,' he told Hatcher.

'It will be,' said Mike. 'I can promise you that. But first we have to move the barge back a bit.'

'It will take too long,' the lieutenant demurred. 'You are not very brave,' he added.

'Suit yourself,' growled Hatcher. 'I'll just tell you that I'm not staying on board if it stays where it is!'

'I'm with you!' said the cook as Hatcher got down into the speedboat, and he jumped in too.

The explosion went off with a mighty roar.

'The barge lifted three feet out of the water,' Hatcher recalls. 'And all the rust, which was about all that was holding it together, fell off. The crane jumped three feet off the deck and when it came down the boom whammed down on the cabin top where the VIPs were gathered and crushed the roof. The counterweight fell off the crane and almost went through the deck.'

The visitors were understandably shaken and visibly pale. The lieutenant's apologies failed to remove their frowns as they called for immediate transport to the shore. Or some safer place.

'In one of the holes there were crates of beer and kegs of White Horse Whiskey,' Hatcher recalls. 'It was still good and we were drinking it on board. The lieutenant insisted that we get a clearance and the local health inspector came out to see whether it was suitable for human consumption.'

Hatcher suggested they do a deal, a 70–30 split, which seemed fair enough to him. The inspector however presumed he would take 70 and Hatcher 30, and when he wouldn't budge Hatcher dropped a charge into the hold, effectively quashing the deal. The inspector, naturally enough, was horrified, and said that he would have negotiated, but it was too late and he had missed his chance.

Eventually the precious cargo of tin was located and the witchdoctor was proven to be right ... depending on which end of the vessel the hole count was taken from. In any event the salvage had aroused a lot of local interest. Kegs of whisky – some still intact – and bottles of beer had been bobbing on the tide and soon enough boats came from the surrounding villages to scavenge what they could. Keen eyes noted the ingots of tin rising in piles on the deck. Tin had been mined in Indonesia for hundreds of years and the locals were well aware of the value, which at the time of the salvage was $US43,000 per ton. This translated into $US26 an ingot, each one about the size of a housebrick. That amount of money could keep an Indonesian family going for months. The temptation was obvious.

'The soldiers were supposed to guard the tin at night but one evening I got up after hearing a noise outside and there were two praus alongside loading tin as fast as they could go. The soldiers were asleep. I yelled out and we managed to grab the closest boat and a couple of the thieves – the others dived overboard. But the other boat, fully loaded, was off down stream. There was a big hole in the tin on deck. I reckoned that they'd got away with about a ton. That was a huge amount and the lieutenant and I were really angry. We'd both been made fools of and $44,000 worth of tin had gone down the creek! The lieutenant began questioning one of the guys they'd captured. He was totally arrogant, contemptuous, in fact. He said they'd never find the tin, he wasn't going to tell them anything and that they had no right to hold him.

'They cuffed him around a bit, but he seemed to almost enjoy it. He was being the Humphrey Bogart tough guy. I could see it was all going nowhere so I stepped up and said I knew how to get him to talk. The lieutenant looked at me in disbelief. But I said "Give me a try" and since he'd failed there was no other option.

'"What do you want?" he said in surly tones.

'"First of all get his pants off."

'They looked at me hard. Indonesians are very private. The divers even shower in their bathing togs. They go to great lengths to avoid being seen naked. I was counting on that.

'"Get his pants off!"

Now the grin had disappeared from the suspect's face and he was looking distracted and unhappy.

'"Have two soldiers hold his arms and get the biggest knife from the galley!"

'The knife was brought and now the suspect turned green. I'm not sure whether apprehension or embarrassment was the stronger emotion.

'"Maybe you'll tell us now?" I suggested, waving the knife towards his family jewels. He still shook his head, but with a good deal less conviction.

'"OK. Off they come!" I cried with the right amount of

Captain Mike Hatcher with a beautiful *Tek Sing* bowl looking as though it came out of the kiln yesterday. *Restless M* is in the background.

(© HUGH EDWARDS)

Brother David and baby Michael Hatcher. (© MICHAEL HATCHER)

Hatcher the impish
schoolboy.
(© MICHAEL HATCHER)

Hawaiian night at the Manly Surf Club. Hatcher, on the left, was the organiser. 'A great night until someone ripped off my grass skirt!' (© MICHAEL HATCHER)

Mike Hatcher and his sister Jessie at her wedding. A red-letter day for both of them. (© MICHAEL HATCHER)

Tally-Ho, the famous British submarine which sank the German U-IT 23.
(© IMPERIAL WAR MUSEUM)

Commander LWA Bennington at the periscope. A lucky shot at extreme
distance sank the former *Reginaldo Giuliani*. (© IMPERIAL WAR MUSEUM)

German submarine U–537 was sunk in the Java Sea. None of the Monsoon Fleet made it back to Germany. (© IMPERIAL WAR MUSEUM)

Een duik in het verlede

Eindelijk weet Hans Besançon waar zijn vader en drieëndertig anderen in de oorlog hun zeemans hebben gevonden. Een combinatie van wonderbaarlijk toeval, een dosis geluk en de hulp van eer derne piratenbende, voerde hem naar dat plekje in de Zuidchinese Zee, waar de onderzeeboot van vader, de K XVII, vijftig meter lager met een kapotte neus in het zand steekt. Een dramatische exped

K XVII

Dutch submarine K XVII, sunk by a mine north of Tioman Island, pictured in *Panorama* magazine. Inset is Commander Besançon. When Hatcher found the sub, Besançon's son Hans made the long journey from the Netherlands to visit his father's sea grave. (© Panorama)

TEKST: REINIER HOPMANS – FOTO'S: MARTIN PATERNOTTE E.A.

Hans Besançon vindt het oorlogsgraf van zijn vader

Harer Majesteits *K XVII* is terecht! Na eenenveertig jaar met man en muis vermist te zijn geweest. De ongelukkige Nederlandse onderzeeboot ligt op de bodem van de Zuidchinese Zee, dik twee uur stomen noordelijk van het eiland Tioman, voor de kust van Maleisië. Op 03° 10,4' noord en 104° 12,89' oost om precies te zijn. Vijftig meter diep. Met in zijn neus een gat waardoor een vrachtwagen naar binnen kan. En met in zijn buik de gebeenten van de mannen die mee naar de kelder gingen.

De tijd verstrijkt tergend traag. Al twintig minuten wachten we op het boven water komen van Mike, die via de telefoonlijn met triomfantelijke stem heeft gemeld: *I've got the steering wheel.* Ik heb het stuurwiel!
Via de luidspreker horen we het gorgelend geluid van zijn ademhaling. De koperen ploert brandt ongenadig. De morsige kotter onder onze voeten deint op de cadans van het water. Duizenden pinkellichtjes plagen de ogen. En moeder wat is het heet!
Hans Besançon staat met de benen een stukje uiteen op het achterdek, het bovenlichaam licht voorovergebogen. Hij zegt niks, maar zijn houding verraadt een zekere spanning. Ik weet waaraan hij denkt.
't Is wat, om na veertig jaar eindelijk vast te kunnen stellen waar je ouwe heer ligt. Een paar dagen eerder had hij het zo gezegd. Dit is geen moment om vragen te stellen. Wat zou ik moe-

Hans Besançon and Mike Hatcher receive local knowledge on the location of submarine wrecks. (© PANORAMA)

Hans Besançon deep in thought as he studies the bronze helm of K XVII.
His father must have handled the wheel many times. (© PANORAMA)

A rock in the middle of the sea off the Malaysian coast ... (© MICHAEL HATCHER)

... became a refuge for shipwrecked boat people from Vietnam.
(© MICHAEL HATCHER)

Hatcher puts a sick girl into a life jacket before plunging with her into the surf towards a waiting inflatable.
(© MICHAEL HATCHER)

Rescued boat people show their joy at their salvation. Many others drowned or were killed by pirates. (© MICHAEL HATCHER)

LEFT PAGE: Raising an anchor from a 17th century wreck in the Malacca Strait.
(© MICHAEL HATCHER)

THIS PAGE: Broken cannon mark the site of a furious naval battle between the Dutch and Portuguese off Malacca in competition for the spice trade.
(© MICHAEL HATCHER)

Mike Hatcher checks the inscription on an ancient bronze gun.

(© MICHAEL HATCHER)

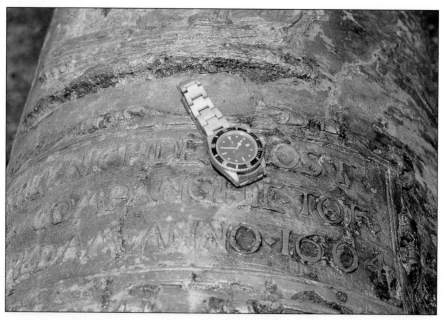

A Malacca Strait cannon dated 1604. (© MICHAEL HATCHER)

Sea growth is cleaned off the bronze guns with a high-pressure hose.
(© MICHAEL HATCHER)

Mike Hatcher beside bronze guns in pristine condition. A joy for divers and
historians alike. (© MICHAEL HATCHER)

Damage to the fore part of the gun shows the force of the explosion which sank the vessel. (© Michael Hatcher)

Latin inscription on a bronze gun with the date 1589. (© Michael Hatcher)

fierceness. I jumped forward with the kitchen knife but as the steel touched the sensitive areas a remarkable transformation took place.

'"No! No!" he cried. "I tell! I tell!"

'His sole condition was that he could have a towel wrapped around his nakedness. Then he sang like a little bird. Of course I wouldn't have made a eunuch out of him, but this was Indonesia. The interesting thing was that the lieutenant and the soldiers were quite unmoved. I'm sure they thought I was fair dinkum. At any rate no-one jumped forward to prevent me going ahead, or even protested. The lieutenant was all smiles at the result.'

The next morning the first speedboat took Hatcher, the lieutenant and the soldiers with their sub-machine guns to the village named by the informant. Predictably, everyone there denied all knowledge, but Hatcher saw a pile of fishing nets, and sure enough, hidden underneath, was the entire ton of tin. The man in a nearby house immediately fled and was given chase by the soldiers who began firing their sub-machine guns.

'I took off after the guy with the soldiers shooting wildly behind me,' Hatcher recalls. 'I stopped to tell them to quit firing – they were more likely to hit me! – and the bloke sprinted to the end of the jetty and dived off. Bad move. The tide was out. When I got to the end of the jetty I saw there was about a 15-foot drop and less than a meter of water. I sort of belly-flopped in and touched something on the way.

'The guys on the jetty shouted down to me that the escapee had "magic" and was going to swim underwater to some praus about half a mile off-shore. "If he's that good," I said, "he can go free." I've often wondered since whether what I touched underwater was the other guy. Whether I could have saved him if I'd realised that at the time.'

The man did not reach the praus and three days later his body floated back to shore. He had either broken his neck or been knocked unconscious in the dive.

'Of course they blamed me as the foreigner,' Hatcher recalls. 'We got our tin back but the local mood had turned sour. We'd just about finished the job when the lieutenant told me that there would be an official inquiry into the death. The only friendly witness on my side would be me, and I didn't trust the lieutenant or his sidekicks. Whichever way you looked at it I was going to be greatly outnumbered when it came to giving testimony. That night I chucked my gear into the speedboat and took off for Singapore. The company put me on a plane for Australia the next day. They said they were looking after my best interests.'

Meanwhile, the salvage had turned out to be a bonanza for the company. The tin was sold for $US seven million, a healthy profit given the cost of the salvage operation was less than $US200,000. When Hatcher rang from Australia to inquire about his share he had thought he was on a retainer plus 17.5 per cent commission.

'No, no, Mr Hatcher,' said the company secretary. 'You must be mistaken. Your share was to be $17,500.'

'There wasn't anything I could do. They had me cold. There was nothing in writing. I was in Australia at a time of poor communications, and they were a world away in Singapore. They could also always bring up the question of why I had left Indonesia without a clearance. I just had to put it down to experience.'

❁

Hatcher soon bought another boat and with Paul Rand, who had been diving with him in Indonesia, formed an Australian salvage company. They landed a contract doing diving work on a new jetty in Mackay, but when they got there they were told that the unions had placed a black ban on them because they had failed to take out membership. Hatcher was less than impressed and immediately upped and left for Singapore once again.

He went through Darwin four weeks before Cyclone Tracy

struck on Christmas Eve, 1974. It registered 262 kilometres an hour winds, the highest recorded on the Australian continent up to that time. The town was destroyed, with 80 per cent of domestic buildings blown away or damaged beyond repair. In Darwin Harbour the cyclone claimed HMAS *Arrow*, a 33-metre naval patrol vessel, as well as ferries, steel trawlers, fishing vessels and other small craft. More than 100 people died and the town had to be evacuated and later completely rebuilt. If Mike Hatcher had been anywhere in the vicinity he would surely have perished along with his vessel. But, with the usual Hatcher luck, he was well clear before the fatal storm.

❀

On the Malaysian coast he eked out a living as a yacht club diver, fixing moorings, retrieving lost outboard motors and doing general diving work. Unknown to him, his first major salvage was just around the corner.

One night he was awoken by a frantic knocking on his cabin roof. He roused himself to find an Indian chauffeur urging Hatcher to follow him quickly. Mystified, he grabbed his diving gear and was driven in a Mercedes far out of town to an expanse of water where a huge tin dredge was working.

'I could see at once what the problem was. The tin dredges are huge, as big as a 10-storey hotel – floating factories with heaps of engines and machinery on top of big pontoons. This one was leaning sideways at a crazy angle and looked ready to turn right over at any moment. Obviously it had a leak in one of the pontoons and this was why I had been summoned. They had pumps trying to get the water level down, but it was coming in from somewhere as fast as they could get it out.' Hatch considered the situation. 'I had grave doubts. It was so big and it looked bloody dangerous. But it was my first big job.'

He agreed to give it a go and got down inside the pontoon. It was pitch black, he had no light and all around him were the creaks and groans of stressed metal, ready to tear apart at any second. Working by feel he eventually located the crack in the pontoon welding which was the major leak. He asked for some bags of local clay, plugged up the crack, then pumped her out, straightened her up, and put a coffer dam around the leak area, eventually welding a patch over it. An excellent result.

Needless to say, the company was delighted and put Hatcher up in a luxurious hotel for the night. The next day, the manager paid him a visit.

'How much do you want?' he asked, after some preliminary niceties.

'What do you think is a fair thing?' countered Hatcher at that point, having no idea of the value of his efforts.

'How about $30,000? After all, you saved her.'

Hatcher fought to control his elation. He had never thought of such a sum. 'Sounds all right to me,' he replied, trying to keep his voice calm.

'You can stay in the hotel again tonight,' said the grateful manager spontaneously, and Hatcher realised he could probably have negotiated for more. In future years he would play his cards better. 'Never settle for the first offer' was a philosophy that from that moment on went into his mental wisdom bank. But there were no regrets. The operation helped to build his reputation and people soon began coming to him with other jobs as a result.

❀

Mike Hatcher has always been interested in 'technical innovations' in the diving and salvage industries. A cement which could be used underwater had been developed in Europe but didn't work well in the tropics because it set too quickly. Hatcher worked out that by carrying it in a bag of ice the setting would be delayed and it could be effectively applied. This seemingly straight-forward technique earned him jobs on Malayan rubber plantations in the 1970s where repairs were needed on floodgates. The planters still lived a lordly life like the 'pukks sahibs' of pre-war days, with spacious bungalows and plenty of servants to do their bidding. One of them introduced Hatch to a different kind of innovation.

'We were sitting out in the garden some distance from the house,' he recalls, 'and the planter was having a gin and tonic at the end of the day.' Hatcher was asked what he'd like to drink and replied that a beer would be good. A few moments later, as if by magic, an Indian servant appeared, resplendent in turban and white uniform with a beer on a silver tray.

Hatcher blinked. 'I say, that's service!' he observed.

The planter smiled knowingly under his moustache. A little while later, his wife came out to join them. Her husband asked her what she would like to drink, and again, almost instantly, the turbaned servant appeared with her drink, and without apparent instruction.

'How do you do it?' asked Hatcher, unable to contain himself any longer. 'How does he know what drinks you want, and when you want them?'

'My dear chap!' the planter laughed. 'There's no mystery, it's quite simple really. A little scheme I thought of to make life easier.' He showed Hatch a button on the underside of his chair and a cable leading to a bell in the kitchen. 'One ring is for a gin and tonic,' the planter explained, 'two rings is a Scotch, three a beer and so on. Works like a dream.'

If I ever get rich enough to have servants, Michael Hatcher thought at the time, I'll remember that trick.

❁

He did get rich, but the dollars were a while in coming and there were some false starts. Hatcher found that while he had the skills and ideas necessary for ocean salvage, he had some hard lessons to learn in business. The fact that land sharks bite harder was one of those lessons.

He decided to form his own company late in the 1970s on the basis that he did the diving and contract work, his partners would put up the money, and they would divide the profits. A reasonable proposal, Hatcher thought, with mutual benefits to be shared by all. He asked some of the planters and businessmen he had met in Malaya to be directors and investors. They agreed and in turn introduced Hatcher to a Malaysian gentleman, the brother of the Prince of Selangor.

'He can help smooth things with the government if there are ever any problems,' they suggested. 'We may be able to get the licence for all Malaysian waters.'

'Good idea,' said Hatch. 'That's the way to go.'

He bought *Seeker I*, a concrete ex-trawler from Vietnam, later named 'The Rat boat', to use as an operations vessel. His share was to be 32 per cent and this time he got it in writing. He had four divers and *Seeker I* was soon engaged profitably in recovering brass and copper from wrecks and oil company charters. One oil company job alone brought in $350,000.

When Hatcher returned to port, after six months spent mainly at sea, he found that the company had set up bright new offices. They had bought the prince's brother a stretched Mercedes limousine and a couple of the other directors were also sporting new cars.

'Where's my dividend and the crew's wages?' asked Hatcher.

'Well at the moment there's no cash in credit,' was the reply. 'But don't worry, it will be taken care of with the next job.'

'You mean there's no money? None at all? You've spent the lot?' Hatcher was incredulous.

'Now don't take it like that, old boy,' the tone was sharper. 'We had to get things on a proper footing. You just let us handle the finances and you'll be taken care of.'

There was a pause while Hatcher's brown eyes turned to ice.

'By the way what *is* your next job?'

'There's none,' said Hatcher, barely trusting himself to speak.

'There isn't one. I'm finished.' He spun on his heel and walked out. Then he took the boat and crew, and blew the 27-ton propeller off a recent wreck in the Malacca Strait. Returning to port he sold the bronze scrap, paid his divers and waited angrily to see what the future held.

❁

Even after parting with the company, the problems were far from over. The company still technically existed and owned *Seeker I* and the salvage gear. Hatcher had nothing. It was while he was still seething with anger and wondering whether there was an honest person left in the world that he was contacted by an urbane Chinese accountant named Soo Hin Ong.

'We own you now,' said Ong by way of introduction.

'What do you mean?'

'My principals have bought the company which employs you and owns the boat. Your directors, by majority shareholding, voted to sell the company. We bought it.'

'The hell they did!'

'Yes. It's quite simple. The question I have to ask, since I understand you have some previous dissatisfactions, is whether you wish to keep operating under a new and perhaps more satisfactory management?'

'What's the alternative?'

Ong shrugged. 'We sell you up.'

'Suppose I agree,' Hatch said slowly. 'What are the terms?'

'Tell me what you want,' said Ong reasonably, 'and I'll see if I can get you a better deal.' He smiled. 'And give you some better financial advice at the same time.'

Ong was a London-educated accountant, and the man he represented – a shadowy figure always in the background – had serious wealth and a possible tax advantage to be gained in an industry as uncertain as underwater salvage. Ong called Hatcher 'the yacht club bum', but, because the company had been sold with the bait that 'Hatcher knows where there is gold!' he was prepared to gamble on behalf of his investor.

'I put it to him straight,' Hatcher says. 'I said it was no use messing about with the kind of second-grade equipment that we had. To accumulate we had to speculate.'

'What do you need?' Ong asked him.

'One of the new side-scan sonars,' Hatch replied. 'And a decent magnetometer.'

'What do they do?'

'The sonar shows you a picture of the seabed and what's on it, including wrecks. The magnetometer registers the presence of iron, even if its buried under sand or coral. Most modern wrecks are steel. Even the older ones had iron cannon and anchors that throw a signal. That, combined with research, is how you find a wreck.'

'And what do these things cost?'

Hatcher told him, and Ong wrote the figures down carefully in a notebook.

'Besides that,' Hatcher continued, 'there's a lot of skill in operating a sonar. I need to go to Norway to do a course. And I need some cash to keep me and the boat going in the meantime.'

Ong considered a moment. 'I think these things can be arranged. I'll come back to you. Meantime here's a thousand dollars to tide you over.'

On those less than certain terms began a partnership which would be rewarding for all concerned.

'We did all kinds of jobs at first,' Hatcher recalls, 'and a lot of them were "no cure, no pay", especially with insurance work. If you succeeded in raising the sunken vessel, found the lost jewellery, or whatever, you got paid. If you didn't, no matter how long you spent at the job or what it cost you, then not a solitary brass razoo came your way. The insurance companies were tough. On one job I was asked to look at a freighter in the Malacca Strait. The claim was for several million dollars. I found that it had been deliberately sunk and the owner had to withdraw his claim or face going to gaol on charges of fraud. It was a big win for the insurance company and they were delighted. Then they quibbled about paying my hotel bill.'

There were countless tragic stories to be found in the shipwrecks. A vessel carrying survivors from the battleships *Prince of Wales* and *Repulse* had been sunk off the east Malayan coast by Japanese aircraft. There was an enormous torpedo hole in the ship's side and within, a mess of wire beds blown into a corner, tangled full of human bones. The occupants had been sunk not once, but twice.

Along the way Hatcher met some memorable characters. One who would loom large in his life, in a literal sense, and despite a less than promising meeting, was a six-foot-seven Swiss surveyor named Max de Rham.

'*Seeker I* wasn't a pretty boat at any time,' Hatcher recalls. 'The basic description "45-foot ex-Vietnamese concrete trawler" says it all. But on this particular day she really looked bad. We were doing a refit and there was rubbish and cardboard boxes and plastic everywhere. She really wasn't fit to go to sea, but a survey charter came up and we had to take it. I was trying to get the boat tidied up when this tall bloke and his offsider appeared on the wharf looking down on us in more senses than one.'

'This boat is filthy – it's a pigsty!' the tall one said in disgust, in heavily-accented English.

'Well that didn't go down too well. Anyway he got his survey gear aboard and continued looking around as though he expected to see snakes and spiders or horse shit or something. Next thing he wants to go out of the harbour to test the gear. "And, by the way," he says, "that won't be part of the charter!"'

Hatcher's short fuse ignited.

'Terrific. Well listen to this! I'm not interested in doing the charter on those terms. You can take yourself and your gear and your handy person off my boat. And good riddance!'

De Rham replied that nothing would please him more. He would be delighted to find another boat, any boat but *Seeker I*. However he did ask whether the gear could stay on board for the moment until he could find another deck to receive it.

'OK!' snarled Hatcher. 'Twenty-four hours, then I start charging storage!' De Rham found a Russian boat at a cheap rate and Hatcher thought no more about it.

Around midnight a couple of days later, Hatch was asleep in his cabin when he was woken by the Malay boatman.

'Captain,' he said, whispering urgently. 'That tall fella is back again.'

'Oh yeah?' said Hatch. 'Then he can piss off again.' He rolled over and prepared to resume his slumbers.

'Tuan, he has brought a carton of beer.'

'Has he indeed.' Hatcher sat up, rubbed the sleep out of his eyes and pulled his shorts on. 'Better see what he wants, I suppose.'

On deck Max proffered a can of Tiger beer. 'I've come to apologise,' he said, 'for the little misunderstanding the other day.'

'Uh huh,' Hatcher replied. 'Misunderstanding? I thought we understood each other pretty well.' However it's hard to drink another man's beer and still stay angry.

'Please let's forget the harsh words.' De Rham was obviously trying very hard.

A couple more Tigers were downed and Hatcher was left wondering what on earth this bloke wanted. Eventually Max came, uncomfortably, to the point. It seemed the Russian boat had broken down and was going nowhere. There was no other boat available in Singapore. *Seeker I* was the last card in the pack. Literally. Would Hatcher reconsider?

'What would you charge me?' Max asked, knowing that Hatcher now had him at his mercy.

'Same price as before,' Hatcher said without hesitation. 'Except that we put these last two days on the charter.'

Later De Rham asked why Hatcher hadn't charged him an arm or a leg.

'That's not the way I do business,' said Hatcher. 'We'd agreed on a fair price before and it was still a fair price. I wasn't going to take advantage of you because of a personal disagreement.'

They finished the carton and in the ensuing months overcame the bad start to become the best of friends. It proved a fruitful relationship. De Rham was an experienced surveyor and had a lot of off-shore oil company work, and Hatcher was able to provide the unlovely but efficient *Seeker I* for his requirements. In time they would be associated with one of the great salvages of the modern era – the 1752 Dutch East Indiaman *Geldermalsen*.

But these were early days.

❀

One incident in particular illustrates the kind of work available to adventurous souls in Singapore in the 1970s.

'We had an oil company survey down Sumatra way,' Hatcher remembers with a smile. 'It was in a wide, shallow bay and Max needed to set up some shore repeater stations for the survey. This involved placing transmitters powered by 12-volt car batteries in the mangroves so that Max could triangulate or whatever it is that surveyors need to do. We were both on a learning curve in the kind of work we were doing. But I'd been at it a bit longer than Max. Learning it the hard way I'd picked up what the locals called a bit more "savvy" than he had.

'The tide was out and I could see a wide band of shallows stretching out from the shore. Max was all for going in right away, but I could foresee some problems.

'"Wait until high tide and I'll give you a hand," I said, "But if you're going in now you're on your own."

'"Why?"

'"You'll see if you try it."

'"Now!" Max insisted. "We get on with it NOW!"

'"OK then. It's your problem."

The tender was taken in to the shallows with Max and the transmitters and the batteries.

'Max hopped over the side. "Give me a battery," he said and then asked, "Why are you laughing?"

'Max started walking ashore, but the further he went the deeper he sank in the blue mangrove mud that lies below the thin surface of sand in many of these tropic bays. This very tall man got shorter and shorter until the water level passed his waist. Finally when I thought we were going to lose him altogether he gasped and let go of the battery. After struggling to extricate himself he just managed to get back to the boat, dripping black mud. One battery was gone forever.

'When the tide came in we took the boat into the mangroves and set the batteries and transmitter up from the dinghy. No trouble. The stations were all chirping away merrily that night. But in the morning there were no signals. The system was dead. Investigation showed that every battery had been stolen, presumably by the locals.'

'The thieving bastards!' Max cried, outraged. 'Let's go ashore and sort them out!'

'Better let me do it,' said Hatch. 'Unless you want to go back to Singapore and get new batteries.'

They went ashore and found the headman of the village and Hatcher told him in no uncertain terms that a very bad man had taken all their batteries. The headman shook his head sorrowfully and agreed that it must have been a very bad person indeed ... a thief of the lowest kind. Hatcher then asked, much to Max's horror, what it would cost to get the batteries back. While Max continued to fume Hatcher negotiated a price of $US100 per battery. It was well over the price of a new battery, but substantially less than the cost of returning to Singapore, which would have been the only alternative.

While De Rham was speechless with anger Hatcher continued his dialogue with the headman. 'And how much would you charge us to see that this theft does not occur again, hmm?'

De Rham found his voice. 'This is blackmail!' he hissed. 'And you are encouraging it!'

'It's the way things have been done here for thousands of years,' said Hatcher. 'We get new batteries, they steal them again. This is the cheapest and best way. We get the job done and everyone stays friends.'

The final blow to Max's pride came after the price for protection had been agreed. After studying his toe-nails impassively for some time, the headman looked up and said, 'OK, but one thing extra. When you go. Batteries stay here.'

'Done,' said Hatcher.

'My God! What a country!' cried de Rham.

The batteries shortly reappeared in their mangrove stations as if by magic, the survey was completed to everyone's satisfaction and the local economy was boosted by the cash commissions and the addition of some high performance 12-volt batteries. The village headman allowed himself a pale smile of victory. The thousand-year-old trading traditions of south-east Asia had been maintained with honour.

CHAPTER FIVE

Diving the Dead U-boats

Mike Hatcher was introduced to the U-IT 23 and the shadowy wraiths of the sunken Monsoon fleet of U-boats through a chance conversation at a dinner party. One evening in 1978 he was invited to the home of Qantas' Singapore Manager John Hill and his wife Evelyn. 'They were really nice people,' Hatcher recalls, 'and it was just unfortunate that all the guests got food poisoning that night.'

Over pre-dinner drinks John Hill and Mike Hatcher were discussing shipwrecks in general, when Hill suddenly exclaimed that there was a book Hatcher just had to read. He went to his study, took the volume down from the shelves and pressed it into Hatcher's hand. Hill reckoned it was a great read, but more importantly, he had a hunch it contained a lot of information about wartime shipping casualties off Malaya that was simply unavailable elsewhere.

Naturally enough, Hatcher was more than a little interested, and after skimming a few pages he asked if he could borrow it. Hill wouldn't hear of it and offered the book to Mike as a gift, wishing him good luck in his hunting.

The book was *The Hunting Submarine* Tally-Ho by Ian

Trenowden, published by William Kimber & Co., of London, in 1974. It was sub-titled *The Fighting Life of HMS* Tally-Ho, and dealt with the exploits of a Royal Navy submarine in the Malacca Strait in 1943 and 1944.

Under a very able commanding officer, Lieutenant Commander LWA Bennington, *Tally-Ho* sank 12,623 tons of enemy shipping, more than 20 per cent of the combined total of all British submarines operating east of Suez. One of her victims was the U-IT 23, sent to the bottom of the Malacca Strait early in 1944. Hatcher knew some of the German subs were carrying valuable cargoes, including shipments of gold and mercury, tin, opium, rubber and wolfram (tungsten), and he wondered whether the U-IT was firstly at a salvageable depth, and secondly whether anyone else had got to her first.

He put her at the top of the list.

He began researching the sub's history, becoming increasingly fascinated as more and more information came to hand. His discreet inquiries – there was no point in letting any of his rivals know of a likely target – seemed to indicate that no-one else had found her down in the murky depths of the Malacca Strait where the currents ebbed and flowed.

The story he pieced together, beginning with Trenowden's book, went back to February 15, 1944. As dawn broke over the Malacca Strait through fine morning mists, the submarine U-IT 23 had surfaced and was steaming up the main shipping channel. She was beginning a 10,000 mile journey to the western French port of Lorient, during the closing stages of the European War. D-Day was only a few months away.

A huge submersible of 1140 tons, she had originally been built in Taranto, Italy, and named *Reginaldo Giuliani*. She had served Mussolini and Italy well in the Mediterranean before the Allies landed in Sicily and Italy and made that sea unsafe for Axis warships. During the war Germany was chronically short of tin, morphine, rubber and wolfram. Japan had plentiful supplies of all these commodities, but she lacked mercury and technology – instruments, machine designs and skilled people.

The exchange of these items between Germany and the Japanese through their captured territories of France, Malaya and Singapore created a unique avenue of trade. At first the goods were transported by merchant ships, but as the Allies gained control of the Atlantic the point was reached where only submarines could get through (or under) the blockade.

Reginaldo Giuliani and four other big Italian submarines, *Capellini*, *Torelli*, *Tuzzoli* and *Barbarigo,* had been sent on outward voyages to Singapore on a non-stop journey from Brest. It was to prove an unfortunate assignation. *Tazzoli* and *Barbarigo* never arrived at all and were presumed sunk by the Allies. *Reginaldo Giuliani*, *Capellini* and *Torelli* reached Singapore to find out that Italy had surrendered. 'Our war was over,' lamented *Capellini's* Captain Auconi to Mike Hatcher. 'We became prisoners and our ships were taken from us.'

Most of the Italians joined Australian and British prisoners in the notorious Changi prison camp on Singapore Island. Their vessels were commandeered, over the protests of Japanese naval officers. The Japanese were unenthusiastic about the large Italian regular navy submarines, considering them too big and unwieldy for the shallow seas of south-east Asia. However the Germans had their own U-boat base at Penang and were happy to receive *Reginaldo Giuliani*. To them size was for once an advantage, since most submarines had very limited space for cargo. Tin, a metal urgently needed in Germany, was usually carried externally, replacing the iron ballast carried by submarines in twin docking keels. The keels kept a submarine level when sitting on the seabed. The blocks of iron ballast were detachable in an emergency when all other attempts to surface had failed.

The Japanese dry-docked the German U-boats, cut tin blocks to the size of the iron ballast, and 'stowed' the cargo in this unusual but very practical manner.

So in 1944, *Reginaldo Giuliani*, re-named the U-IT 23 and complete with a German Kriegsmarine crew, was steaming up the Malacca Strait, beginning the homeward voyage. Her crew of 60 would have been concerned with the way the war was going for Germany and they would have been aware of the dangers involved in the last few hundred kilometres approaching the coast of occupied France. But they must also have been looking forward to being re-united with wives and children, sweethearts, families and friends. 'There's no place like home' rings true irrespective of cultural or geographical boundaries.

The Malacca Strait was mirror smooth 32 miles off shore that morning. The nearest point of land was the island of Pulan Jarak. The U-IT 23, refitted at Port Swettenham in Malaya, was making good speed, 14 knots on the surface, steering a dead straight course of 360 degrees. The fact that there were no zigzags in her wake indicated a lack of any sense of danger.

But crossing the Strait on a course of 089 degrees, almost at right angles to the path of U-IT 23, was the shadowy form of another vessel. She was the British hunting submarine *Tally-Ho*, named personally by Winston Churchill, and based at Tricomalee in Sri Lanka. Now she had come to stalk victims in the Japanese enemy's own territory – the Malacca Strait between Malaya and the huge island of Sumatra.

Tally-Ho had retired to the middle of the Strait to charge her batteries during the night, and now, at first light, she was heading towards the Malayan coast looking for targets among local coastal traffic. Suddenly a quite unexpected sight appeared ahead of her.

'U-boat!' exclaimed the young officer of the watch, Michael Clark. From the peak of the conning tower he had sighted the low, black silhouette of the enemy almost dead ahead. 'U-boat!' he repeated, hardly able to believe it. 'Fine on the starboard bow. Doing about 14 knots, sir!'

'Alter course to 090 degrees!' *Tally-Ho's* senior officer Lieutenant Commander Leslie William Able Bennington responded at once. At 32 years of age he would have seemed incredibly young today for such a position of responsibility. But in wartime men who were young in years became 'old' very quickly. Aboard *Tally-Ho* Bennington was the 'old man' in both senses of the word – he was of the most advanced years and 'old man' was the Royal Navy's traditional name for a skipper. Most of his officers were under 24 years of age and the crew were all aged around 20. This was not entirely accidental. Older men, the Submarine Service considered, tended to think more and to think in reflective terms. In the claustrophobic world of a submarine, between long periods of boredom and sharp moments of extreme danger, that kind of thinking was not conducive to good morale. The young thought they were immortal. Older men knew they were not.

To Bennington's sharply focused mind the slim shape ahead was simply a target. Not only that but she was a U-boat – one of the highest priority targets of all. As he crouched over the torpedo deflection sights he had all the thrill of the hunter aiming for a kill. But the kill was quite dispassionate. There was neither hate nor sorrow. No thought of the men inside that other submarine, men like those beneath his own feet in the potential steel coffin of *Tally-Ho*. And if it had been the U-IT 23 which had *Tally-Ho's* lean silhouette in *her* sights the attitude would have been no different.

'Fire three on a 120-degree track,' Bennington ordered. Down below in the torpedo room the firing team moved swiftly and there was a whoosh of compressed air as the explosive-headed, one-and-a-half ton, 20-foot-long 'tin-fish' were launched. The distance of 3000 to 3500 yards was at the extreme range for torpedo accuracy, and as Bennington prepared to fire, the U-boat was lost in an isolated patch of mist. He fixed his gaze on the spot where the U-boat had vanished. He had to aim at a target he could not see, fire at maximum range, and while he hoped for a result, realistically the odds were against him.

As soon as the torpedoes were fired their tracks divulged *Tally-Ho's* existence; her cover was blown and she was now vulnerable to counter attack. All those on the conning tower clattered down the steel rungs of the ladder. The hatches were slammed shut and locked.

'Dive!' Bennington ordered. 'Turn 90 degrees! Take her down to 80 feet!'

Then there was dead silence as all aboard listened intently. The distant sound of a muffled explosion, the noise of the target's engines (heard on *Tally-Ho's* hydrophones) cutting abruptly, would signal a strike. No sound at all would mean a miss. Then perhaps the other submarine would search for *Tally-Ho*, or worse, radio for aircraft and destroyer support.

Bennington's eyes were fixed on his watch. The torpedoes seemed to have been running a hell of a long time.

Suddenly there was the muffled thump of an explosion.

Bennington wrote in his log, 'There was a torpedo explosion two minutes and twenty seconds after the firing time for the third torpedo. HE [hydrophone effect] stopped immediately. A few minutes later periscope observation showed nothing in sight. It is considered the U-boat was hit and that it sank.'

He was correct in his assumption.

The U-IT 23 had received a direct hit under her conning tower. As she began to sink by the stern, men scrambled out of her for'ard hatch and while 40 managed to escape, the 30 in the stern and in the forward torpedo compartment were trapped below. The former *Reginaldo Giuliani* raised her bow, mortally wounded, and slid stern-first down into the murky depths of the Malacca Strait in a trail of oil and bubbles, coming finally to a shuddering, bumping stop in the mud 170 feet below.

It appears some of those men trapped below survived for a time on small pockets of oxygen. The chief engineer was found lying down with his bible closed on his chest. It would seem he had read a little before blowing his brains out with his Luger pistol. Others remained in their bunks or on top of the engines above the level of water which had part flooded the submarine. Thirty-five years later when Mike Hatcher entered the wreck they were still in the same positions.

In the forward compartment the first to die were crew who had been sleeping on top of the cargo of bales of rubber. The rubber floated as the water came in, jamming them up under the ceiling. On board *Tally-Ho*, the crew were enjoying their issue of rum, traditional after a successful strike.

On the surface, another drama was unfolding. The U-IT 23 survivors – those who could swim or had grabbed life jackets in their hasty exist – were floating, devastated and disoriented by the suddenness of the attack. The nearest land was some 32 miles away, too far for anyone to swim, so they stayed together in a group. Some prayed. Some wept. Some waited stoically for their fate. After all they were submariners. In their service death was always grinning, just around the corner, always unwelcome but never entirely unexpected.

Then came a sound from above, an engine aircraft. They began waving and cheering and saw a float plane circling, preparing to land. It was German and had come from the U-boat base at Penang, sent out to check on the U-IT 23 when no transmission had been received. But there were too many water-logged survivors to carry on board at once, so the pilot took the wounded and as many others as he could in the cabin. Others clung to the floats and he taxied them to shore. He returned again and again until all 40 were saved, a rare occurrence in the grim undersea world of submarine warfare where crews usually died with their boats.

For those saved the reprieve was temporary. The survivors were transferred to another U-boat which was sunk with all hands by a mine laid in Sunda Strait by the British submarine *Porpoise*. In turn, the British boat herself would become a victim, sunk with all her crew by aircraft in the Malacca Strait.

The *Tally-Ho* strike had been a lucky one. On two other occasions she'd had U-boats at ranges of 1200 yards and less – much easier shots – and had missed them both. Remarkably, after the war, some of *Tally-Ho's* crew met some of their German counterparts from the 'missed' subs at Galloway in Scotland where captured U-boats were assembled. They were able to tell the German sailors how lucky *they* were.

❀

On February 24, 1944, nine days after her triumph over the German U-boat, *Tally-Ho* came near to joining the U-IT 23 at the bottom of the Malacca Strait. Travelling on the surface at night she was surprised and rammed by a Japanese Hyabusa-class torpedo boat. The torpedo boat's propellers shredded *Tally-Ho's* external ballast tanks on the port side, cutting a series of huge holes over a distance of 96 feet.

Down below, the noise of the alien propellers chopping through steel sounded like the hammers of hell. 'We've 'ad it now!' exclaimed engine room artificer 'Taffy' Hughes. The others clung, white-faced for balance as the submarine was thrown sideways by the impact, waiting for the dreaded sound of a rush of water. But it never came. Fortunately for the British submarine the Japanese craft had shredded her propellers and wrecked her steering gear in the impact and was immobilised.

Left wounded and vulnerable, *Tally-Ho* escaped miraculously in the darkness, limping back to Trincombalee with a marked 12 degree list (tilt) to port. When she was eventually dry-docked she looked not unlike a toast rack. But she was one of the survivors of the war and was credited with sinking a formidable list of enemy shipping, including the Japanese cruiser *Kuma*.

Lieutenant Commander Bennington was awarded the Distinguished Service Order and Bar and the distinguished Service Cross and Bar, and went on to a celebrated naval career before retiring in 1960, laden, as the saying has it, with his country's honours. He never knew, during the war, the identity of the submarine he sank that day in the Malacca Strait. Because of her unusual size, he assumed that she must have been one of the Japanese I-boats.

The ship's cat, 'Snoopy', accompanied *Tally-Ho* on all her patrols and after the war returned to England where he was cared for by Bennington's mother. He went on to live to the grand old age of 12.

❀

Meanwhile, at the bottom of the Strait, the U-IT 23, laying at a slight angle, gathered weed and barnacles and became festooned with torn fishing nets, gradually becoming a part of the sea, her dead entombed within her. Mike Hatcher found that Trenowden's book was meticulously researched, with interviews with all the important characters, including Bennington. It also carried a good deal of information not usually found in popular reading, such as Bennington's own attack plan of February 15, 1944 on the U-IT 23.

'I went to Bennington's house outside Southampton,' Hatcher recalls, 'to ask him about the U-IT. He was retired at the time. He gave me pretty short shrift. I didn't even get inside the front door. He was well into his sixties, and was very Pukka ex-Navy. A crusty old bugger, obviously in no mood to talk to salvage divers like myself.

'Maybe he had an opinion about disturbing war graves or non-service types messing about in areas that he reckoned didn't belong to them. He certainly wasn't going to talk to me about things he thought shouldn't concern me. What really capped it off was when I asked him whether the position he had set down for the place of the action was correct.

'"*Of course* it's accurate!" he shouted at me, as though I'd accused him of violating Holy Orders or something. The door closed and that was the end of the conversation!'

It turned out that the U-IT 23 had in fact gone down 10 miles away from the position recorded by *Tally-Ho* in her log. It was natural, though frustrating, that in the tension and drama of *Tally-Ho* firing her bracket of torpedoes and the jubilation of the hit, there could have been some discrepancy in the navigation.

'I could understand that,' said Hatcher. 'But it didn't help me much. We spent eight months up and down the Malacca Strait looking for her. I even offered one of the local fishermen a new boat if he could find it. They often get the positions of wrecks because they're good fishing spots. But they didn't get her. We found everything else – cargo ships, dead junks, fishing boats, aircraft, barges, you name it. The Strait was full of dead ships. Then we put a new Simrad Sonar into *Seeker I* and bingo! We got it in no time at all. My sonar training course in Norway really paid off.'

On the first dive with his new diver of the time, Abdul W Rahim, Hatcher thought, initially, that he had found another cargo boat.

'I went down the buoy line and there was what appeared to be a mast all draped in fishing nets. It was hard to make out any shape because of the nets and the fact that the water was deep [170 feet] and murky. Then I realised it was a periscope.

'"We've got her!" I yelled. "We've finally got the bastard!"'

Dropping deeper he found that the sub's forward gun had been removed and the emplacement stacked with ingots of tin. There turned out to be four and a half tons valued at $43,000 a ton. In addition, all the underside of the outer casing was jammed with bales of rubber. This would yield 25 per cent of the new price because the rubber was unaffected by sea water or immersion. She was discovered in November, 1979, and the excavation took three months from January, 1980. The job was worth $US7 million.

The salvage was conducted in what was to become standard practice for Hatcher. A salvage barge with decompression chamber, lifting machinery and all the necessities for 30 men living aboard was moored above the wrecksite with four anchors holding it steady. *Seeker I* was the tender and supply boat. The task of the divers was to dig a trench alongside the vessel to provide access to the keels and the ingots of tin below the hull.

Tapping on the hull revealed that some areas were still 'dry'. A flooded compartment gives a dull and different sound to the ringing echo of a dry section of the ship. A half-empty kettle gives a similar sound above and below the water level.

'We had to find out what was inside the sub,' Hatch recalls. 'The divers were naturally nervous about going in there. Between the machinery and controls there's very little room to spare. Always the fear of your light going out or getting the airline caught on something. Or the airline becoming cut on broken glass or some sharp object. We also knew that there were likely to be bodies in there. Our crew and divers were mixed – Malay, Singaporean, Indonesian, Chinese. Good divers, but naturally there was a lot of superstition and fear of spirits in their backgrounds. They were mortally afraid of ghosts. To tell the truth none of us were very happy about what we might find in there, but it had to be done. We had a couple of Aussie ex-pats. Mickey Heuston from Perth was one of them! Maybe we were a little harder. Or maybe we didn't let it show as much.'

To gain access to the submarine Hatcher used plastic explosives to cut a 'door' at the bow and another at the stern. The forward torpedo room contained the bales of rubber, and on top, human bones and bodies. Rahim made this sad discovery. Deeper inside the submarine was a huge dry area in the conning tower and a load of tin was retrieved from here. She was completely unarmed – her torpedo tubes had been removed and the compartments had been stuffed with tin and other cargo.

There were some scary moments, Hatcher recalls. 'We had a system where one guy went in and the other stood watch at the "door", feeding the lines in and out. Any slack on the lines and they could have looped around machinery wheels and levers and have the diver caught up. The diver inside had a light on his helmet and voice communication to the surface and to his co-diver. Even so things could go wrong. Once when I was well inside the sub the light went out.

'There was a moment of blind potential panic. You're thirty fathoms down, inside a natural grave, and it's blacker than anything you've ever known before. Lose your way and you're dead. Keep calm and just follow the lines, slowly, slowly. Don't let the tension go off. Just keep following, feeling by touch, and you must get back to the door. I did, and I've never been so glad to see anything as that square of light. It still makes the hair stand up on the back of my neck to think of it today.'

However he was to endure an even worse experience.

'The U-IT was leaning over to starboard where she lay on the bottom. This was convenient because we had to get right under her to reach the keel ballast. We used an airlift to dig a trench, and when we tunnelled under there, sure enough there were the blocks of tin. All shiny and beautiful. A little bonanza.

'We had to use explosives to free the tin blocks and the bottom was soft and mushy. With that combination we were always worried that the sides of the trench might collapse while someone was under the sub. One day it did happen and the diver who was buried alive was me. It was the most terrible feeling. There was a soft rumble and suddenly there was no light. I knew at once what had happened. I became disoriented not knowing which direction was which.

'I had to speak sharply to myself to avoid panic. That would be fatal. At least I was in Kirby gear with the air circulating inside the helmet. And my line of communication was still open. With scuba gear I would have been a goner. I told the others on the talk-back what had happened. The major problem was that I was at 170 feet. That's a deep dive on air with the certainty of decompression sickness if you stay long enough and the possibility of getting "narked" [suffering nitrogen narcosis] which can affect your judgement and capacity to act effectively. Though I could keep going as long as the air supply continued – and God forbid anything happening to that – time was the major problem.

'"What can we do?" they asked from above.

'"Nothing. I'm going to try to dig myself out," I replied. I still had enough room to move my arms.

'So I dug, and dug, and bloody dug like a blind mole. Finally at last there was daylight and I emerged beside the submarine. Blessed relief!'

Then there was horror. Hatcher realised that he was on the wrong side of the submarine. Disoriented, he had dug and clawed in the wrong direction. Now he was in the open but his air and telephone lines led back under the submarine, tethering him like a dog on a lead. His only option was to come back the way he came.

So he did. Burrowing, scraping and praying that he didn't become lost again. Blind down there in the mud. Finally he was exhausted, arms aching, unable to go any further, still with no idea how far he had to go.

'Pull on the lines,' he gasped. 'I can't go on any more.'

'But if we pull the fittings out of the gear you'll drown,' they replied from above.

'It's the only way,' he repeated. 'I'll just have to take the chance.'

There was silence from above.

'Pull you bastards! PULL!'

The pressure increased on the lines. At first nothing happened and Hatcher braced himself, dreading the thought of the airline parting or the fittings pulling out of the helmet. The lines grew rigid with the tension. Then he began to move. Slowly at first but with increasing speed. Finally he burst out of the mud slurry on the correct side of the submarine in an explosion cloud of silt and mud and debris.

'I came out like the cork out of a champagne bottle,' he recalls. 'The daylight never seemed so bloody beautiful!'

❀

Later, Mike Hatcher met some of the men who had served in the World War II submarines. He has an undisguised admiration for them.

'They had a hell of a war,' he said. 'Maybe they made things tough for a lot of merchant seamen. But it was total war and bastardry was practised by both sides. You have to respect men who regularly face death in one of its most unpleasant forms. Getting a bullet in the gut is one thing, but going down trapped like a rat in a steel coffin with no way of ever seeing daylight again is something I wouldn't like to face.

'We left the U-IT 23's dead in their bunks exactly where they were and treated them with respect. At the end of the salvage the team had a little service for them and threw a wreath on the water. The service was in the Christian, Hindu, and Muslim religions, from each nationality.'

The divers brought up some flags and memorabilia from the submarine and sometime after Hatcher journeyed to Europe to return them to their point of origin.

'Gus Britain of the Grosport Naval Museum arranged for me to go over to Germany with the gear,' he recalls. 'We stayed at the Altona Hotel in Hamburg, owned by an ex-submariner. Hamburg was an original home port for most of the U-boats. There was a conference room in the basement with flags and memorabilia from the U-boat days. It was their regular meeting place. I met all the captains. Some had sunk more than 200,000 tons of Allied shipping. Things were pretty formal at first – stiff, you might say. Among the U-boat commanders I met were Captain Dommes, Captain Schuiz and Commander Schnee. Then one of the senior Admirals, the president of the association, arrived. Everyone stood to attention. Rigid.

'"Where is the Engländer?" he asked. I was pointed out to him and he came over and shook hands and thanked me for coming and from then on things eased up. We presented the memorabilia and assured them that we had treated the U-IT 23 and her men with respect. They appreciated that and a lot of them came and shook my hand. Then there were a lot of drinks.

'The next day we went out to the Admiral's estate. There were deer grazing on the lawn I remember, and an indoor swimming pool. I remember thinking that that was better than being on the bottom of the North Atlantic or the Malacca Strait.'

The compass cover with the name *Reginaldo Giuliani* was sent to the Italian Navy's Submariner's Association. Hatcher had spoken to one of the Italian captains of the subs that were sent to Singapore and though clearly distressed at the memory, he was elated to have the memento. Like most, he had lost much in the war and some of his men had died in Japanese camps.

❀

The submarine was to prove as deadly a weapon in south-east Asian waters as it was in the Atlantic. Though casualties went both ways. In former submarine commander Richard Compton's comprehensive book *The Underwater War 1939–1945*, he records that three British and four Dutch Submarines were lost in operations. However the Allies sank two Japanese cruisers, two destroyers, five U-boats, 13 small vessels, 47 large merchant ships and numerous small craft. Seven other large merchantmen were sunk by mines laid by the submarines.

The really telling blow was the later activity of American submarines. They virtually destroyed the Japanese merchant fleet, cutting off supplies to beleaguered troops on Guadalcanal, Saipan and Okinawa. In the end they operated even in Japan's Inland Sea in Operation Starvation from March 1945. Compton-Hall suggests that they were as important a factor in forcing

Japan to submission as the two atomic bombs on Hiroshima and Nagasaki in August, 1945.

For the record, Germany built 1162 U-boats in World War II and 785 of them were sunk. Though they sank more than 14 million tons of Allied shipping at a cost of 50,000 lives, they paid a heavy price. Of the 55,000 crew who went to sea in U-boats 27,491 of them died. This was one of the highest death rates in any service of any country in the war. None of the German U-boats of the 'Monsoon fleet' operating from Penang ever made it back to Germany, nor did any of the Italian 'Mercator' boats. Most of them lie in the shadowy twilight at the bottom of the sea ... along with the ghostly form of the U-IT 23 and her submariners. At peace and at rest. Forever.

CHAPTER SIX

Death Visits the Dive Team

Mike Hatcher lost two divers on the U-IT 23 salvage, deaths which he regards as both stupid and unnecessary. Twenty years later he is still sad and angry at the memory. He has never fully recovered from that loss and the death of another diver, a young man called Kamal, everybody's favourite, on another U-boat in the Java Sea.

Were the U-boats unlucky?

Hatcher shrugs. 'Diving accidents can happen anywhere, any time. They're mostly human error and luck doesn't come into the equation. Potentially there's always a risk. By training and sound practice we try to keep the danger level down as much as we can. But you can never eliminate it entirely. Diving, let's face it, is a dangerous game and the deeper it gets the more dangerous it becomes.'

The two divers who perished on the U-IT 23 were performing a comparatively simple task by professional standards. About two weeks into the job a buoy line attached to one of the four anchors holding the barge broke away and a new line had to be fitted. The anchor was at 170 feet so it was a deep dive and there was too much distance to use surface supply breathing equipment. But the procedure was straightforward. The line was attached to the wire rope leading to the anchor by a sliding shackle.

'All the diver had to do was slide the shackle down the wire until he reached the anchor, then attach it,' Hatcher recalls. 'Then he could return to the barge by the wire, or surface beside the float.' He clears his throat. 'In fact, if the diver had any problem at any time all he had to do was come up the buoy line to the surface. I sent one diver down to do the job and another to keep him company. A third diver went halfway down the wire with a spare scuba tank in case there were any problems.

'They all went down together, the buoy started to move off in the direction of where the anchor lay. Then for no apparent reason it stopped short of the mark. We waited, not with any degree of worry at first because it seemed such a straightforward task. But then the stop diver came back with the spare tank, rolling his eyes and saying that the other two had disappeared and he did not know where they were. I yelled at him for coming back with air in his tank and more importantly with the spare before his stop time was up.

'But probably whatever had gone wrong down there had already happened. The two divers never did come back. We looked for them on the bottom and with *Seeker I's* sonar. We thought we had them on the sonar. Two single blips not moving, just drifting away on the tide into the deeps of the Malacca Strait. Because of the depth of water we couldn't do a visual diving search too far away from the orientation point of the anchor. The other divers were demoralised. It was bad enough to lose two of them. I didn't want any more to die on the job.

'Eventually it became clear that the two weren't coming back. Their air couldn't have lasted any longer. They were dead. Finished. That was a bad moment. A really bad moment. One of the worst I've ever had. There was only one thing I could do myself if I wanted any of the others to dive again. I had to take a scuba set, go down the wire on my own, pick up the buoy line where it was hanging loose, and slide it down to the anchor.

'I did it because (a) the job needed to be done; (b) for crew morale; and (c) for my own satisfaction in knowing that it wasn't an unreasonable thing to have asked of my divers. I've never ever asked anyone to do anything I wouldn't do myself.'

Exactly what went wrong remains a mystery to this day. One diver may have lost his air and tried to get his companion's mouthpiece to buddy breath. Perhaps one of them panicked and both drowned or perhaps both went down with insufficient air, though this seems inconceivable. The first thing a professional diver, any diver, does before going deep is to check the amount of air in the tanks. Even if one forgets it seems hard to believe that both would do so.

It was unlikely they had been taken by sharks or marine monsters either. Sharks tend to shy away from scuba bubbles and generally stay clear of work areas. Though it's not something that can be entirely dismissed. If a shark appeared it might have panicked the divers, though they were professionals and had trained for such occurrences.

The Malacca Strait certainly has currents and sometimes they're quite strong, but they weren't running hard on that particular day. The divers were going down a wire which gave them something to hang on to and in any case, Hatcher had done the same dive without any difficulty.

The mystery remains.

❈

The death of Kamal, a diver on the U-IT 23, and a veteran of salvage work with Hatcher despite his youth, was even more painful. The fatality occurred in the Java Sea on another German submarine of the ill-fated Monsoon Fleet.

As the war in Europe drew to its sad and bloody conclusion, Admiral Donitz, head of the German Naval High Command, ordered the Germans at Penang to come home. There were four submarines remaining and it was arranged that they should refuel from a tanker off the Cape of Good Hope. Unknown to the Germans the Allies had cracked their 'Enigma' code earlier in the war, and were able to decipher their radio messages and intercept their submarine supply vessels and tankers. At the critical moment of refuelling a British warship pounced and sank the tanker, her fuel lines still trailing over the side.

The submarines dived and escaped, and the British vessel, with U-boats in the area, wisely decamped at full speed. Three of the subs, now refuelled, continued on their way, though none of them reached Germany. The fourth submarine, the U–168, picked up the tanker survivors and then, with insufficient fuel herself, turned back for Indonesia. She reached Batavia (Jakarta) on the last smell of diesel fuel in her tanks. She needed new batteries and work done on her generators before she could attempt the long voyage to Europe once more.

En route to Soerabaya for dry-docking, she was ambushed in the Java Sea by the Netherlands submarine *Zwaardvisch* (Swordfish) operating out of Fremantle. It was another case of a position betrayed by the cracking of the Enigma code.

'We were waiting for her behind a headland,' the Dutch captain, Hans Goossens, told Hatcher when he met him in Holland. 'In the distance we saw this big trail of black smoke and her engines were making a regular racket. We thought at first that she was a merchantman. Then when she got close we realised that her diesels were out of tune. She was a funny one. We hit her in the bow with the first torpedo. She went down bow-first and stayed with her stern sticking out of the water and her propellers still turning.'

Her crew scrambled out through a rear hatch and in a rare act of chivalry (for submarines usually went directly for deep water after a sinking in case a radio warning had gone out) the Dutch captain picked up survivors. But naturally he kept them on deck.

'If I am under attack, I will have to dive,' he warned them by loud hailer from the conning tower. 'As submariners you will understand that.'

They were lucky. Swordfish deposited the Germans, their war effectively over, on the deck of a passing fishing boat. In later years Mike Hatcher would meet the U-boat captain in Germany. 'I lost my boat in the Java Sea,' he lamented.

'I know,' said Hatcher with a grin. 'I salvaged her.'

This salvage went somewhat differently to the U-IT 23. Again tin was the object and at $43,000 a ton it was exceeded in metal value only by gold and silver. Hatcher spent six months 'lawnmowing' before he found her, in deeper water (200 feet) than he generally liked. He decided to apply slings and wind her up to the barge, then lift her up from the bottom and take her into the shallows where it would be easier to work on her. The scheme was partly successful. The U-boat was raised, but the weight jammed the lifting tackle and prevented a release.

'We had to run her into the bottom to shake her loose,' Hatcher recalls. 'It wasn't pretty. But it worked. She was supposed to be full of tin and mercury, but she had a pig iron keel and I knew that meant there wasn't too much of anything else. Sometimes bad luck seems to come in runs. In the Java Sea I was stumping about with a broken leg in plaster. No fun on a salvage barge where the accommodation is up and down steep steel stairs. It was one of a row of bad things that happened. We'd been looking for a Jap freighter called *Disan Maru* sunk by a Yank submarine in the South China Sea. She could be easily identified from railway equipment on deck. She was also supposed to have been carrying 1200 tons of tin. Multiply that by $43,000 a ton and see what you get!'

Seeker I picked up the silhouette of the sunken vessel on the Simrad sonar late one afternoon.

'We anchored up. It was six o'clock at night by the time we'd done that. Too late to dive. In any case we were in a mood to celebrate – we reckoned we were all millionaires! Boy was it a party!'

The hangovers hardly improved with the bad news in the morning. Abdul Rahim was the first diver down.

'Nothing,' he reported over the talk back phone in his helmet.

'Nothing? What do you mean *nothing*?'

'That's it. Her hold is empty. There's no tin. Just some railway engines and carriages on deck and a big hole in her side.'

'At least we've got the right ship. Have another look.'

But the wreck was, as Hatcher sorrowfully described it, 'bare as Mother Hubbard's cupboard'. It transpired she had hit a mine off Brunei and had put back into port. The cargo of tin was unloaded and she was trimmed so that she was bow high with the mine damage clear of the water. She then tried to limp across to Palembang to unload the railway engines and gear before going to Singapore for repairs, but en route a US submarine got her.

After that disappointment the next target on Hatcher's list was the Swordfish's U-boat victim in the Java Sea. But before *Seeker I* could transfer to the new field of operations, he required a permit from the Indonesian authorities in Jakarta.

'There was a military speedboat going from Sumatra to Jakarta. They offered me a lift, and that seemed a good idea. Fast transport wasn't easily come by in that part of the world where they still mostly travelled by ox-cart. But roaring down the river at a great rate of knots the idiot driver fell asleep and the speedboat veered off into the mangroves. We hit with a hell of a thump. A tree branch broke the windscreen and a log came through the bottom of the boat and hit me on the leg. When I looked down my foot was sticking out at right angles. You could have used it for a putter.'

Everyone agreed that it was dislocated. But how would they get it back on a north-south line when it was facing the opposite direction?

'They found a *bombo*, a local witch doctor, in Jambi, a place in the middle of Sumatra. He fed me opium pills and Bintang beer. When he judged I'd had about enough he put a rolled-up towel between my teeth and told me to hang on to the iron bed frame behind my head. Then he gave my foot a huge twist and tug. My teeth met in the middle of the towel and I pulled the iron bed-frame out of the bed and over the witch doctor's head and laid him out. That was the end of *that* treatment. True the foot had come around to a better angle. But it was blue and swollen and still hurting like hell.

'"No more messing around with witch doctors," I said. "Get me to bloody Singapore before they have to amputate."'

When Hatcher arrived there his ankle and foot were almost the size of a basketball and shiny in brilliant technicolour hues. At his first sight of it the doctor in the hospital did seriously consider the possibility that an amputation might be necessary in order to save the patient. Hatcher wanted none of that but implored the doctor to do what he needed to do quickly. An X-ray revealed three separate breaks plus the dislocation and the doctor suggested he would have to insert a metal plate.

'You can't do that!' Hatcher yelled.

'Why not?'

'I travel a lot. Every time I go through a security system at the airport the alarm system will go off.'

The doctor laughed. 'Don't worry. We'll use stainless steel.'

By the time Hatcher got down to the Java Sea with his leg in a plaster of Paris cast the crew had been on their own for some time. Discipline had become a little lax.

'They'd gone ashore and come back with pets, for heaven's sake. There was a bear on board, a bloody crocodile, and a fledgling sea eagle called "Rod the rocket". Rod was still learning to fly. He could lean into the wind and flap his wings and get up OK. He'd soar around for a while, but when he wanted to land he'd sometimes miss the boat altogether and crash land in the water. The speedboat would have to go out and pick him up. You've never seen anything that looks as sad as a waterlogged eagle. He eventually got the hang of landing properly and ended up in the Singapore bird park.

'The bear was called Jo Jo, and he was really cute. The divers used to walk with him like a baby, paw in hand, to take a shower. Everyone loved him. He was especially the favourite of Kamal. The problem with pets is that they distract people in a working environment. Salvage barges aren't a good place for bears. If something happens to a pet everyone gets miserable. The work suffers and before you know it you can have an accident. Jo Jo liked to chew on things. One day he chewed on a life-buoy, swallowed a piece of styrene foam and choked to death. The crew were inconsolable. Especially Kamal.

'I don't say that the bear was a factor in what happened later. Though the crew tended to link all the bad things together. Including my leg.'

Kamal's death came at the end of a beautiful sunny day and the circumstances understandably threw both Hatcher and the salvage crew into a state of total shock. The divers had finished their work and had been through the decompression chamber. It would be another 12 hours before they could go back in the water, which was 170 feet deep. Kamal was the stand-by diver and he had his wetsuit and weight belt on, but no mask or fins.

The airlift was still running. It was a big one and with the air bubbles accelerating from 170 feet down it made a hissing pool of bubbles five metres wide on the surface.

'Kamal was laughing, skylarking about,' Hatcher recalls. 'Suddenly he said, "I'm going to have a bubble bath" and before anyone could stop him he jumped into the middle of the pool of bubbles.'

He vanished. A minute went by. Then two minutes. Divers began to look for a head in the water behind the barge with growing concern.

No head appeared.

At three minutes there was consternation. Still no head. Divers began to look for equipment that had been put away for the day. The compressor that operated the Kirby suit surface supply had been turned off. No-one was ready for such an unexpected emergency.

By the time Mike Hatcher had been summoned, Kamal had been gone 10 minutes. Every diver there wanted to go back in the water regardless of the fact that they would have almost certainly suffered the bends in a repeat dive. Hatcher had to physically restrain them, yell at them. Kamal was dead.

Eventually they were calmed somewhat and they accepted that to go after Kamal would risk other lives. The stupidity of the death hit everyone hard.

'Kamal was always kidding about,' Hatcher says. 'But he was always such a lovable, likeable guy, that no-one could mind. It was just so tragic that it could cost him his life.'

❁

At first light two divers went down to look for the body. One was Hashim, Hatcher's chief diver. Hatcher told him in no uncertain terms that he had 15 minutes bottom time and not a second more. Hashim said that he had had a dream that Kamal had come to him in the night and told him where he was. 'I want you to come and get me,' he'd said.

'They found him right away and brought him up on the stage with them,' says Hatcher. 'There was a terrible scene when they brought the body to the surface. The divers were crying. Mickey Heuston the Australian wanted to rush forward and embrace the body. I yelled at him to get back. Kamal was Muslim. "You're unclean. You can't touch him!"'

They covered the body with a sheet and the divers came past to pay their respects. Then Hashim was led straight to the decompression chamber. The Muslim boys washed Kamal's body in the traditional way. His religion decreed that his burial service had to be that day. He was taken into Samarung, a town in central Java and Mike Hatcher, Hashim and two others went ashore to attend the service in the mosque.

'There were only four of us able to go ashore,' Hatcher recalls. 'I felt bad about what I thought would be a lonely funeral. But local people came from everywhere. I never found out how they knew what had happened, but there must have been 300 to 400 people, the women and children with their white veils. It was one of the most moving and beautiful things I have ever seen. After the service we had Kamal embalmed with all their usual unguents and oils and spices. We sent his body back to Singapore for burial by his family. Hashim and I went formally to his father to apologise for his son's death – if you can ever apologise sufficiently to a father for a tragedy of that magnitude.'

The father was very dignified, very solemn, very correct.

'You cannot blame yourselves,' he replied, lifting his hands in absolution. 'My son is in paradise now. What happened to him was the Will of Allah.'

Hatcher discovered only later that before the feast of Ramadan Kamal had telephoned his parents from Java to say that he was 'sorry for his previous disobediences'. He had told them that he wanted to clear himself because he'd had a premonition that he was going to die.

The death left a deep emotional scar on Mike Hatcher. He felt Kamal's accident more keenly than the others because the lad had been one of his personal 'family' of divers and he had watched his career blossom. While there was nothing he could have done to prevent his death he still agonised over the responsibility he felt on the matter.

'I asked myself a hundred times a night what I could have done to prevent it and every time I came up with the same answer. Nothing. But that didn't take the question away. I guess it will always be there.'

What did happen to Kamal?

Nobody can be certain. But anyone who has been caught in a 'dumper' in surf knows that you cannot swim in bubbles. Aerated water has no buoyancy. The 'bubble bath' into which Kamal jumped may have been akin to jumping into a hole in the sea and he probably 'fell' far deeper and far more quickly than he could have anticipated. The airlift, the source of the bubbles, was 170 feet below him. He had broken, in his light-heartedness, a couple of cardinal rules – he had no fins and he was wearing a weight belt.

The weight belt would have carried him down to the point where he realised what was happening, and then he would have jettisoned it. Too late, perhaps. Without fins it may have been too far down for him to regain the surface. Or he may, in a desperate effort to reach the top, have come up under the ladder or the barge and struck his head and become unconscious. There was a mark on his forehead when he was found.

The tragedy illustrates how easily diving accidents can happen, even to a good swimmer and professional diver like Kamal.

'The Will of Allah,' his father said.

CHAPTER SEVEN

The Rat Boat and the Refugees

Mike Hatcher's worldwide fame would come not from salvaging modern wrecks, but from the centuries old cargoes of a 1680 Chinese junk, the 1752 Dutch East Indiaman *Geldermalsen* ... and from a gunboat incident in the Gulf of Thailand.

The world loves a treasure story, preferably one with the ingredients of gold and confrontation in it. Both vessels contained fine porcelain while the Indiaman had the added bonus of gold. On the downside, Royal Thai Navy gunboats provided more confrontation than Hatcher needed and cost him a fabulous cargo.

Hatcher's accumulating fortunes didn't appear overnight, and were built gradually on more humble salvages. Income and reputation came from submarines and tin ships, general salvage work on modern vessels and oil company charter work. Hatcher and his team advertised themselves with their boat, *Seeker I*, as being available for any kind of charter that was practical and legal, and prided themselves in taking on work others wouldn't touch because it was felt to be too hard or inconvenient. You could say they enjoyed a challenge.

In the process *Seeker I*, no beauty at the best of times and sometimes the despair of the more fastidious Max de Rham, became known as 'The Rat Boat'. The unlovely title was bestowed by Fergus Hinds, an ex-Royal Navy Officer who had been engaged in salvage work in the East with the famous British firm of Risdon Beasley. The name seemed to suit the vessel and was confirmed when a crewmember was bitten by a rodent on the toe while steering!

Fergus and Hatch's backgrounds were poles apart and ordinarily they would have been the most unlikely combination in business. What brought them together was the significant dollar factor and it went some way in overcoming Hatch's deep-seated suspicion of senior service types. (He was still smarting from his brush with Lieutenant Commander Bennington.) At any rate he chose to ignore the sage old yachtsman's advice: 'There are three things you should never take on board your boat – a wheelbarrow, an umbrella, or a Royal Naval officer.'

Risdon Beasley had closed down in the Far East and Fergus had stayed on. He knew the position of a couple of tin wrecks on which the firm had worked, but which had not been 'completely cleaned out', as he put it. It seemed to him that the information should be worth a few bob. He admitted frankly in his book *Riches from Wrecks* that he tried most of the other established operators before he turned to Michael Hatcher. Those who had the capital and resources to do the job didn't always have the inclination to undertake what they saw as an enterprise attended by risk. And those who would like to do it more often than not weren't adequately equipped or resourced. In the end there was only Mike Hatcher. A fortunate choice as it turned out.

'It can be said that of all the resident Far East expatriates in this business [salvage] Hatcher alone has achieved anything,' Fergus Hinds remarked. 'He has been up against all sorts of competition from bands of friends setting out on a shoe-string on the one hand to the world's leading offshore companies on the other. None but he has anything to show for it. He does not owe his success to inherited capital, nor to education, nor to influence, nor to favours. His has been a harsher experience than most of us have had to contend with and this may explain a fairly unremitting concern for his own interests.

'Mike has a manner of speaking which makes it difficult to know what to believe. He talks in an imprecise way that allows nothing he says to be verified, a great asset in a business where confidentiality is everything. Anyone who has given business lunches or run a hospitality suite or drunk with clients until three in the morning knows quite well that it is impossible to socialise without talking and impossible to talk without saying something. But Mike's talking is seemingly so muddled, careless and inaccurate that nothing can be made of it and one even gets to wondering if he can see the salient points himself. He can, of course.'

From a financial point of view, the deal between Fergus Hinds and Michael Hatcher proved to be more than satisfactory. The target was a Japanese freighter called *Taigyo Maru*, one of many torpedoed by allied submarines in the latter stages of World War II in the South China Sea. Risdon Beasley's research had turned up details of her loss, and their vessel *Ashford* made the first salvage of her cargo. Her manifest said that she was carrying 217 tons of tin. Risdon Beasley salvaged twice that amount from her holds and went away well satisfied.

When Risdon Beasley closed their Far East operations Hinds gave the information and the position of the wreck to Hatcher for a share of the profits. Perhaps keen to watch his own interests, Hinds also stayed on as a participant in the venture. Fergus believed that perhaps 50 to 70 tons may have been left in the wreck when the monsoon closed their season. At $US43,000 a ton, 50 tons of tin was still worth pursuing.

The salvors were in for a pleasant surprise. They found an untouched hold in the sunken ship that had been missed by Beasley's men and recovered not 50 or 70 tons of tin, but 600 tons of ingots worth $US10 million. Fergus was wearing a broad smile at the end of the recovery. The operation was an eye opener. Risdon Beasley had generally undertaken much higher profile activities with ocean-going vessels and had employed what they considered to be a more professional approach. But 'big' is not always 'better', and humble equipment can sometimes operate with comparable efficiency, especially when applied by a consummate shoe-string operator.

In a letter to his children, Fergus Hinds described his first impressions of the salvage of *Taigyo Maru*.

'All the gear on the ship [*Seeker I*] is just barely adequate, some things we can not do at all, some only just, and none at all easily, it is a hard grind. The ship has cockroaches everywhere, some as big as kittens. There are rats above the ceiling over my bunk by day and chewing the stores under it by night. We got two of them but that is not the lot. When it rains my bunk gets wet. We had no fresh vegetables on a trip for 20 days after day five. Tinned carrots, tinned cauliflower (horrible stuff) and the odd frozen sprout thereafter. The oranges went bad about day 10. A supply of vitamin tablets is supposed to take care of all the dietary deficiencies.

'We are very tight for fresh water. Washing takes place in a plastic bucket on deck using salt water from the engine cooling system which runs across the deck in a grubby hose when underway. Or from a bucket of cold sea water from over the side when not travelling. We have masses of shampoo which will lather in salt water after a fashion. You rinse in about a quart of fresh water from the shower. The bog [toilet] is a horrible penance. The shower overhead drips on you as you sit, and the door has to be held shut. If the boat rolls in the slightest, air puffs up round the bend and sprays you with sea water or whatever else has just gone down there every five seconds or so. Except when the engine is running you have to flush the thing with buckets of water from over the side. For this you use the bathing bucket which also serve as a dhobi [washing] bucket and container in which raw meat and vegetables from the deep freeze thaw out in sea water. As you can see it is a pretty important bucket (in a vile corset-pink colour) so when it got a split in it, it had to be patched up inside and out with sticky tape – less than ideally hygienic.'

Life on the Rat Boat.

Fergus was especially nervous aboard *Seeker I* because of her odd construction – a skeleton of steel reinforcing rods and chicken wire which had been plastered with concrete on both sides. Coming alongside a jetty or another boat with a bump tended to crack the concrete skin. While this could be readily repaired with another bag of concrete, the more serious consequence was the passage of sea water into the interior reinforcing rods. This began a process of rusting out the rods and the wire which was almost invisible as the outer crust of concrete concealed the extent of the damage. Would the hull collapse one day in a puff of concrete dust and rust flakes? There was no way of telling.

'I once ran that boat,' Fergus Hinds recalled, 'loaded down to a foot of freeboard with $600,000 worth of tin ingots for 300 miles across the South China Sea. I was conscious every yard of the way of the nearest shelter to make for should even the slightest puff of breeze ruffle the mill pond flatness we set out on. It was not at all wise. But the cargo was the first earnings of a long season and cash flow considerations were pressing!'

And the rats?

At one time *Seeker I* was tied up behind another boat for nearly three weeks. There was nobody and no food aboard and the crew hoped that the remaining rat would starve or die of thirst. No such luck ... it ate Fergus' flannel, some of his shoes and even somebody's sun cream. The rat was probably still aboard ('unmanifested livestock' as Fergus put it) when *Seeker I* was finally sold.

The rodent equivalent of the Flying Dutchman.

❀

There were other aspects of the Hatcher operation which Hinds describes with a chuckle. In addition to the usual salvage barge, in this case the 'Anchorer' positioned over the wreck as the divers' base of operations, there was another vessel called *Sea Runner* whose sole job was to tow the barge when it needed to be moved. Built in the Philippines she would never have passed survey in any other port.

'This ship had about 10 links to its single anchor cable, the rest being a seven-fathom-length of wire,' Fergus recalls. 'She would drag her anchor even in Singapore Roads! When not required *Sea Runner* remained tied to a buoy. To prevent her crew absconding she was never given enough fuel to steam more than 50 miles and from their position in the South China that wouldn't have been enough distance to get her into water where her anchor could even touch the bottom, much less hold her!'

The *Taigyo Maru* salvage turned out to be a happy event for both Hatcher and Fergus Hinds. There was a degree of luck involved, but they also had spent an entire season diligently searching. Hatcher's good fortune has saved him many times over the years, and often at the 11th hour when enterprises which seemed doomed suddenly blossomed into bonanzas. In spite of fortune, whether good or bad, persistence and self-belief inevitably played important parts.

The coast of Vietnam and the east coast of Malaya, both washed by the South China Sea, were waters where tragedy was played out in the late 1970s and the 1980s after the fall of Saigon. About a million people tried to flee the country and the new regime, buying passage in rickety fishing boats which were often hardly fit to go to sea. In desperation, some reached Australia, navigating by the pages of school atlases because no charts were available in Vietnam. It has been estimated that half of the refugees who set out perished at sea. The real figure will never be known, since the voyages were clandestine and illegal so far as the Vietnamese regime was concerned.

According to Australian Department of Foreign Affairs information, in the two years prior to 1987, 46,000 boat people, mainly of Chinese descent and discriminated against in a Vietnam hostile to China, fled the country. In 1987, a further 23,000 were expected. Recorded figures showed that 7000 people a year were arriving at Palau Bidon in Malaysia. They were the lucky ones. Australia accepted more than 100,000 refugees from 1975 onwards.

Despite this phenomenal exodus, as many as 500,000 people may have died in one of the great maritime disasters of all time. The chief cause of casualties was undoubtedly the unseaworthy condition of the boats in which the refugees set out. There was also a lack of adequate supplies of food and fresh water. However, a significant number of boat people fell prey to Thai pirates who patrolled the refugee route south to Malaysian waters. These pirates were in normal circumstances ordinary fishermen, but in the unusual situation of the exodus of the boat people they became ruthless predators, their high-powered vessels waiting in the sea lanes like hungry sharks.

Many of the refugees were carrying valuables, gold, silver and jewellery to give them a start in a new country. The pirates stole what they could, sometimes torturing the boat people or threatening to kill children to make them reveal where they had hidden their valuables. They took rings from women's fingers and when the rings would not come off they would excise the finger.

Many of the women and girl children, some as young as 10 or 11 years old, were raped. Some of the more attractive young women were taken away to islands to become sex slaves for the pirates or forced to work in brothels for passing fishermen. If there was any resistance when the pirates boarded the refugee boats the men were killed or thrown overboard. Sometimes the boats were simply sunk on the basis that 'dead men tell no tales'.

These outrages were widely publicised in the world press, but most of the regional governments refused to recognise the situation or take action. The Vietnamese regarded the refugees at best as escapees from the responsibilities of re-building a war-ravaged country. At worst they saw them as traitors. The Thai government did not want boat people coming ashore and saw the pirates as a practical self-regulating deterrent. The Malaysian government allowed some of the desperates to land, but under-resourced themselves, they kept them confined in camps while destinations in more affluent countries such as the United States, Britain, Canada and Australia were found.

A good deal of the practical assistance given to the boat people came from private sources – from oil companies, survey vessels and salvage operators who happened to be working in the area. Helping the refugees, often in unstable or sinking vessels, was a natural humanitarian thing to do. But that generosity could result in major problems for these good Samaritans.

Most of the boat people were in craft that were unfit to go to the river mouth let alone venture on the open sea. When they came alongside an oil rig platform or another vessel the first impulse was to jump onto the rig or the more seaworthy craft and make themselves the responsibility of the captain and crew. Sometimes they deliberately sank their rickety vessels so that the craft they approached would be obliged to rescue them and look after them. Since the authorities of most neighbouring countries refused to accept boat people, the reluctant hosts could be stuck with their unwanted cargo for an indefinite period.

There was strong sympathy for the boat people among the operators of working craft in the area, but most were on contract to do a job. They could not break off to ferry unwanted passengers long distances to Singapore or other ports. The refugee craft carried from 30 to as many as 300 people and work boats did not have the facilities to look after those sorts of numbers. Nor could they afford to be tied up days or weeks in port while officials argued over the fate of the miserable human cargo.

It was an unhappy situation all round.

Fergus Hinds' old firm Risdon Beasley had some unfortunate experiences. 'The region was infested with revolting Thai pirates who preyed mercilessly on any refugees they could catch,' Fergus recalled in *Riches from Wrecks*. Several times boats came alongside the salvage vessel *Ashford* seeking protection from pirates at night, 'which could hardly be refused'. On one occasion 39 people were taken on board for what was intended as temporary refuge. 'Their boat was taken in tow, but the weather being bad and the condition of their boat deplorable, in the morning *Ashford* found herself towing nothing but a plank. Her visitors had become residents.'

Ashford was obliged to take her boat people on to Singapore. There the authorities would not let them land until the British High Commission confirmed that the United Kingdom would accept them. This meant that *Ashford* was tied up in port for three weeks having to feed and look after the extra people.

Oil companies with platforms and rigs on the east coast of Malaya were particularly vulnerable. The boat people could see the flame of the rigs from 50 miles away at night and used them for navigation. 'Once you see the flame of the oil rig you are safe,' they were told. The temptation to jump from their unsafe craft to an oil rig or another boat was often overwhelming. But of course a rig could not operate with a milling mass of refugees aboard.

Some of the oil companies adopted a compromise policy. All the rigs were required to have safety vessels in attendance and Mike Hatcher's *Seeker I* and later *Restless M* was often chartered for that purpose in addition to the regular survey work. When a refugee boat was sighted the safety boat was sent to meet it, offering food and water and directing it to a buoy in the vicinity of the rig. There it would be protected from pirates.

'We would wait until we had a number of boats tied off the buoy,' Hatcher recalls. 'Then we or the Malaysian Navy would tow them into sheltered waters where they would go on to a gazetted receiving point.'

He witnessed a number of incidents during the period, some of them disturbing. 'Once on a wreck-searching survey we anchored off an offshore rock. I thought it might be worth a check in the morning for possible wrecks. The rock was called Ko Hosin and was 40 miles off Malaysian shores. It had a beacon on it but no light. In the morning I got up and looked up and then stared in sheer amazement. The rock was covered with people all waving at us.'

During the night a boat containing a dozen refugees heading south from Vietnam had seen the riding lights of *Restless M*. Heading towards them they had failed to see the unlit rock and their boat had hit it and sank.

Phil Vidal, a member of Hatcher's crew, wrote a graphic description of the rescue. 'The rock was barely eight metres wide, and only two metres above sea level, washed by the waves. First we took bread and condensed milk to the castaways and Mike Hatcher in a wetsuit swam the food in to the refugees. There were men, women and children, cold and in a pathetic state. We assured them they would be rescued and we returned to *Restless M* to assess the situation.

'We needed advice to see how we could best help them. The political aspects of refugee resettlement were complicated. A wrong decision could ruin or delay the refugees' chance of resettlement. We could be quarantined or even turned away from port ourselves. We had all heard stories of these boat people being turned back into the sea. And where would we take them? Thailand, Singapore or Malaysia?

'Every morning there was a south-east Asia network on ham radio run by Rowdy (Rowdy's net). So when the emergencies at sea were called, Mike checked in. There he talked with Rowdy and Chuck in Hong Kong who rang the United States and British embassies for legal advice on the situation. Since *Restless M* was a British registered vessel we had to have an assurance from a high commission that they would take the refugees. We had a satellite communication system on board and Mike pressed the "Emergency at sea" button which was hooked in with the rescue control centre in Norway. Within a short period we were able to confirm that if we picked up the refugees they would be taken from us in Singapore.

'That was all we needed. We went back with a buoyancy vest and rope. Mike swam over to the rock again. Starting with the smallest children, he put the vest on them. There was terror in their faces as Mike leapt over the barnacles with them into the churning water. Hashim manoeuvred the dingy in as close to the rock as possible, careful to avoid the razor sharp barnacles as one contact could slice open the inflatable and sink it.

'Even the youngest children had iron grips as we pulled them into the dingy and when we had the 10 women and children, we raced them back to *Restless M.* There the crew had prepared an area on the bow where they could wash. The second load was the men and except for a couple of the boys none of them could swim at all. It was their first bath in 10 days and the soap suds and shampoo flew for the next hour. Then all their clothes went over the side to be replaced with fresh T-shirts, shorts and underwear donated by the crew.

'You could see the colour returning to their faces as they drank hot coffee with the realisation that they were almost free and safe. They all had barnacle cuts on their hands and legs which were attended to. It was amazing that no one had any serious injury. Two of the girls were obviously not getting their colour back and were very sick and dehydrated. We stretched out mattresses on the floor of the lounge. Laying them down comfortably, we took their temperature, blood pressure and pulse. It was then that we realised how close to death they were. So we declared a medical emergency. It was an effort to make them drink but we forced glucose and vitamins into their bodies. There they lay unconscious for the next 18 hours. One had a husband and he sat at the door all day and night silently weeping as he had given up hope of her survival. The other girl tossed and turned and wept in her sleep. We did all we could to get her temperature down.

'The girl who could speak a little English, "Anh Kim", then related to us her story of how they had been rowing for the last eight days. They had left the southern tip of Vietnam 10 days before and their engine broke down two days later. Their boat was very small and they had run out of food on the seventh day. They had seen the lights of our boat around midnight and were heading to it when they hit the rock. Their boat had been taking water and this was the last straw for it. They were extremely lucky the seas were fairly calm and it was low tide so they were able to scramble up onto the rock without much difficulty before the boat sank completely.

'We picked up anchor and started our trip for Singapore. A little while later we received a telex from the United Nation's Refugee Centre advising us to head for Pulau Bidong. Pulau Bidong was two hundred miles south of Ko Losin on the Malay Peninsular and we told them we would be there the next morning. The night was a long one and we were all praying for the girls as the boat steamed on. We arrived at Bidong at dawn. And as the United Nation Refugee Centre had promised, doctors were standing by. The refugees were transferred to shore by a Malay fishing boat and the doctors hospitalised the two girls at once. They went straight onto an intravenous drip and the doctors said they were lucky to be alive.

'We told our story to the United Nations officials who received them. They assured us they would do all they could to get these people into a respectable lifestyle in society.'

❋

By the time the refugee boats reached the Malaysian coast they had been two to three weeks at sea. Often the people aboard were starving and out of fresh water. Sometimes they had dead bodies on board. When asked why they didn't throw the bodies overboard, the usual response was that the dead were relatives and that it was hoped they could be buried on shore. With no facilities for washing and usually no toilet on what had been subsistence fishing boats with crews of only five to 10 men, the overcrowded vessels were a sea-going nightmare for the refugees.

'You could usually smell them before you could see them,' Hatcher recalls. 'Especially if there were bodies on board.'

When they reached the oil rigs buoy the refugees were brought aboard *Seeker I* in relays and given a chance to wash down with the deck hose and eat the first food they may have had for days. The pirates were so bold that they sometimes pursued the refugees right to the oil rigs, knowing that *Seeker I* and the other boats could do little.

'On one occasion we had a number of refugee boats on the buoy and another one appeared in the distance,' Hatcher recalls. '*Seeker I* and other safety boats went out to pick it up and found it had just been the subject of a raid by two pirate boats. There were the usual piteous scenes. The pirates were totally arrogant. One of the boats took off, the other stayed with the crew jeering, making obscene gestures, and firing pistols in the air. When we went alongside the refugee boat to give assistance to the injured, the pirates circled around deliberately so that the wash banged the vessels together.

'It was too much for the crew on the boats nearby. The refugee boats often carried basic arms, pistols, AK 47's and rocket-launchers, left over from the Vietnam war. Usually we made them throw them overboard, but some did keep a few pieces in case the pirates ever gave them a personal problem. On this day the pirates finally went too far. Some of the pistol shots began zinging dangerously close to our guys trying to help the refugees. One of the crewmembers on the boats ran out of patience. He picked up a rocket-launcher – we'd all wondered how effective they were – and aimed it at the pirate boat. The Thais rolled around laughing because they never believed he'd have the guts to pull the trigger. Big mistake!'

BANG!

'The rocket snaked out across the water. Then there was a double explosion as it hit somewhere around the stern of the pirate boat. A huge cloud of black smoke and debris went up in the air. When all the bits splashed back in the water and the smoke had cleared there was nothing. No boat, no people, just a dirty patch on the water. Obviously the rocket had hit a fuel tank. The refugees cheered themselves hoarse. For once the victory was on their side. I have often thought about that incident since. I'd like to be able to say I felt sorry for the pirates and that I had some regrets. But I don't. Those people deserved everything they got. If anything it was a kinder departure from this world than the evil treatment they had meted out to those poor refugees.'

Musing on the incident, Hatcher later reflected, 'Pirates sometimes gave you no choice. If you didn't respond quickly and effectively you were dead meat yourself. A truly dangerous situation needs courage and quick thinking to resolve it. A lot of Europeans were reluctant to make the first move and a few of them paid a heavy price. One yacht was boarded off Penang. The skipper had a revolver and the pirates were only armed with knives and machetes. But he was reluctant to fire. They got on board, half-chopped off his arm with a machete blow, raped his pregnant wife and stole everything they had. The skipper and his wife lived but they never recovered from the experience. It ruined their lives.'

❦

Not all confrontations ended so dramatically and many ended in laughter. Often pirates would come up alongside the tankers and other commercial vessels (including *Seeker I*) in fast outboard boats, with one man on the foredeck swinging a grapnel which he'd hook on to allow the rest of the gang to swarm on.

While doing standby duties for an oil-rig in the Malacca Strait, a couple of grapnel boats appeared out of nowhere and started approaching *Seeker I* from astern. Mike Hatcher's boat was fitted with a large fire pump which doubled as a bilge pump and when the watch alerted him there were fast-approaching pirates, he ordered the pump to be readied. As the pirates closed in, Hatcher let them have a couple of thousand gallons of greasy bilge water under high pressure. The jet blew the man right off the foredeck, grapnel and all, and half sank their boat!

Another incident Hatcher recalls involved *Seeker I* towing a line of refugee boats ashore. Because the boats were in such bad condition Hatcher allowed the women and children to ride on *Seeker I* until they were close to shore. A girl came up to Hatcher and in good English (mostly the refugees spoke only French or Vietnamese) told him there was an old man aboard Hatcher's boat who had taken all their money. He was the organiser of the voyage and they had paid him an agreed amount, but when it was time to go on board he demanded more. He had stolen her engagement ring and money and jewellery from the other passengers. It was extortion, plain and simple.

Officially, Hatcher couldn't interfere, but there were only supposed to be women and children on board, so he went down to the stern and sure enough found the man hiding under a tarpaulin clutching his bag of ill-gotten gains. He told him he had to return to the refugee boat.

'I can't,' the old man replied. 'They will kill me.'

'If you stay on board here you have to give back the rings and things you have taken from them,' Hatcher said.

'It was a contract,' he insisted.

'No. You haven't fulfilled your contract. I am taking these people ashore. Not you.'

He shook his head stubbornly.

'Right!' Hatcher said to the crew. 'Slow her down and make ready to transfer this heap of crap back where he belongs!' Seeing Hatcher was serious, the old man finally gave in, handed over the bag and the goods were duly distributed.

When Hatcher reached the end of the tow, he looked for the old man, but could not find him. He could only assume he had not made it to the end of the voyage, the victim of his own greed.

❀

While Mike Hatcher was on the east coast of Malaysia he was asked by a fisherman working out of Mersing to free his trawl which was stuck fast to an obstruction on the bottom. The fisherman couldn't afford the cost of a dive, but in the area where the trawl was caught the most likely obstruction was a wartime wreck.

He went down and discovered a very large (73-metre) Dutch submarine with a hole in the front you could have driven a truck through. Most probably she had hit a mine while running on the surface. She had the word *DICHT* on a crate and they thought at first she was German.

Research showed that five Dutch submarines had left Soerabaja in Dutch Colonial Indonesia in December 1941 to join British forces in Singapore after Pearl Harbor. They were given the task of patrolling the east coast of Malaya and the Gulf of Siam. The O-XV1 had a brief burst of glory, sinking four Japanese transport ships, but on December 13, returning for more torpedoes, she was sunk, probably by a British mine. Another submarine, the K XVII, simply disappeared and was never heard of again.

Mike Hatcher reported his find and the first thought was that it was the O-XV1, whose single survivor, quartermaster Cor de Wolf, had described the sinking. But it was the wrong place for the O-XV1. Sometime later Hatcher was contacted by Hans Besançon, a former navy officer now retired in Holland, whose father had been the captain of the K XVII. He wondered whether the submarine might be his father's ship and had been researching the records in Holland trying to discover what happened back in 1941. The two talked for a while and Hans mentioned he could get the backing of a Dutch magazine, *Panorama*, to pay his way out to Singapore and to charter Hatcher's boat. He wanted to know whether they could mount an expedition to go out to investigate his father's grave and to try and determine exactly what had transpired.

The wreck lay north of Tioman Island in 150 feet of water. Getting *Seeker I* there from Singapore was not difficult, but it would take some days to arrive and complete the dive. *Panorama* magazine sent reporter Reiner Hopmans and photographer Martin Paternotte out to Singapore with Hans Besançon to go to the sunken submarine.

'I never really thought about the death of my father until a few years ago,' Besançon told Hopmans. 'I was 11 years old when it happened. My father was an officer in the marines and in my eyes he was a kind of hero. But the family did not discuss the matter very much. I joined the marines myself and met a few old colleagues of my father. But no-one ever spoke of the fate of the K XVII. The old men did not like to talk about the war. It was painful for them how they had survived the war and my father had not ...'

In 1981 *Seeker I* took Besançon and the *Panorama* team to sea. First they went to the island of Palau Aur, where Cor de Wolf, the sole survivor of the O-XV1, had come ashore after swimming for 35 hours. His was a remarkable story. De Wolf was lucky enough to be on the bridge in the conning tower as the O-XV1 headed back to Singapore to rearm with more torpedoes. Her crew was in a buoyant mood after sinking four Japanese troop transports. The Pacific War was only five days old. De Wolf reported:

'About half past two at night there was a big explosion, an enormous bang. I saw the boat split in a half before my eyes, a huge amount of water poured over the bridge followed by the smell of warm diesel oil. The commander and the oldest officer tried to kick the trap door shut but in vain. I am attached with my oil skin to the mines harness, but I managed to free myself. The boat sank within a minute and I found myself in the water. I looked around but in the darkness couldn't see anything. I called out but did not get a reply, however after a time I saw others floating in the water and swam towards them. We called out to the commander and heard a reply, but he couldn't come to us and must have been a long way away. After that I didn't see him again.

'We swam next to each other, sailor van Tol losing strength. We had taken our clothes off, except for van Tol who was wearing a short coat and couldn't get it off. I couldn't bear it and swam back to help him and succeeded in getting it off. It was getting light and a few moments later van Tol sank. In the distance we saw some islands and this gave us hope. I encouraged the people to keep on swimming. About 8 am Jeekle also drowned. I asked Box and Kruidenhof if they were managing and they replied "thirsty". We were able to see the mountain tops more clearly, help might be near, a plane flew over us but did not notice us.

'At 9 am sailor Kruidenhof drowned. I know the time as my watch stopped at 10 am. I was still together with Box. We swam further but I noticed that the current would take us east of the island. We swam against the current until we were in front of the island. Another plane came near, a Dutch plane, but this one also did not see us. We swam all day. A terrible thirst came over us as the sun set after 17 hours. After this Box said to me, "I can't get on, if you stay alive please give my love to my wife and two children". Then he disappeared in the deep water.

'Finally after swimming 35 hours I reached the island on Tuesday at 12 o'clock. I was thrown onto the rocks where I lay bleeding from my legs and back. The sun burned my body. I had to have water but there was no water. I kept falling over and this lasted about five hours without result until I climbed down and found a crack in the rocks with water leaking out. I lay down and drank and fell asleep. When the sun came up I tried to walk around the island, but there were a lot of rocks and it was not easy. Finally I reached the other side of the island and I saw a native man in a little boat. I shouted loudly and the man heard me.'

The island where de Wolf came ashore after his remarkable feat of endurance is still uninhabited, but Hatcher was able to introduce the Dutch party to the brother of the man who had cared for the exhausted submariner. The hut where he spent several days recovering was still there.

❁

Seeker I moved on to the K XVII wrecksite. It was hoped that it would be possible for Hans Besançon to dive on the wreck even though he had not used underwater equipment before. However, because of the depth of 150 feet and because the surface was disturbed, Besançon was not confident of making the dive and declined with regret. Instead, Hatcher's divers Hash and Zac brought up a porcelain insulator from the radio aerial to show him. They said that old fishing nets caught on the submarine made the dive hazardous. Mike Hatcher went down and tried to free the compass but did not succeed. The divers reported that the deck gun still had its stopper in the barrel, indicating that no action was expected. All the submarine's deck hatches were open, showing that she must have been running on the surface and sank very quickly. The bow damage was almost certainly caused by a mine. In a similar situation the O-XV1 sank in less than a minute.

Finally Hatcher managed to free the bronze helm, the steering wheel, and brought it up for Hans Besançon. A number on the wheel would later identify it as coming from the K XVII.

'I am satisfied,' Hans said. 'This is my father's ship and this is where my father died. It was worth coming all the way out from Holland for this moment.'

Some other aspects were less satisfactory.

Hans Besançon was unhappy that he had received no government assistance with his pilgrimage and that for a relatively small price the resting place of the O-XV1 might have been discovered as well as more information about the K XVII. In addition, *Panorama* magazine failed to pay the costs they had promised though it was the major story in their November 1982 edition.

'Apart from that somewhat sour note I was really glad we were able to sort things out for Hans Besançon,' said Mike Hatcher. 'The wheel was a nice memento for his family.'

As it turned out the expedition to the sea grave of the K XVII would pay its own dividends before too long.

CHAPTER EIGHT

A Cargo of Porcelain

Michael Hatcher's act of kindness in bringing up the helm from the sunken Dutch submarine K XVII for Hans Besançon was repaid, literally, in gold. The wreck of the 1752 Dutch East Indiaman *Geldermalsen* with its fabulous cargo of Chinese porcelain and gold bars would make him famous around the world.

The seeds of the discovery were sewn on the return trip to Singapore aboard *Seeker I*. As they travelled Hatch was lamenting to Hans Besançon the scarcity of modern wrecks suitable for salvage. Most of the easy ones had been worked through, the difficult ones didn't get any easier, and the fall in the price of tin had made them even less attractive.

Hans asked why Hatcher didn't consider looking for some of the really old ships, the 17th and 18th century vessels laden with treasure.

'I'm not sure how I'd go about it,' Hatcher replied doubtfully. 'They were lost so long ago, how would you find them?'

'It can be done and I can help,' said Hans. 'I'm in the Netherlands with access to all the old records of the Vereenigde Oost-Indische Compagnie [the VOC].'

'The Vereenigde *what*?' Hatcher asked, screwing up his face.

'The United East-Indies Compagnie,' said Hans patiently. 'The Dutch East India Company operated in these waters from 1600 until the 19th century. Hundreds of their ships sailed through here with rich cargoes for over 200 years. Not all of them made it home. There were hazards of reefs, cyclones, pirates, warfare with the English and Portuguese.' He looked out across the waves. 'Quite a number were wrecked or sunk in south-east Asian waters. Some not so far from here.'

'What kind of cargoes did they have?' asked Hatcher, his interest now aroused.

'Silver and sometimes gold,' said Hans. 'Silks and spices, tea and tin. There were mixed cargoes. Everything from peacock feathers to fine ceramics.'

'Sounds interesting,' Hatcher mused. 'Can you find out about them? Is it possible to get information about probable positions, depths and cargo descriptions?'

'I can certainly try,' Hans replied. 'The company kept meticulous records. Everything was written down in duplicate and often triplicate. A lot of the records still survive. When I get back to Holland I'll have a look in the archives.'

Some weeks later Hans called. 'I've got something that I think will interest you,' he began, and proceeded to rattle off an extensive list of ship's names and dates. In particular, he mentioned a ship called *Risdam*, sunk in the Malacca Strait, as well as *Geldermalsen*.

❁

In 1983 the Hatcher team tackled the 17th century *Risdam*. It was their first choice since it was in the most convenient location. They were successful in finding the wreck and rang Hans and the Dutch government with the idea of launching an archaeological programme, but because of bureaucratic delays in Holland the project turned into a disaster and the name *Risdam* left a bitter taste.

'It was a stuff-up from start to finish,' Hatcher recalls tersely. 'When we went back to port the cook sold the position to a Singaporean group who went out and blew the tripes out of the wreck with explosives to get at the tin ingots in the cargo. It caused a hell of a fuss. But the negotiations with the various governments, Dutch and Malaysian, took so long that the looting was inevitable.'

The wreck was only two miles offshore, well within Malaysian territorial waters. The Malaysian authorities were furious when they found out. They arrested the rival salvors and threw them unceremoniously in gaol.

The incident and accusations of 'looting and pillaging' caused a furore in Holland where a 'Save the *Risdam*' campaign was mounted. Hatcher was included in the wrath of the academic historians and archaeologists and the experience left a dark legacy of anger and mistrust which would surface again when the *Geldermalsen* cargo arrived in Holland two years later.

Geldermalsen was supposed, from the survivors' accounts, to have been lost on the Geldrias Shoal south east of the position of modern Singapore, and that was the position Hans suggested from his research. But Mike Hatcher believed that it was more likely to be on the Admiral Stellingwerf Reef because that coral ledge better fitted the *Geldermalsen* story of a reef out of sight of land.

On Monday, January 3, 1752, a top-sail came in sight, a vessel bearing south from China down the South China Sea on course for the Gelasar and Sunda Straits. As the sail grew closer she could be seen to be a Dutch ship, three masted, and pushed along by a light northerly wind. The sun sparkled on her green and gold upper works and red lion figurehead, and the red, white, and blue Netherlands flag flying at her stern.

Geldermalsen was a near-new Indiaman and had been built in Middelburg for the Dutch East India Company Chamber of Zeeland in 1746. She was a large vessel, 150 feet in length, and she carried 31 cannon, 112 people and a valuable cargo. In the five years since her launching, she had been engaged in trade between the Dutch port of Batavia and India, Malacca and China. In 1752, with her holds full of cargo, she was homeward bound from Canton in China to her home port in Zeeland.

A port which she would never reach.

It was not the kind of day on which anyone would expect to be shipwrecked. Perhaps that was a part of the problem.

Her skipper, Jan Morel, a German aged 33 years, had enjoyed a good lunch and had left the navigation at a critical point to men whom history would show to be less than reliable. The sea was calm. Though it was the time of the north-east monsoon and the wind was blowing out of that quarter, it was comparatively light. About 4 o'clock in the afternoon the skipper came up on deck. He asked the boatswain Christoffel van Dijk whether Red Island, known to the Dutch as Het Ruyge Eiland, had been passed. The island was an important orientation point on the voyage south. Once it was passed the sea was clear of reefs and a ship could proceed south with confidence. The boatswain replied that the island was in sight to the north-west of the ship. On the basis of that information, which would soon prove to be disastrously wrong, Morel ordered that the ship's course be changed to due south.

At 6 pm three crewmen were sent to the masthead to see whether they could sight land. They reported open sea ahead. But just after sunset a Corsican seaman, Urbanus Urbani, who was checking the anchors, noticed breakers ahead. He screamed out to turn hard a' port and to put the helm down hard over but it was too late to change course and *Geldermalsen* crashed head on onto the reef.

By backing his sails the skipper managed to work his ship free of the corals but a few minutes later *Geldermalsen* struck again, this time with such a force that the main top mast fell down, killing and injuring a number of sailors. The rudder was knocked out of its

The Corel model of a VOC vessel from the *Geldermalsen* period. (© COREL)

Survey tower for the *Geldermalsen* search. In later years global positioning systems using satellites made fixed datum points unnecessary.

(© MIKE HATCHER)

Admiral Stellingwerf Reef — scene of the 18th century *Geldermalsen* disaster.
(© Mike Hatcher)

Broken blue-and-white pottery marks a ship's sea grave south of Singapore.
(© Mike Hatcher)

Salvage basket brings up treasures from the *Geldermalsen* wrecksite.

(© MIKE HATCHER)

Chamber-pot made to order in Chinese porcelain for Dutch customers. (© Mike Hatcher)

Immortals. Figurines found on *Geldermalsen* were probably the private property of the people aboard. (© Mike Hatcher)

Geldermalsen cargo in the warehouse in Amsterdam. At auction it brought $US20 million. (© Mike Hatcher)

The *Geldermalsen* auction in Amsterdam was an outstanding success. Many items fetched five times the pre-auction estimates. (© MIKE HATCHER)

A blue-and-white vase depicts a Chinese rural scene. (© MIKE HATCHER)

A bird statue survived the shipwreck to become a valued item at the Amsterdam auction. (© MIKE HATCHER)

Beautiful blue-and-white objects typified all that was best in Chinese porcelain manufacture. (© MIKE HATCHER)

The ship's bell from *Geldermalsen* was presented to the town of Middelburg by Hatcher and de Rham. (© MIKE HATCHER)

Gold ingots fetched prices of up to $US50,000 each at auction.

(© MIKE HATCHER)

Thai fishing boat with Thai Navy personnel approaches the salvage vessel *Australia Tide* in the Gulf of Thailand. (© Mike Hatcher)

Thai Navy marines approach *Australia Tide* with revolvers and automatic weapons. (© Mike Hatcher)

A Thai Navy vessel orders Hatcher to sail to a Thai port. He refuses and a stand-off ensues. (© MIKE HATCHER)

Surrender. Hatcher finally agrees to hand over the cargo to protect the crew. (© MIKE HATCHER)

The shark-tooth peak of Condor Reef comes within two metres of the surface. (© HUGH EDWARDS)

A massive anchor on the top of Condor Reef came from an 18th or 19th century wreck. (© HUGH EDWARDS)

Unsuccessful search on Condor Reef. There was plenty of evidence of other wrecks, but not of our target. (© HUGH EDWARDS)

At full sail, the junk *Song Saigon* looked magnificent. But looks can be deceiving … (© HUGH EDWARDS)

Broken porcelain shards salvaged from Condor Reef. But where was Ralph Lambton's cargo? (© HUGH EDWARDS)

Smiling faces from a past era greet today's travellers at Angkor Wat.

(© HUGH EDWARDS)

Angkor Wat's magnificent ruins stir visitors with their beauty and symmetry.

(© Hugh Edwards)

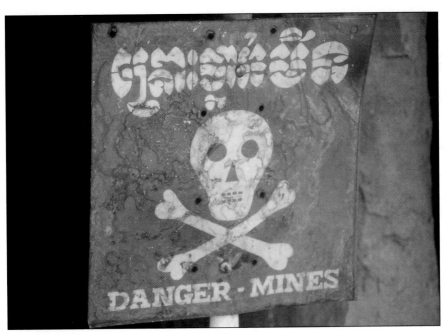

Landmine danger is ever-present in post-Khmer Rouge Cambodia. This sign carries a grim warning in two languages. (© Hugh Edwards)

The rebuilt Lord and Lady Lion. Local residents demanded an increase in the size of Leo's wedding tackle! (© Hugh Edwards)

Fishing boats at Lake Tongle Sap where Cambodians eke out a meagre living. (© Hugh Edwards)

Landmine victims are encountered everywhere in Cambodia, a country with no pensions or welfare.
(© HUGH EDWARDS)

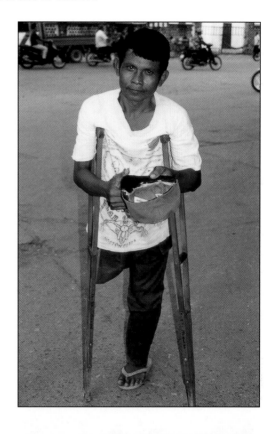

A street vendor in Siem Reap watches the passing parade. (© HUGH EDWARDS)

A solemn-faced Cambodian soldier aboard *Song Saigon*.

(© HUGH EDWARDS)

Mike Hatcher gets a laugh out of a soldier's automatic weapon aboard *Song Saigon*. (© HUGH EDWARDS)

pintles and the tiller snapped off at the head. Again the ship drifted free. But she was mortally wounded and water was pouring in through a massive hole in her bow timbers. Two anchors were dropped, the line breaking each time, before a third eventually held firm. *Geldermalsen* was now stabilised, head to wind, but she was taking water faster than the pumps could discharge it.

The two boats, a longboat and a gig or 'cockboat' (standard on VOC vessels) were launched. But as it became clear that the ship was sinking and there was only limited room in the boats, discipline broke down. There were no lifeboats as such in the 18th century and Indiamen usually carried one large boat for transferring cargo ashore and one smaller one for going between vessels at sea. At best the two boats of the *Geldermalsen* could have carried only half of the people aboard. As with *Titanic* in 1912, a seat on board a boat was the difference in the end between life and death.

The skipper assembled the main group of people on the poop, hoping that the ship would float until daylight, hoping against hope that there might yet be a chance to save her. The boats – so the boatswain reported – remained nearby. But it may be that those in them, fearful of being overwhelmed and swamped by a concerted rush of panicking people, put some distance between themselves and the ship.

At midnight a dreadful cry arose from those still aboard the ship. *Geldermalsen* lurched, half rolled on her side and quite suddenly disappeared below the waves. Few sailors could swim in 1752 and the choking cries of those in the water were soon silenced. Eighty people drowned that night, including Captain Morel, who had a wife and child in Holland and a son he had never seen; an English passenger named Richard Bagge; all her officers and most of her crew, among them 16 English sailors who had enlisted in Canton.

Only 32 of the 112 aboard survived in the two boats, though there was room in the longboat and cockboat for at least another

20 men. At daylight, the boatswain van Dijk reported that there was no trace of the vessel or crewmembers. Only the top of the mizzen mast broke the water.

Suffering dehydration and exposure, the survivors finally reached Batavia after some eight days at sea. The Dutch authorities there were furious at the loss of a fine ship and full cargo. They were also suspicious of the stories of the survivors. Van Dijk, in particular, was severely questioned. The authorities wanted to know whether those in the boats had left too soon, thus abandoning the others. Had they made an adequate search for survivors? In particular, what had happened to the chest of gold?

'Chest of gold?' van Dijk said, taken aback. 'What chest of gold?' He knew nothing, he said, of any gold.

The authorities were confident that the first thought of the captain would have been to see that the chest was placed in one of the boats, given the critical situation of the ship at the time. What had become of it? Stern faces frowned as the inquisition continued. Van Dijk still denied any knowledge of the gold but Morel's own steward, a man named Arnold, said that he and another crewmember had been ordered to bring a chest up from the captain's cabin. It was small, but very heavy. They had taken it to the ship's side and were preparing to tie a line to it when *Geldermalsen* rolled on her side and went down. Arnold swam to the boats and was saved.

The authorities continued to hold their suspicions. They demoted van Dijk to the rank of ordinary seaman and sent him back to the Netherlands in disgrace. The whole thing, they agreed, was very unsatisfactory, but at that point there was nothing else that could be done. Except, of course, to record the tragedy and the loss in company correspondence to Zeeland and Holland.

Years passed. *Geldermalsen* and her drowned captain and crew were forgotten. Teredo worms and other marine creatures bored holes in her timbers until the ship's structure collapsed and only the cargo and hard artefacts, such as the cannon and anchors, remained.

And the gold.

Centuries went by. Until one day Michael Hatcher, armed with Hans Besançon's information and a hunch of his own, went to the Admiral Stellingwerf Reef to search for her. It was a reef Mike Hatcher knew well. Situated in the southern approaches to Singapore it had fine staghorn corals and was a natural ship trap for vessels travelling north or south. He had found tin ingots and silver coin there in past years.

❁

In 1983 Hatcher was excited to find shards of blue-and-white pottery at Admiral Stellingwerf Reef. Nearby were some better preserved whole pieces. To Hatcher they did not look especially valuable but he took some in as general souvenirs. That year he had to make a business trip to Amsterdam and he took some of the blue-and-white pieces with him. The auction house Christies had an office in Amsterdam, specialising in Chinese porcelain.

'How much do you think this is worth?' the lady valuer asked him of a particular piece.

'About two quid,' said Hatcher, flashing his crooked grin.

'Try two thousand,' was the response.

Hatcher was amazed.

'How many pieces do you have like this?'

'About 30,000.'

Now it was the valuer's turn to be amazed.

For the first time Michael Hatcher became aware of the true value of Chinese porcelain. He realised he had a lot to learn on the subject and with typical thoroughness where cargoes of value are concerned he set about studying the subject.

'I had to ask myself why the porcelain was valuable. What sort of quantity was still out on Stellingwerf Reef, and where we should go from there?'

Just why was wreck porcelain – the cups, saucers, bowls, plates, jugs – intended for general domestic use in Holland in the 17th and 18th centuries, so valuable in modern times? Ironically, Chinese porcelain was not at all expensive at its time of manufacture. It was pragmatic ware, intended for practical use. Chinese blue-and-white pieces were minor items in terms of the value of cargoes brought back from the East to Europe aboard Dutch East India Company ships.

Although tea was the most valuable cargo, porcelain, because of its weight, had a practical use as ballast. It was loaded at the bottom of the holds in crates with the plates and bowls often packed in tea. It formed about 5 per cent of the cargo's value. The VOC usually auctioned the fine China at the wharf when a ship came home, making a tidy profit of 75 to 100 per cent. However tea was always the star trade performer, making up 60 per cent of the cargo of a ship like *Geldermalsen* and returning a profit of usually more than 90 per cent.

It was tea drinking which created the first fashion and the demand for Chinese porcelain. In the 1730s and 40s tea drinking became a craze in well-to-do Dutch homes. Coffee and chocolate also became popular. All the beverages had to be drunk from blue-and-white porcelain cups (different ones for each kind of drink) and a new word 'China' or 'Chinaware' entered the English language.

Women began to hold tea parties and they became a popular excuse to get out of the house and go visiting, to socialise and show off their porcelain. Because it was so pretty, and so light and attractive to the eye, blue-and-white China also had a decorative appeal. Paintings of the period show interiors with shelves lined with blue-and-white. In Holland it created a new industry in cabinet making with glass-fronted cabinets displaying house-proud burghers' wives' collections for visitors to admire and envy.

Prior to 1600 Europeans ate off wooden or pewter platters.

Chinaware was a revelation. At first only the rich could afford it but as demand increased prices became reasonable, and by the mid 1700s Chinaware was as affordable as the Korean and Japanese stoneware plates and table settings in supermarkets today.

Before too long a bewildering number of styles and shapes became available – 50 to 70 variations incorporating dinner plates, cuspidors, chamber pots, fish bowls, fish plates, beer mugs, milk jugs and butter dishes. There were soup plates and dessert bowls, saucers, cups and complex dinner services with scores of individual pieces.

Blue-and-white took Europe by storm.

It had such a marked effect that when European potters like Josiah Wedgewood began making similar goods using machine processes in the 1800s, they blatantly copied many of the Chinese 'Willow pattern' designs, and of course they called their product 'China'.

Despite its fragility (indicated by the old saying 'A bull in a China shop') a good deal of 17th and 18th century Chinese porcelain survives to this day, and is eagerly sought by collectors. As with coin and stamp collections, the value of each piece depends on rarity, fashion and the whims of the collectors' world. The chance discovery of an entire cargo of undelivered porcelain on the seabed by divers such as Mike Hatcher can set the antiques world abuzz and send prices rocketing.

❀

Although Hatcher now had an estimation of the value of *Geldermalsen's* cargo, there were still innumerable obstacles before him on the road to recovery. The most obvious problem was that even though Hatcher had brought a fair range of samples to Amsterdam for valuation, 90 per cent of the cargo was still on the seabed, fair game for anyone else who might happen along. Despite the depth of 130 feet (40 metres) of water, now that he had some inkling of the value of the porcelain Hatcher was naturally nervous. Possession, out in the South China Sea, was not just nine tenths of the law. It was 100 per cent.

At that time, Max de Rham was aware of *Geldermalsen* and had been making his own independent searches as a rival. Stellingwerf Reef was an obvious location. What if he came across the porcelain while searching for the Indiaman?

For their part Christies had their own degree of nervousness about Michael Hatcher. To them he was a sometimes-controversial salvor whose reputation had not been enhanced by the furore over *Risdam*. Hatcher resolutely refused to give any indication about where the porcelain had come from, though barnacles and sea growth indicated that the source obviously lay underwater. There was a question mark over Hatcher's legal title to it. There was nothing unusual about that. The law of the sea and salvage varied from country to country and was open to legal challenge even where explicit statutes were laid down.

Treasure trove has always been a controversial issue. The discovery of items of enormous wealth, such as the Central American the 'Ship of gold' in the United States, was inevitably followed by prolonged sessions in the courts and a bonanza for lawyers. A situation which has sometimes been likened to a piranha feeding frenzy.

In Australia the Commonwealth Government claims ownership of all wrecks within its territorial waters, regardless of whether (as in the case of the 1629 *Batavia*, 1656 *Vergulde Draeck*, 1712 *Zuytdorp*, or 1727 *Zeewyk*) the vessels were wrecked centuries before the east coast was discovered by Europeans and the country settled.

The world picture is confused, with different regulations in different countries. In some areas of the Mediterranean for example, it is a crime even to dive on an ancient shipwreck site. Regulations are one thing, legal rights another, and moral issues (whether a wreck is a sea-grave) for instance, a third factor. Salvors' views are naturally oriented towards their own interests. They tend to claim that a wreck, particularly a very old one, is abandoned and should therefore be the prize of whoever has the skill and courage to go after it. 'My motto,' Hatcher always says, 'is finders keepers!' Though he now makes agreements of convenience with governments he has never changed that basic belief.

The principle worked with tin wrecks and the relics of World War II where the cargoes were sold quietly to scrap metal merchants. But when it came to historic wrecks such as *Risdam* and *Geldermalsen* it became a heritage matter. The academic historians, the archaeologists and the public became involved. A controversy not easily resolved.

Christies were concerned about the title of the Hatcher porcelain they were handling. They were naturally cautious about items which their experts delicately described as 'having a doubtful provenance'. They tried placing 100 pieces at the end of an already planned auction of Chinese porcelain in 1983. The results were mixed. Some pieces brought fair prices, others failed to sell. But the fact that there was a return at all, combined with his increased awareness of the value of porcelain, sent Hatcher back to the Admiral Stellingwerf Reef. There he brought up the remainder of the cargo from the un-named ship which he believed was most likely to be *Geldermalsen*.

Up until that time Christies had been auctioning the pieces of blue-and-white purely on their collector value. Their romantic origin – that they had been brought up from the bottom of the sea – was glossed over for the reasons just described. But with the 1984 cargo the experts were concerned that the release of a large quantity of porcelain onto a capricious market would lower its value. Rarity was the essence, it was suggested. If the bowls and plates and cups became common as fish and chips, surely the prices must tumble.

It was decided to try a new tack. The fact that the material came from a shipwreck became the focus of publicity and

Captain Michael Hatcher was promoted as a swash-buckling treasure salvor. The result was a rush which exceeded all expectations. In a series of auctions throughout 1984 Christies saw porcelain prices climb far beyond the norm.

Anthony Thorncroft in his book *The Nanking Cargo* recalled that some plates, normally priced at about $1,000, were selling for $8,000 a pair. A peach-shaped wine ewer brought five times the anticipated price. Most significant of all, a bottle-vase covered in barnacles which the 'experts' expected would go for about $100 attracted a bid of $1,400.

The auction netted Michael Hatcher more than two million pounds sterling, a result which he saw as satisfactory at the time even though later events would indicate that much higher prices were obtainable using the right sales pitch.

The message was clear – publicise the wreck and promote Hatcher.

It was noted that most of the buyers were international dealers such as Axel Vervoordt of Antwerp, Elizabeth Gertz of Dallas and David Howard of London who on-sold their acquisitions to their clients at prices far above those realised at the auction. 'Far from flooding the market,' Thorncroft reported, 'the Ming cargo was actually acting as a stimulant. The romance of an ancient shipwreck obviously enhanced the value of porcelain. The lesson was taken on board and Hatch, instead of being a mysterious stranger to be treated with caution, became the hero of Christies.'

There was one other important realisation. The porcelain cargo, now marketed as 'The Hatcher Collection', was *not* from *Geldermalsen*. Characteristics of the pottery identified it as coming from the Ming period of Chinese history. This ended in 1643 when the reigning emperor was cut down by his own guards in a palace coup, terminating the dynasty. A date, 1643, on one of the pieces confirmed the period of manufacture. The unlucky *Geldermalsen*, departing Canton in the last weeks of 1751, would have been carrying porcelain from the Qing period, dated 100 years later.

Max de Rham, who attended the auction, was swift to pick up on the point. He had given up his search for the Dutch East Indiaman believing that Hatcher had already found it. In fact Hatch had shown Max blue-and-white porcelain in Singapore when he himself had thought that *Geldermalsen* was the source. Now it seemed the shipwreck was an un-named Chinese junk, 100 years older than the Dutch East Indiaman.

'You bastard!' said Max at the auction. 'It's not the G is it?'

Hatcher grinned apologetically. 'No,' he agreed. 'It's not. I thought it was at the time.'

There was a silence while the same thought ran through both their minds. *Geldermalsen* was still out there. Awaiting a discoverer.

There were two possibilities. They could compete. Or combine. They decided on the latter and thus began the real search for *Geldermalsen*.

CHAPTER NINE

The *Geldermalsen* Gold

When *Geldermalsen* rolled wearily on her side and sank in a cloud of bubbles in the green water off Admiral Stellingwerf Reef in 1752, she took her cargo, her captain, and 79 other men with her to the bottom of the South China Sea. Sharks and fish took care of the bodies within days. The ever ready requiem squad of the deep.

Over three centuries, the 18th, the 19th and 20th, the ship and cargo settled deep into the bottom sediments. The upper works, which included Captain Morel's cabin and the quarters of the English merchant, Richard Bagge, and their personal luggage, soon collapsed in the play of the currents, tumbling like a house of cards. The masts and rigging fell, rotted away, and left only iron rings on the sand.

Hungry teredo worms honeycombed the timbers. They tunnelled into the pine, fir, elm and oak, far from their native earth of northern Europe, allowing the salt water into the fibres of the wood until the once strong beams and plants rotted and became dust, mingling with the coral and shale bottom sediment.

By the time the 19th century came around, with New Year 1800 and the Napoleonic Wars, there was no ship to be seen, simply a mound rising gently from the seabed.

❀

In March 1985, armed with his new knowledge of Chinese porcelain, a new partner in his old friend, Max de Rham, and a new vessel in *Restless M*, Hatcher was back at the Admiral Stellingwerf Reef. Once again it was a case of patient search by 'lawnmowing'. As a marine geophysicist, Max De Rham was in charge of the survey. A temporary datum point of building scaffolding (Hatch was the master of improvisation) was erected on the high point of the reef. This was the area where *Geldermalsen* must have received her fatal injury 233 years before, stopped dead in her tracks by the corals, before drifting off into the night.

The quarters for the divers and the machinery for what was hoped would be the ultimate salvage were aboard a contract barge called *Costay Nile*. Max had brought his own yacht, *Star Ferry*, and *Restless M* was to be the lawnmower.

There was initial success at Stellingwerf with the recovery of two anchors. They were huge, wrought by blacksmiths in the classic 18th century shape with spade flukes and arms five metres across, and a shank more than six metres in length. They were located in shallow water buried under a metre and a half of dead coral. They were picked up by the magnetometer towed behind *Restless M* which registered metal anomalies, even though they were buried in the reef, and they raised hopes that they might be a part of the missing wreck.

A high pressure water jet, known as a 'stinger', cut through the coral and exposed the anchors. But there was no other associated wreckage to be found. It was back to lawnmowing for *Restless M* and as the weeks went by, the crew and Hatcher became increasingly despondent.

'We'd given the area a pretty good going over in the year we found the junk,' Hatcher recalls. 'As time went by with nothing new coming up on the sonar screen or the magnetometer readings, it began to look as though we'd drawn a blank.'

The exercise had cost the better part of a million dollars. They were already into extra time and over the costs they had allowed themselves. Were they simply throwing good money after bad?

'I was for packing it in,' Hatcher admitted later. 'The crew were bored out of their minds with inactivity. We'd been out there two months straight. Day after day with a big round zero for our efforts was pretty discouraging. Was it worth mortgaging ourselves any further? That was the question we had to ask ourselves.'

Max de Rham was on his first search and was keen to continue. 'Give me three more days,' he pleaded over their evening game of backgammon and bottle of red wine. 'We'd kick ourselves if someone else came out here and found it.'

'Two days,' agreed Hatcher. 'And that's the ABL. The absolute bloody limit.'

'Okay,' said de Rham. 'We'll find it tomorrow.'

They both smiled at the jest. The experience was one which would be mirrored in the junk discovery in 1999. Aside from the problem of running out of money.

The good weather period, the 'window' in the wind between the southerly and northerly monsoons, was drawing to an end. Every night the storm clouds built up in dark ominous peaks and castles in the sky and sheet lightning flashed between the cloud banks in a spectacular display. There were fierce sunsets in red, crimson and gold. For the time being it was only 'show time' – dry showers and the occasional hot gust of wind, indicators of more ominous things to come. The skies would clear by morning, but Hatcher knew the real storms would begin soon and when that happened it would be too difficult to work the wreck. The barge had already been damaged in an earlier storm and following machinery repairs and problems the crew had re-named *Costay Nile* 'The Costly Nile'. A rubber diving dinghy had also been washed overboard and lost. Further damage would create serious financial problems for the partners.

The crew were tired of fish and rice and they were looking forward to getting back to their wives and girlfriends in

Singapore, 100 miles to the north east. They were on a 'no cure, no pay' basis and it looked increasingly as though they had drawn a dud. Some were worried about their finances, anxious to find another job quickly in order to put food on the table. To take their minds off their problems, Hatcher took the diving crew over to the shallows of the high reef for a bit of spear fishing and surfing – two of the things they enjoyed most. There was also the thought that in the past the reef had provided ingots of tin and silver coin embedded in the coral. Perhaps a one-in-a-million chance might see something else turn up. The reef had been swum many times, chances were slim, but it was better than sitting on the barge staring out to sea.

Restless M meanwhile was patiently patrolling her invisible lines. She was an 80-footer, built in California and at the time of her construction she had been the largest fibreglass hand-laid hull in the world. An American owner had fitted her out to travel the world, but had tired of the nautical life by the time he reached Singapore. Hatcher bought her for the very reasonable price of $250,000 in 1983. She replaced the unlovely 'Rat Boat' *Seeker I*. Nonetheless *Seeker I* had done Mike Hatcher proud through the years. She had carried millions of dollars worth of tin, and few craft of her humble construction had ever earned as much money.

Restless M was a far prettier vessel with a dark blue hull and white upper works. Strangely enough the name which was so appropriate for her new owner Mike Hatcher, certainly a restless soul, had come with her from America.

'It helped with the sale,' Mike later admitted. 'How could I resist? I saw it as an omen.'

Now, as Mike Hatcher dived in the corals of Stellingwerf Reef, his hunch was about to be proven. He heard the sound of a fast-approaching outboard motor and by the time the boat arrived he was on the surface, mask pushed back, waiting.

'What's up?' he asked Max de Rham as the rubber dinghy stopped alongside him.

'Mike, we've got a signal on the mag,' said de Rham. 'And some interesting shapes on the bottom. MJ [the sonar operator] thinks it's worth a look.'

'Let's go then!' Hatcher heaved himself on board the 'rubber duck' diving tender and they zoomed off towards *Restless M* a mile away. A small buoy had been deployed marking the 'strike' point. De Rham told Hatcher that the depth was around 120 feet and that the visibility was pretty good. They pulled on the shoulder straps of the two scuba tanks in the bottom of the diving tender, fitted fins and face masks, and fell backwards over the gunwales into the water.

The sonar print-out of the bottom had shown lines and some strange depressions. It was a pattern quite unlike anything else they had seen anywhere in the vicinity.

BJ, a Singaporean Indian with considerable experience in operating sonar and magnetometers with de Rham, felt instinctively that the picture represented something significant. But to avoid disappointment, a low-key approach was taken. Max tried to hide his excitement until he was actually in the water, though, like BJ, he also had the feeling that they had registered something worthwhile. At the same time the magnetometer began clicking away 'like a cicada' indicating that iron objects were scattered about below. The two divers swam down the buoy-line, the water becoming increasingly dark as the sunlight receded behind them.

They had passed the 100-foot mark before they saw the bottom. It was grey and featureless, pale sand with dark streaks. Max swam towards one of the depressions which had shown on the sonar. It was about two metres across and a bit more than a metre in depth. A moray eel lived in the hole and in a fierce territorial display opened its mouth to show its nasty teeth. Max ignored the creature, reaching down past it towards something he saw indistinctly in the bottom of the depression.

Picking it up disturbed a cloud of sediment, temporarily

obscuring his vision, but as his fingers closed around the object he knew with heart-palpitating certainty what it was. As the fog of sediment finally cleared away there, in his hand, was a small white cup encrusted in sea growth ... a porcelain coffee cup that could only have come from China.

I think we've got it! Max told himself, then swam towards Hatcher, eager to show his prize.

Mike had already headed off towards where he saw fish hovering. A sure sign of a reef, or a shipwreck. As Max caught up with him they were both startled to run into what appeared to be a brick wall. It was made of small flat bricks of a kind once common in Jakarta. The bricks would later turn out to be part of the ship's galley. While they wondered about the bricks on that first dive they saw other shapes and their heartbeats increased with excitement as they identified cannon and anchors – one anchor identical to the others on the high reef.

Because of the depth and the danger of overstaying their bottom time they had to leave for the surface long before they were ready to do so. The urge to remain to examine, to explore, was almost irresistible.

It was a wreck and an old one. No question about that. But was it a Dutch wreck? Was it *Geldermalsen*? Or was it some other unfortunate and unnamed victim of the Admiral Stellingwerf Reef? A ship perhaps in ballast, or carrying valueless cargo? It would take time to survey it properly, to dig down into the cargo and they had already been down too deep, too long. Despite the temptation to linger, commonsense prevailed. There would be other dives. On this the first occasion they had time only to grab some broken shards of pottery and then reluctantly fin back towards the surface and the sunlight high above.

On deck, still in their dripping wetsuits, they examined their finds while the crew and the other divers peered eagerly over their shoulders.

'Look at that! Bloody beautiful! It's blue and white!' cried Hatcher, rubbing the sea growth off the broken shards he had brought to the surface. 'It's porcelain! We're in business, Max!'

Max de Rham gave a huge grin and made an imaginary toast with his coffee cup. 'We've got her!' he repeated.

Then, they stopped and stared at each other.

'What now?' asked Max. Suddenly all the plans they had made, the expectations of returning home, were tossed overboard. 'Where do we go from here?' he queried. This was Hatcher's area of expertise. He was the experienced salvage operator and on the way up from the dive his mind had already begun to race. He knew what equipment would be required, what stores, what difficulties might be encountered. However, there was a need for caution first. Hatcher held up his hand.

'Let's not jump the gun,' he said. 'The first thing is to check her out properly. To see if there's a cargo. Then if there is we go for it!' He was acting cautiously, much to the displeasure of many onboard, but he also recognised the importance of moving quickly.

'A secret doesn't care who had it in the first place,' he recalled later. 'We'd had the bad experience on *Risdam* when we went into port for stores and the cook sold the wreck's position to the opposition. They blew it apart and got the archaeologists and the authorities mad as hell. If this was a cargo we had to do the job properly and in one hit. I knew that someone would surely talk when we got back to shore. Once that happened all sorts of people from professionals to happy amateurs would be out there to see what they could get.'

There was also the question of government interest. The wreck was in international waters, but it was not far from the island of Bintan which was a part of Indonesia. Some nations were now claiming waters up to 200 miles from their tidemarks as 'zones of economic influence'. Strictly speaking this applied to all rights and resources such as fishing grounds. Wrecks weren't mentioned, but government departments in some countries appeared to make their own rules.

A court decision on the matter could take years of legal argument and appeals. Meantime the contents of the wreck would be dispersed by illegal operators while lawyers wrangled.

'If it's good we do it *now*!' Hatcher re-affirmed.

The wreck *was* good. An airlift probe disclosed the edges of plates and dishes still as pristine as they were when they were packed in chests in Canton in 1751. There was a good chance that most of the porcelain could be recovered intact, provided the weather held.

At that point there was no clear identification of the shipwreck. The iron guns and anchors suggested a European origin and this was soon confirmed by the finding of a brass candlestick, as well as wine bottles and glassware. The wreck was 36 metres in length and the buried timbers were intact up to the level of what would probably have been the waterline. It was surprising how well objects buried below that level were preserved. For example, some of the wooden crates containing porcelain were in such good condition that they actually had to be prised open.

Hatcher saw at once that a rapid excavation – necessary because of the impending monsoon – would require more divers and more equipment than they currently had on site. He made a trip into Singapore and returned with an extra barge, *Engineer*, a 50-ton crane, air compressors, a tug with a six-man crew and four more divers.

The two barges *Costay Nile* and *Engineer* were lashed together to form a stable base above the wreck. The machinery was set in place and a diving program organised. Before work could begin one of the factors which had most concerned Mike Hatcher came into play ... the weather.

A major storm came raging in across the mountains of Sumatra, bringing high seas and strong winds. The barges took a buffeting, machinery broke loose, and the team were forced to let go their anchors and cut and run for cover. They licked their wounds in more sheltered waters, repairing the damage and waiting in frustration for the weather to clear.

When they returned to the site they found that the storm had washed away their marker buoys. In the days before GPs (Global Positioning Systems) it looked as though they would have to begin the search for the wreck all over again. They groaned at the thought of more 'lawnmowing'. But luck was on their side. A crewmember sighted a fleeting glimpse of red far below the surface. A mere flicker of colour. But it was enough. It was one of the buoys which had been carried down by currents and entangled in the anchor lines.

The delays had cost a frustrating three weeks since the first sighting of the wreck, but finally, on May 28, 1985, recovery of the porcelain cargo began in earnest. Once the system was established the plates, dishes, bowls, and cups of the cargo came up from below as fast as they could be handled by the deck crew above who were engaged in cleaning off sea growth, scrubbing and washing.

The divers used surface-demand Kirby Morgan gear complete with full fibreglass helmets and microphones allowing communication with those above. As emergency back-up each diver carried a small 'pony' scuba tank. They worked in pairs, doing two shifts a day, the first pair entering the water at daylight, the last surfacing at last light. Their first dive was 50 minutes at 130 feet (46 metres), the second a shorter period of 40 minutes at the same depth.

As soon as they surfaced each pair of divers went straight into the decompression chamber for a spell of half an hour, breathing pure oxygen through a mask. This was a time of tedium and boredom which all the divers disliked, but it was essential to purge their systems of the nitrogen which had been absorbed into their bloodstreams under pressure more than 40 metres below.

The dishes and bowls were carefully placed by hand in plastic bins in a large steel basket. A winch on the barge then hauled it up to the surface by a wire rope running over an A-frame. The divers were raised and lowered in a lift, complete with emergency air tanks, which formed their underwater base of operations. The divers clipped their air lines to the lift and had a 45-foot radius in which to work. When the airlift was sending its clouds of bubbles skywards and sediment was billowing below, the visibility was sometimes reduced to an arm's length.

The airlift was a large pipe through which compressed air was pumped. As the air rose in a rush of bubbles to the surface it expanded in a thick white column and created an intense suction at the mouth of the pipe. Working like a giant vacuum cleaner it sucked away dirt and debris exposing the rows of plates and dishes and other objects of interest. However the airlift had to be used with care. The suction was so powerful that it could easily pick up and smash fragile porcelain. It could also painfully 'grab' a diver's hand. But a skilled operator could use it as a delicate tool, removing the over burden while leaving the cargo lying undisturbed.

Much of the porcelain initially retrieved was chipped or broken, most probably as a result of the enormous impact as the ship sank. But once the divers got below the surface layer most of the cargo was in pristine condition. It was a mixed blessing that the porcelain was packed in tea because as it was lifted out carefully the tea rose in a black cloud, sometimes reducing visibility to zero. It could be minutes before it settled enough to be able to see. Since time was precious the divers worked mainly by touch. This too had its disadvantages. Hands became scarred with cuts and grazes from broken pottery with sharp edges and wounds which refused to heal with continued work in salt water. If the divers wore gloves they lost a good deal of their sense of touch and most preferred to take the risk.

Day after day the items were loaded into the plastic bins in the lifting basket and were hoisted dripping up onto the deck.

Besides the hundreds of bowls and saucers, plates, cups and standard table ware, there was an amazing assortment of other objects – butter dishes, beer mugs (which brought a cheer from the crew), chamber pots, soup tureens, and some strange items later identified as vomit bowls. Like the Roman nobles of Nero's time, it seemed that the good burghers of Amsterdam at banquets sometimes ate to bursting point and then made themselves regurgitate in order to be able to eat again!

Most of the porcelain was the now-familiar blue-and-white variety, decorated with pictures of Chinese pagodas, rural scenes of peasants, flowers, animals, social life and stylistic patterns. But some items were different. There were pale-green celadon vases and bowls, items older than the general cargo and extremely valuable in their own right. There were also statuettes of gods and ancient figures dubbed 'immortals' by the crew as well as parrots, birds, buffalo, and mischievous small boys with blue shirts, no pants and tiny penises. One of the fascinating aspects was the fact that many of the jars and vases often contained smaller items which tumbled out on the sorting table. These included small figures, jewels and pill boxes. Some of the most magnificent pieces were huge fish dishes, 45 centimetres long and decorated with spectacular designs.

About 180,000 items were raised in total, and once on deck they were washed and the sea growth removed. They were then sorted into their various categories before being packed carefully away into containers for transport to Singapore.

Even with such exciting material, continually handling plates underwater, day after day, tended to pall. To prevent boredom the divers held competitions amongst one another. The best effort was 12 basketfuls of dinner plates, representing several hundred pieces, in one 50-minute dive.

For a time the cargo seemed to be almost inexhaustible but by the end of June it was mostly on the barge above. The divers were weary. Everyone in the crew was more than ready to go home. They had now been months at sea without a break, working seven days a week.

The only one, it seemed, in no hurry, was Mike Hatcher.

'Let's make sure we've got it all!' he said. 'We don't want to leave the job unfinished.' He proposed to airlift a trench around the wreck to check for cargo 'spill'. There was some grumbling out of earshot but Hatch's experience on recoveries and his gut instinct once again proved invaluable.

The trench progressed down the port side until one of the divers who was working around the bricks of the collapsed galley encountered by Max and Mike on the first dive, made a surprise discovery. The galley had burst through the port side of the ship, perhaps as a result of the impact when she struck the bottom, but more likely due to the vessel's timbers rotting, weakening and finally collapsing. The chief diver, Hans, was on the monitor and the intercom at the surface when a diver's voice came through.

'Surface! Surface!' he called, a new note in his voice.

'What's the problem?' There was sudden tension. Was the diver in trouble? Was the back-up diver ready to attempt a rescue if need be?

But the next words to come through sounded like heavenly music to the ears of Mike Hatcher and Max de Rham.

'GOLD!' shouted the diver. 'I've found gold!'

CHAPTER TEN

A Twenty Million Dollar Sale

'Gold!' The cry echoed around the barge. Pandemonium broke loose. All the divers were at the intercom trying to ask questions of the man down below. Amid the hub bub neither the diver below nor the questioners could be heard.

'Quiet!' shouted Hatcher in exasperation. 'Everyone shut up!' They all fell silent, waiting, wondering.

Finally the diver surfaced, a triumphant grin flashing white behind the glass of his helmet. When he unzipped his suit 17 small copper-coloured ingots fell to the deck with a dull clatter.

Gold! The divers pounced on them and rubbed them for colour, holding them up to the light, balancing them in their palms for weight. Gold! It was almost too good to be true!

The ingots, the diver said, when he came out of the decompression chamber, were lying outside the ship. Undoubtedly they were from the chest brought up on deck by the captain's steward, Arnold, when the ship was going down. The very same chest about which the VOC officials had questioned the boatswain Christoffel van Dijk so severely. A 234-year-old mystery had been solved. The gold had not been stolen after all, as the VOC officials feared.

Max de Rham was the next diver down, and he too found

142

gold bars. There began an excited competition to see who could bring up the most gold in a single dive.

The divers recovered a total of 125 bars, Mike Hatcher had a personal tally of 29. Later individual ingots, some cast in the Chinese 'lucky' shape of a shoe, and carrying various stamps, would fetch in the region of $US100,000 though their bullion value was only about $4000. It was the final triumph, the glitter which made *Geldermalsen* a $US20 million dollar prize.

With the lessons of the junk auctions behind them, Christies, Hatcher and de Rham began making plans for effectively marketing the G's porcelain and gold. The cargo was originally intended for a quayside auction in Amsterdam (back in 1752) so it seemed only fitting that the Dutch capital should host this new auction as well. One thing the junk auctions had taught them was that the history of the ship and the cargo were of great importance.

Where collectors were concerned with condition, rarity and age, the public was attracted by the romance of the story. In fact they were seeking souvenirs rather than collection pieces. But before the auction the extent of public participation was an unknown quantity. Since the porcelain was not as old as the collection from the junk and was of a lesser quality and a vastly larger quantity, there were more than a few who shook their heads before the auction.

'Christies, the auctioneers chosen by Hatcher to organise the sale, were racked by doubt as to whether there could be enough buyers for such a vast and unprecedented quantity of Chinese porcelain,' Anthony Thorncroft wrote in *The Nanking Cargo*.

'A number of dealers were also unimpressed,' Hatcher recalls. 'They reckoned we'd flood the market and destroy the value of what they already had for sale. They were very down-in-the-mouth about that.'

As it turned out, the cargo wasn't from Nanking at all, though the name proved a drawcard for sales. In the 18th century, all

Chinese porcelain had been advertised in Europe as being from Nanking though that was not geographically correct. Canton was more often the port of lading. The porcelain was spun, moulded, painted and fired far inland. By the time each individual piece reached Canton it had been repacked a number of times and had passed through many hands.

The history of porcelain manufacture in China is a fascinating story. Most modern-day Europeans have heard of 'Ming' porcelain and associate it in their minds with exquisite plates and vases affordable only by the very rich. In fact most of the export porcelain made during the Ming and succeeding periods was not highly priced. There was a distinct difference, of course, in quality between porcelain manufactured for the Emperor's court – delicate marvels of the potter's craft – and the bulk orders to be sent overseas.

Strangely, some of the earliest porcelain was designed not for the living but the dead. Funerals for important personages were elaborate affairs in which the deceased was finally laid to rest in a tomb with statues of servants, soldiers, concubines, horses, oxen and carts. There were models of most of the items in their contemporary life. Beautiful bowls, vases and plates were among the equipment taken into the next world by the deceased at the end of their earthly journey. Sealed in the tombs, some of the most exquisite examples of early porcelain art unearthed in modern times give a graphic picture of life at the time of the funeral. And, of course, they evidence the artistic skills of the potters of the time.

The name 'porcelain' is a European term. There is argument about whether it comes from the Venus or porcelain-like bi-valve shell so often depicted by painters of the Middle Ages or whether it is derived from the Latin *porcus* for swine, because the fine, white, smooth texture of good porcelain is not unlike the fine and smooth skin of young European pigs.

The Venus possibility is undoubtedly the more romantic of the two! The scallop shell of Venus, (recognisable in the Shell Oil

Company sign), does have the smoothness, strength and light weight nature of porcelain. Though the colours may pose a question. The pig image is probably closer to the mark. Pigs have been amongst the more useful domestic animals through human history, but they have been rewarded sadly with abuse and unflattering terminology. Perhaps we could (for once) let them live with a compliment.

The Chinese called porcelain *tzu*. According to George Savage in *Porcelain Through the Ages* this was because it gave a resonant note when struck. The striker, of course, had to take care that the resonant note did not become the dreaded tinkling sound of a fractured masterpiece.

'There are some variations on the term,' Savage added. 'Such as *pai-tzu* which signifies that the substance is white as well as resonant.'

'A rose by any other name,' said Shakespeare, 'would smell as sweet.' Should that also ring true for porcelain? Early Chinese pottery and patterns may have been influenced by Persian, Sumerian and Moorish Islamic designs which had incorporated ideas and conceptions from abroad. But by 618 AD Roman ladies were wearing Chinese silks and there was trade going in both directions in goods carried over the caravan routes made famous in legends such as *The Arabian Nights*. Chinese pottery and porcelain fragments from the year 883 AD have been found in excavations in the ancient city of Samara in modern Syria. By the Middle Ages Chinese silks and porcelain were regularly reaching the Middle East on camel back by the caravan routes, trans-shipping through Arab ports and through Venetian sea traders in the Mediterranean.

The marvellous pale-green celadon vases and plates were especially popular with European princes and potentates. It was a time of volatile politics and the plates were highly prized as they were supposed to change colour if poisoned foods were placed upon them. Back in England, Savage records, Archbishop

Warham bequeathed a bowl of Chinese celadon to New College, Oxford, in 1530.

Until the advent of aggressive European traders in south-east Asian seas, beginning with the arrival of the Portuguese Vasco da Gama in India in 1496, Chinese porcelain was largely manufactured for domestic use only. The Emperor's court was the major purchaser of fine-quality wares. In 1433 the Emperor's eunuch officials placed an order for 443,500 pieces from 58 designated 'official' kilns. Curiously, sales of what could have been an important export item were severely curtailed prior to the arrival of the Portuguese, Spanish, Dutch and English in eastern seas.

The Chinese had been a great sea-going nation. In 1405 a fleet under the eunuch Admiral Zheng He left China with 62 vessels and 28,000 men. Their junks were said to be 400 feet in length, with as many as nine masts to carry the enormous sails of silk. The stuff of legends, and legends traditionally tend towards exaggeration. But whatever the size – and there can be no doubt that they were far bigger than anything sailing European waters at that time – they made some impressive journeys.

On Zheng He's expeditions his fleets visited Malacca, Ceylon, India, the Persian Gulf and the Red Sea, before sailing down the East African coast as far south as Zanzibar. In waters closer to home they visited Sumatra, Java, Borneo and the islands of the eastern Indonesian Archipelago as far as New Guinea. It has even been suggested that Zheng He in his seven great expeditions may have sighted Australia. At the time the Ming navy totalled perhaps as many as 3,500 vessels and was the largest and by far the most powerful navy in the world, one quite capable of reaching Europe or the Americas had their commander continued pushing back the oceanic frontiers.

The question remains, what happened to Chinese sea power?

It collapsed entirely, defeated by scholars armed with nothing more than their quotations from Confucius.

By the 1500s and less than 100 years after Cheng He, the Imperial fleet had dwindled to a few score smaller vessels, poorly manned and maintained. The building of ocean-going ships had been forbidden. The Imperial court also forbade the Chinese people from private trading abroad or even leaving the country. The penalty for disobedience was death. It was a triumph for the numerous and widespread scholars and Confucian-educated bureaucracy of the Ming period. They despised the merchant classes and restricted them wherever they could, convinced they had become too prosperous and too prominent through the exercise of sea power. Taking away their ships cut them down to size.

Other arguments advanced were that the Zheng He expeditions had been horrendously expensive and that the money previously allocated to navy shipbuilding and maintaining a large contingent of vessels and men was needed for defence on the northern boundaries. The threat of the Mongols, the Huns and other barbaric tribes was a constant concern for the emperors in Peking. The Great Wall of China still stands today as testament to their caution, or paranoia, depending on how you look at it.

Finally, it was decreed, trade with countries outside China was unnecessary. Foreigners merely brought trouble and polluted the purity and virtue of Chinese life. Trade was despised as greedy and undignified. 'Profit is the concern of the little man,' Confucius said. A virtuous man put his mind to higher things. The Confucians extolled honour, noble birth, culture, arts, painting, poetry, the things of the mind. They also eulogised the importance of ancestors, respect for elders, parents and the family. The English aristocracy held similar attitudes, though instead of reading Confucius they rode to hounds.

While the essence of some of the purist Confucian theories of the scholars and mandarins and the officials of the Imperial court may have been admirable in abstraction, they failed to take into account a number of significant factors. Without a navy the government was henceforth unable to keep the unwanted ships of the Europeans, the despised 'Long Noses', from the coasts of China. Men on horseback could not supervise the activities of ships operated by Chinese subjects once they were at sea. The coastal provinces had poor hinterland country and had depended on their junks, shipbuilding and trade for their livelihood. They needed the sea for survival and in the end it proved impossible to keep them from it.

As soon as there was a relaxation of the harsh Imperial edicts and a lack of attention in the face of other serious threats to the emperors in Peking, the coastal people were building ships and sailing again. But the navy was never replaced and the end result was that the Europeans forced themselves and their unwelcome trade (including the noxious opium) upon the reluctant Chinese.

With improved designs of ships, superior firepower and irresistible self-confidence, the Europeans became the masters of not only Asian seas but of the oceans of all the world. For 400 years from the time of da Gama's arrival in India, the only serious opposition they struck was from ships of their own region where Catholic and Protestant were mortal enemies. In their home territories the Spanish, Portuguese, French, Dutch, and English all fought wars against each other.

With the martial skills and improved weapons developed in this inter-nicine warfare, the Europeans went forth with their cannon, their swords and the cross of the Christian religion and proceeded to conquer the world. For those 400 years of colonisation they remained constantly at each other's throats in an unending series of wars which continued into the 20th century.

But where China was concerned they were united. They would trade with Chinese whether or not the Emperor consented. Unable to prevent European ships calling, the Court decided to try to control their access. They allowed the Portuguese to establish a base at Macao which lasted until 1999. The Dutch established themselves at Fort Zeelandia in Taiwan and the

English and other nationalities succeeded in gaining admission, under restricted conditions, at Canton on the Pearl River.

Every European ship, or 'Indiaman', was a fortress in its own right, carrying up to 40 cannon – gunnery was their speciality. No Arab, Indian, or Chinese craft could stand against them on the water. However, they did not have the numbers of men or cavalry for serious military expeditions ashore. Their power tended to end at the high-water mark.

In China they were forbidden to venture beyond the boundaries of their 'factories' and for the most part, since they did not wish to actually live in China, they were content with the trading arrangements. Tea and porcelain were among the major exports carried in the holds of Dutch, Portuguese, and British ships to Europe.

The 1600s and 1700s saw the gradual establishment of the European powers on the Chinese coast. In the 1800s Britain located her own major base at Hong Kong and the English were able to live and do as they pleased in a Crown colony all of their own. In time Britain would become the superpower of Asian seas, and indeed of the oceans of the world. 'Britannia Rules the Waves!' expressed the sentiments and satisfaction of a dominant nation as the year 1900 came around.

But back in 1752 when *Geldermalsen* sailed from Canton with her cargo of tea and porcelain, the Dutch East India Company was still a major power in eastern seas. At the time of her loading, lying at anchor in the Pearl River in the roads off the VOC factory at Canton, the Dutch were placing regular orders for huge quantities of blue-and-white porcelain. An order for 250,000 pieces was registered in the *Geldermalsen's* year alone.

The loading of the ships was an exercise in practicality. Dry Pearl River gravel would be laid over the ship's ordinary rock ballast to make a smooth floor, then porcelain would come next packed with tea in chests. A layer of planks would be placed over the chests to form a new floor and then the major cargo of tea would be brought aboard by sampan and loaded in layers of chests until it was impossible to pack another tea leaf in.

The porcelain orders were very specific and had to be ordered at least a year in advance. The Chinese were conscious of the spirit of the earth, and few other industries were as dependent on natural resources as the manufacturer of porcelain. The first requirement was a deposit of the white kaolin clay, an extremely pure aluminium silicate. It was a substance which was malleable enough to be worked on the wheel or in moulds and strong enough to hold its shape while being fired.

Equally important was the feldspar rock which was ground to powder and mixed in with the kaolin. At high temperatures it fused with the kaolin to provide the glaze. The combination resulted in porcelain. It was light, reasonably strong and resistant to penetration by liquids – the perfect eating or drinking vessel and the basis of all 'Chinaware' today, the name applied regardless of whether it is manufactured in China, Japan, or Europe.

The clay was mined and ground to a fine mix in mills powered by water-wheels. This process was carried out in winter when the rains fell and the streams ran strongest. In a good winter with the rivers roaring down, the wheels spun fast and the mixture was ground the finest. If the rains were sporadic the mix was coarser. Thus seasons with good or bad rains could affect the quality of that year's porcelain.

The kilns required very high temperatures, of as much as 1450 degrees centigrade and heat control and consistency was a major part of the potter's art. The furnaces consumed a huge amount of fuel, and a continued supply of firewood, and its dryness and quality were also important to the industry. Labour was integral too, since the porcelain manufacturing process was labour intensive. At Jingdezhen, which became the main centre for porcelain manufacture, more than a million people were involved in the various aspects of the industry. It was said that there was no night in Jingdezhen because the glow of the furnaces and kilns resulted in permanent daylight while firing was in progress.

Here again nature became involved. While the grinding of the kaolin and feldspar was a winter occupation, the firing of the kilns had to be done in summer. Low winter temperatures resulted in a milky glaze. The throwing of the clay on the wheel, the moulding and the painting, and the final firing were therefore summer occupations. The finished product was carefully packed and transported by water from Jingdezhen to the coast. First the porcelain was carried downstream through rapids, then it had to cross the huge Lake Poyang, an inland sea. At the conclusion of that journey it was taken by coolie porters over the 300-metre-high Meiling Pass in the mountains. Then it was loaded into watercraft again for the final broad stream stages to Canton. In total it travelled more than 1000 kilometres by several forms of transport.

Again the seasons and good rains were important because there had to be enough water in the streams to circumvent the rocks in the 28 rapids between Jingdezhen and the lake in the first stage of the journey.

Finally, after this exhaustive winter-summer process there was another seasonal factor. The ships leaving Canton, loaded with tea and porcelain, had to wait for Christmas time and the north-east monsoon to make their journey down through the South China Sea to the Sunda Straits and the Indian Ocean.

By the time a piece of porcelain reached Europe on the other side of the world, it had been through many hands at critical seasons over at least two years. The kaolin miner, the potter, the painter, the firer of the kiln, the various boatmen, the beasts of burden, the human porters, the merchants and the captains, all played their own part before the porcelain reached some proud housefrau's living room or kitchen in Holland. 'There's many a slip twixt the cup and the lip,' is a saying that dates from the time.

❊

If Mike Hatcher had really discovered *Geldermalsen*, and given the importance of such a cargo, Christies wanted to be sure that all legalities of ownership were settled before the auction. They also requested a positive identification of the vessel, the two requirements going hand-in-hand.

Who owned the cargo?

Originally it belonged to the Dutch East India Company, defunct since the 1790s. However, the current Dutch Government were now the legal heirs. The question was whether *Geldermalsen* was abandoned and therefore it was a matter of 'finders keepers' for anyone salvaging the cargo, or whether the Dutch still had some claim. While the wreck was in what had once been international waters by virtue of the generally accepted 'three-mile limit', more and more nations were claiming 'exclusive economic zones' up to 200 miles from their shores.

On that basis it was possible that either Singapore or Indonesia could make claims even though the definition of 'exclusive economic zones' as defined by the United Nations convention on the Law of the Sea, referred only to oil and mineral deposits. There was no reference to shipwrecks. But some countries were disposed to claim anything. If the matter went to court, depending on which court and in what part of the world, it could have dragged on for years. And any decision could have been challenged. A legal nightmare for salvors and auctioneers alike.

Hatcher and de Rham decided to approach the Dutch Government. A deal was agreed whereby the Dutch – who originally wanted 25 per cent – settled for 10 per cent of the money raised from the sale of the cargo because of the distance of the wreck from Europe. The study of *Geldermalsen's* cargo of porcelain became the particular preserve of Dr Christian Jorg of Groningen University. He was concerned that while the cargo almost certainly came from *Geldermalsen*, conclusive proof of the ship's identity was lacking.

Anxious because of the unsatisfactory result of the un-named junk's cargo at auction, Christies suggested that Hatcher and de Rham go back and see whether they could find something which would positively identify the ship. 'Bring us back the name plate or the bell,' they said.

In early 1986 the partners returned to the site and did indeed come back with the ship's bell. They also found two bronze cannon and a personal seal with the initials FB. The bell did not have the ship's name on it, but it did have a date – 1747. That was the year in which *Geldermalsen* was launched. The bronze guns bore the VOC mark of the Dutch East India Company and the initials on the seal may have been those of Frederick Berkenhouwer, the ship's senior master, who did not survive the sinking.

The discoveries, as it turned out, would prove crucial to the success of the auction. Dr Jorg was able to provide full details of *Geldermalsen's* history including cargo lists carrying the signature of the ship's long-dead captain, Jan Morel. He had already written one book on the subject entitled *Porcelain & the Dutch China Trade* in 1982 and *Geldermalsen* gave him material for another book, *The Geldermalsen, History & Porcelain*, in the auction year of 1986.

He wrote: 'For an art historian such an exact dating – assuming that the porcelain shops in Canton have a fast turnover and therefore get new supplies regularly – is a delight. Here we have no less than 150,000 "guiding fossils" [the cargo], a fixed point of reference in time. We can place another piece of porcelain beside it and compare the stylistic characteristics, thus making a much more exact dating [of other works] possible. This is of great importance because of the ordinary Chinese export porcelain only a few pieces can be dated with certainty.'

Dr Jorg's research turned up the full list of porcelain carried on *Geldermalsen* in 203 chests. The list shows the amazing variety of tableware. Evidently fine and formal dining was practised more frequently in 1752 than it is today. The well-equipped household must have needed extensive glass cabinets and shelves to house it all.

Below is an inventory of the *Geldermalsen* porcelain:

171 dinner services – Dutch name *tafelserviessen*

62,623 tea cups and saucers *theegoed*

19,535 chocolate cups and saucers *koffiegoed*

578 tea pots *trekpotten*

548 milk jugs *melkkommen*

14,315 flat dinner plates *tafelborden*

1,452 soup plates *soepborden*

299 cuspidors (for spitting) *quispedoren*

606 vomit bowls (spew pots) *spuijpotjies*

75 fish bowls *viskcommen*

447 single dishes *enkele schalen*

1,000 nests of round dishes *nest ronde schalen*

195 butter dishes *botervlootjies*

2,565 bowls with saucers *kommetjies en pieringen*

821 English beer mugs *Englese bierkannen*

25,921 slop bowls *spoelkommen*

The Dutch allowed for five per cent breakages, and often ordered extra cups because these were the most frequently damaged items.

Other aspects of the recovery were less of a delight for Dr Jorg and other academics. In *The Nanking Cargo* Anthony Thorncroft wrote 'Dr Jorg cannot hide his irritation that a more meticulous archaeological search was not made. He was grateful for the discovery of a candlestick and one is listed among the cabin goods. But was it a candlestick used by Captain Morel and Richard Bagge as they mulled over their evening brandy? If its exact location on the seabed had been passed on more information on social life on board a merchantman would have been collated.'

As the auction drew near and the news of the extent and variety of the 150,000-piece cargo of *Geldermalsen* spread through Europe's universities and museums, academic fury against Hatcher began to mount.

'A bigger threat to the success of the sale,' Thorncroft wrote in *The Nanking Cargo*, 'had been the strong opposition mounted towards it by the [Netherlands] Rijksmuseum and its curator of marine archaeology, Mr Bas Kist. He considered that the *Geldermalsen* had been salvaged too quickly with all the concentration on bringing up the saleable cargo at the expense of serious historical investigation of the site. He called a press conference to publicise what he called the inadequate funding of marine archaeology by the Dutch Government. "... We fear that in the rush of romantic excitement part of the national heritage will be lost," said Kist.

'But when Mike Hatcher attempted to put his point of view [at the press conference] he was refused entry. The Rijksmuseum refused to take any part in the bidding. But in the event the Rijksmuseum's disapproval had no effect on the auction.'

The auction was six months in the planning and was the biggest porcelain sale ever attempted by Christies. All involved knew that a successful publicity and marketing campaign could mean the difference between success and failure. Hatcher had learned a few lessons from the junk. With the *Geldermalsen* recovery he took photographer John Bremner along to take still photographs and video footage of the operation.

Christies appointed Mark Wrey to handle publicity. 'Nanking Cargo' was decided as the title for the sale, the name coming from 18th century auctions which advertised the porcelain as 'Nanking Ware'. It was the inspiration of Christie's Chinese Department Director Colin Sheaf who would later write a book of his own, *The Hatcher Porcelain Cargoes*.

One of Wrey's first moves was the compiling of a video of Bremner's footage. Four hundred advance copies were made and sent to dealers and to Christie's salerooms in London, New York, Amsterdam and Paris.

A major press conference was held in Amsterdam for international newspaper and television journalists, with Mike Hatcher on show together with a range of artefacts from *Geldermalsen*. In March there was another conference with the bell and the two bronze cannon to announce the positive identification of the vessel. During this time Mike Hatcher also gave a series of lectures and television appearances which kept the names *Geldermalsen* and Nanking Cargo in the public eye.

The publicity machine was extremely effective. In the week before the auction 20,000 people queued in the rain to file through Christie's Amsterdam salesroom to view the Nanking Cargo. But Christies were still nervous about the coming sale. They estimated the potential sale at about $US6 million. Hatcher, always the optimist, thought the figure would be higher.

'I had a gut feeling that it would be good,' he said later. 'There was no particular reason. Just instinct and a feeling from the response I'd had that the public were really going to go for it.'

At 10.30 am on April 28, 1986 the real test came. Christies' Amsterdam manager took the rostrum in the ballroom of the Hilton Hotel – suitably decked out in blue-and-white decorations – and banged down his gavel. The sale was on.

There were 2,746 lots to be sold in 11 sessions over five days. Mike Hatcher got the auction off to a good start, bidding for a 1750 German stoneware jug. Christies had estimated that it would probably fetch about 1000 guilders or $US500. Hatcher took the bidding to 11,000 guilders before the jug was finally knocked down to him.

'I found it on the wreck myself,' he said afterwards. 'It was the first thing I brought up and I badly wanted to keep it. But we'd told all the divers that everything was to go in the auction and if they wanted something they could bid for it. I had to set the example, though I didn't imagine it was going to cost me over 5000 bucks.'

'There followed five days of intense excitement,' Anthony Thorncroft wrote in *The Nanking Cargo*. 'Every lot sold, on average, at prices of four or five times its estimate.'

Hatcher, Max de Rham, Soo Hin Ong and his wife, and the divers sat in the front row, AW Rahim amongst them with his wife. Ong and the crew bid successfully for a number of items. Everyone else was dressed in their best and wearing ties. Mike Hatcher had a smart casual jacket with an open-necked shirt. No tie. 'I'm the same man with or without one,' he said with a grin. 'If it worries anyone that's their problem not mine.'

By Friday, May 1, 1986, Christies had sold almost 160,000 pieces of porcelain and 126 gold ingots for a grand total of 37 million guilders. That translated into £10 million sterling, or $US20 million. An extraordinary sum and beyond the wildest expectations of Christies and Max de Rham.

'I wasn't all that surprised myself,' said Hatcher. 'I'd had that good feeling all along. It was a fantastic week. The sort of thing you remember all your life.'

The Hilton Hotel put out a 'Hatcher' cocktail, blue of course, and the sale turned into a week-long party for dealers, private bidders, auctioneers and Christies' staff.

The gold naturally attracted some of the highest bids for individual pieces with $US104,000 for one ingot against its bullion value of $US4,000.

Mr Ong paid $US56,500 for a single dish, and $US82,000 for a gold bar. Max de Rham bought two gold ingots, one for each of his children. Two blue-and-white butter-tubs sold for more than $US22,000, a figure that was 22 times the original estimate of their value. A dinner service brought the highest price of all with a final bid of $US440,000.

Seven auctioneers worked in relays, and others took bids by telephone. There were some crazy bids, such as $US15,000 for a shell-encrusted cannon ball originally estimated as worth about $400. Because iron tends to flake, crumble, and fall apart after a prolonged period underwater unless it is exhaustively chemically treated, it was a dubious purchase.

It was the auction to end all auctions. A record for any similar sale in Holland, the second highest total from any Christie's auction to that time. While the highest bids naturally attracted the most attention many pieces went for modest prices well within the reach of ordinary people. Almost immediately after the gavel came down for the last time porcelain was on sale in London and elsewhere from dealers who had bought lots. Antique dealer David Howard spent $US1,300,000 at the auction and $US700,000 after it. He was offering tea bowls and saucers at $US150 a set and sold most of his stock in London.

Harrods offered Hatcher blue-and-white for sale from lots bought by an agent – in windows decked out with fishing nets and nauticalia. Bloomingdales' New York store had a display, opened by Hatcher himself. The Ritz Hotel in London purchased a 20-piece dinner service for $US60,000 and charged guests $US20 apiece to eat off it. An eminently practical use for the porcelain. Among the Ritz guests who used the porcelain was none other than Michael Hatcher!

One of the most interesting aspects of the whole operation was the scale and speed of the dispersal of the cargo. Items went all over Europe, to wealthy houses in the United States, to museums and art galleries around the world, with Britons the major buyers. For those who could afford only to look, the British Museum bought a representative range of the porcelain.

The G's cargo, one dealer had pessimistically estimated, represented five years' normal supply on the market. Far too much to ever be absorbed he'd said, with a shake of his head. On past history he was probably right. But this was a different kind of sale.

In fact the connoisseur collectors only took a small proportion of the cargo. Aside from the wealthy purchasers of dinner services and other expensive items, the bulk of the 160,000 pieces eventually went to ordinary men and women who had never purchased porcelain before.

Many were undoubtedly entranced by the 'Hatcher factor', but their pride in their piece of blue-and-white was sincere, and they probably valued their own piece of the past as much as anyone else. 'It's like touching history yourself,' one woman explained hugging her cup and saucer. 'After all, they've been two and a half centuries at the bottom of the sea!'

David Howard of Heirloom and Howards in London told of a London taxi driver putting a passenger down outside his Grafton Street shop, then emptying out his cash box and coming in to buy a piece of 'Nanking'. He also recalled receiving an order from a home in a London suburb. In the following week he received an order from the house next door. By the end of the month he had despatched 21 pieces to that one suburban street.

And what of the cause of all the excitement? Michael Hatcher, man of the moment and London's newest multi-millionaire? How did it all affect him?

'It was all a bit like a dream,' he said. 'Hard to believe at first. For the first time in my life I had almost more money than I could spend, and I didn't quite know what to do with myself.' He had to hide away from all the people who wanted to sell him get-richer-quicker ideas. Dodge the professional beggars, those with hard luck stories, the schemers and dreamers eager to share the Hatcher bonanza. His mother tried to contact him for the first time in 40 years.

'It was a little late,' he said tersely. 'The contact never happened.' Nonetheless it brought back some disturbing memories. 'The most difficult thing was the fact that I had this bagful of money, about four million quid, and I thought, Hey, I don't have to do anything more. If I use it properly, I'm made for life. Then I took another look at myself and realised that I didn't want to stop doing things. "Stop" was a four letter word for me. I didn't want it to be all over at 45. I wanted to find more wrecks, to go back to sea, to dive and do all the things I enjoyed so much before the money came in. I didn't want any of that to change. It was at that point that I realised that the adventure meant more than the money.'

There was another small problem. The Ritz Hotel had a strict dress code and princes and commoners alike were required to wear a tie to meals. It was hotel policy, they said. Absolutely no exceptions.

'I haven't got a tie,' said Hatcher stubbornly. 'I don't possess one.' [The statement was not entirely true. In the publicity lead-up to the *Geldermalsen* auction he had been prevailed upon to wear a tie for photographs, usually taking it off and putting it in his pocket afterwards. But ties did not feature in what he considered to be his private life.]

'No tie? Not to worry, sir,' said the restaurant manager. 'We can find you one until you have a chance to get one of your own. We'll bring you a choice.'

'You misunderstand me,' said Hatcher. 'I don't have a tie because I don't want to wear one. Not my tie. Not yours. Not anyone's.'

'But sir, I'm afraid ... '

Hatcher looked around at the opulence, the beautifully dressed men and women, the svelte luxury and red-carpeted plushness of the Ritz. His face remained expressionless. 'Don't worry about it,' he said, 'I'll eat somewhere else.'

'Showtime was over I realised,' he recalled later. 'This wasn't my natural world.' He got his suitcase, took a taxi to a quieter part of London and found a cheaper hotel where no-one wanted him to wear a tie. A place where he felt at home.

And as he sipped a drink there, collar unbuttoned and feeling content, his mind went back to the sparkling blue waters of the South China Sea.

CHAPTER ELEVEN

Expect the Unexpected

At the conclusion of the Nanking Cargo auction in May, 1986, Mike Hatcher and Max de Rham were in a state of euphoria. The sale had exceeded all expectations, the partners were hailed as heroes, winning wealth from the deeps against all odds and for a brief moment they were the darlings of the press and the public.

But by the end of the month, Mike Hatcher was an angry man, and the corners of Max's usually cheerful mouth were turning downwards. The academics, predictably infuriated by the success of the sale, had gone on the attack. The Dutch academic establishment was particularly bitter at the loss of what was described as their 'historical heritage' and the lack of representation of *Geldermalsen* material in their maritime museums. It was true, as Hatcher pointed out, that the Dutch authorities or their representatives could have bought pieces at the auction like everyone else. Surely they could not expect that porcelain that had taken three years to discover, hundreds of thousands of dollars to recover, and had been transported half-way around the world would be handed out like visiting cards?

Besides, he said, the Dutch Government, heir to the once-mighty VOC company had benefited by 10 per cent of the sale.

Why had they not put their two million dollars into purchases of heritage items?

Unfortunately the cynical answer is that governments of any political persuasion in any country tend to put money where they see political advantage. Antiquities are usually perceived as luxury items, non-essentials which do not rate high on the list of taxpayer expenditure, as opposed to demands of a more immediate public nature.

The British Government brought a representative collection, though *Geldermalsen* was far less significant for Britons than it was for the Dutch. They bought nothing despite their windfall from the sale. The Rijksmuseum refused to bid or be involved in a purchase out of purist principle. The Groningen Museum pleaded poverty.

Before the controversy arose in the wake of the auction, Michael Hatcher and Max de Rham had already made a donation of a representative range of 150 *Geldermalsen* pieces to the Groningen Museum. They also generously presented the ship's bell with its significant date of 1747 to the city of Middelburg where *Geldermalsen* was built and where her first and fatal voyage began.

Dr Christian Jorg of Groningen University, an acknowledged authority on the VOC, was given the opportunity to study the cargo in its entirety in the weeks leading up to the auction. The result was one of the most complete and detailed reports on the wreck of an East Indiaman and her cargo ever tabled.

These positives, and the lack of governmental response, were ignored by the academics. They simply saw Hatcher as the personal epitome of all the elements they most detested in the wreck-hunters' world. There was also more than a small element of jealousy involved. His success, in their eyes, was unforgivable. They concentrated their vilification on him and took their accusations to extraordinary lengths.

For instance when a young Indonesian archaeologist, Dr Santoso Pribadi, drowned looking for the *Geldermalsen* site, it was put about that Hatcher had booby-trapped the wreck to frighten away competitors and had thereby caused the young man's death. The suggestion was so outrageous when it was first put to him that Michael Hatcher could hardly find the words to respond.

'It was a monstrous suggestion,' he said angrily. 'It quite took my breath away. I couldn't believe that anyone could be twisted enough to think that way. In any case, for anyone who knows anything about diving it would be technically impossible. How would you booby-trap a wreck level with the sea floor like *Geldermalsen*? God knows, diving is dangerous enough in any case. The question I would ask is how competent was the diver in question? How come he was diving on his own to 40 metres with no buddy diver, no surface supervision and no back-up?'

To this day he still shakes his head. 'I was very sorry for the young man and for his brother and parents. It was an accident of course, and one that should never have happened.'

Nonetheless the story of a sinister cause of death gained wide credence and was reported in the Indonesian press. The local Jakarta newspaper *Sinhar Harapan* first raised the *Geldermalsen* issue in Indonesia and it caused a furore. President Suharto ordered a national inquiry, and Justice Minister Ismail Saleh stated categorically that the wreck belonged to Indonesia.

The *Sunday Times* of September 7, 1986, ran a story with photographs of Hatcher and the *Geldermalsen* ceramics.

❈

HE STOLE OUR TREASURE

JAKARTA ACCUSES BRITISH DIVER

Nearly 235 years after sinking with its treasure the Dutch ship *De Geldermalsen* is again in the eye of a storm. British treasure hunter Michael Hatcher has been accused for the first time by Indonesia of stealing treasure from the wreck.

Hatcher, who lives in Singapore, says *De Geldermalsen* sank in international waters. Jakarta claims the ship lies in Indonesian waters east of Batam. Jakarta correspondent Yang Razali Kassim says Indonesia is determined to stake its claim to the treasure. But how it makes its claim stick is the big question.

The article quoted President Suharto's order for an investigation into how the *Geldermalsen* treasure slipped through Indonesian fingers. Justice Minister Ismail Saleh produced a report stating that after three weeks of investigation, Indonesian authorities had established beyond doubt that the treasures belonged to Indonesia. The basis of the report was the recovery of ceramics said to be similar to those from *Geldermalsen* recovered by Dr Santoso Pribadi before his tragic death on August 25, 1986.

An expedition under Admiral Anwar Effendi had gone to the site of what they believed to be the *Geldermalsen* wreck. They recovered nine Ming Dynasty bowls, 18 fragments of dishes from the same date, a cup from the Ming or Qing period and a modern basket said to have been used by Hatcher in the salvage.

The *Sunday Times* added, 'Significantly this is the first time since the issue surfaced after the [*Geldermalsen*] auction that the government is accusing Mr Hatcher and his associates of running away with stolen property. The possibility of charges being laid against them for violation of Indonesian territorial waters, theft, and even smuggling, the last of which potentially amounts to an act of subversion in Indonesia, has not been ruled out. The disappearance of Mr Santoso Pribadi was mentioned at length, though with great caution by the Minister in his statement.'

The *Sinhar Harapan*, which first flew the speculative kite on booby-trapping, was less circumspect. It was careful not to make a direct and therefore legally libellous statement. But the message was there for readers to interpret. The inference fell little short of an accusation.

A translation from Indonesian to English of the story on September 1, 1986 read as follows:

'Apart from the internal factors [a description of the search for the body] there is a possibility that the disaster that had befallen Santoso Pribadi could also be due to external factors. According to the information known if Santoso Pribadi's health was not affected, which is an internal factor, then definitely the disaster had been caused by an external factor.'

What 'external factor' could be responsible?

The *Sinhar Harapan* looked briefly at the possibilities of an equipment failure before concluding, 'Underwater sabotage by Hatcher's syndicate, so often found in films of underwater treasure-hunting, is another possibility.'

The influential *Jakarta Post* ran a story on September 12, 1986:

POLICE AWAITING SALEH'S WARRANT TO ARREST HATCHER

Indonesia police are still unable to ask the International Police (Interpol), to declare him an international fugitive.

The story was somewhat muddled. Looking through it the reader discovered that there was no actual warrant. Instead the *Post* passed the football back to the ever-ready *Sinhar Harapan*.

The daily *Sinhar Harapan* reported Monday that the Indonesian police have prepared to ask for help from Interpol to capture Hatcher. But the police are still unable to send the request pending a warrant from the Justice Minister ...

No warrant was ever issued. The suggestion that Hatcher was an 'international fugitive' was absurd, since he was at an identified address in Singapore and speaking (tersely) to the paper at that point by telephone on an almost daily basis. Nonetheless, as the old adage has it, if enough mud is thrown some of it is bound to stick and the controversy was undeniably damaging to Hatcher's reputation.

Hatcher found it so hard to believe the various statements that he had a sworn translation of the *Sinhar Harapan* articles registered with the Supreme Court of Singapore nine days after the article was published. His threat to prosecute for defamation was published in the *Sunday Times*. However an action in an Indonesian court would have been playing into the newspaper's hands. There was also the factor that it was obviously not a good time for Hatcher to visit Jakarta.

However, he defended his right to *Geldermalsen* on the basis that it was 'in international waters' and that he had made a deal with the Dutch Government as legal heirs to the cargo. He pointed out that there were many wrecks in Indonesian waters. The wares recovered by Admiral Answar Effendi's expedition were Ming Dynasty, a period much earlier than the Qing porcelain on *Geldermalsen*. They may have been looking at a different wreck, he suggested.

The *Jakarta Post* produced an article on September 22, 1986 on much more moderate lines than its publication of September 12. It was titled:

LET COOL HEADS PREVAIL

We are referring of course, to *De Geldermalsen* and the national furore it has caused because its cargo was recovered and sold for a considerable sum of money, not a penny of which went into Indonesian coffers.

However it differed from the other reports in giving Mike Hatcher a chance to put his point of view.

It would be clear that there is another side to this story. This paper's interview with Captain Hatcher has put the story in a better perspective.

The *Jakarta Post* went on to make some sensible suggestions. Instead of crying over spilt milk, the Indonesian Government should be liaising with the Netherlands on the location of VOC wrecks and establishing its own agency, with sole authority over the salvage of historical 'wrecks' to provide material for Indonesian museums.

> We think it is time for cool heads to prevail so that any remaining bones of contention can be worked out amicably. We see no need to launch time-consuming and expensive litigation that will only cause further bad feelings. Especially if such actions are based on ill-conceived notions of national prestige.
>
> We would, however, like to see the hitherto mute Dutch Government make some kind of statement on the whole affair and perhaps offer to share some part of the proceeds from the sale of the cargo, so as to assuage the more outspoken critics here.

The Dutch Government issued a press release in Singapore and Jakarta simultaneously on September 23, confirming its arrangement with Michael Hatcher. The statement also contained a surprise which most of the papers missed or ignored. Probably because it would have made them look rather silly.

> Prior to concluding said contract the State of the Netherlands informed the Indonesian Government about this fact on 28 January 1986. On this basis an exchange of thoughts is still going on between the two governments. As long as this exchange is not finalised no further information can be given.

So the Indonesians had known about the *Geldermalsen* discovery all along, well before the Amsterdam auction. Why then had they not objected earlier? Why all the post-auction fuss?

The sad conclusion is that while it was purely a historical matter an auction half-a-world away may have appeared unimportant. But when it became a question of $US20 million proceeds *Geldermalsen* appeared in a new and far brighter light. As Anthony Thorncroft remarked in *The Nanking Cargo*, 'It clarified their thinking wonderfully.'

So much for governments. What about the academics and the archaeologists? They can and do differ in their views. Historians for example are a notoriously quarrelsome breed, and have traditionally spent more time shooting down the theories of people in their own fields than taking on outside targets.

Most major innovations in science or philosophy have had to overcome widespread initial hostility within their own disciplines, simply because they were radical or different from currently accepted views. Science needs to be conservative to be certain of its findings. It also needs to be innovative to advance. A conundrum.

Archaeology at the time of the *Geldermalsen* discovery was no different from any other scientific practice in terms of internal squabbles. For many years land archaeologists refused to admit that underwater archaeology was a science at all. They were contemptuous of the pioneering efforts of such now-famous names as George Bass. Their roots were in a study of classical times and unless the object of attention was a couple of millennia old it was more often than not deemed uninteresting. Shipwrecks dating a mere two or three hundred years were hardly worthy of consideration, they suggested.

The dinosaurs have now largely died out and marine archaeology has rightly taken its place in the scientific world. But attitudes of suspicion of non-anointed (non PhD) practitioners remain. Whatever their opposite views on other matters (for instance, should wrecks be excavated at all? Should every fatal wrecksite be treated as a sacrosanct sea-grave?) most marine archaeologists tend to regard commercial salvors such as

Hatcher with emotions ranging from sadness to something approaching hatred.

Most of them, of course, have never met the man.

If they had it is just possible that they might have found some elements and interests in common. As with most of us who feel we 'know' famous figures, the familiarity is largely artificial, coming from press and gossip sources. When we see enough stories and pictures we eventually accept the popular concept. We feel we 'know' the person behind the story and the picture in a personal sense, accepting the information fed to us without question.

In Hatcher's case, while the *Geldermalsen* auction presented an initially flattering picture of the adventurer, the negative reports by the end of the year painted a portrait that was quite the reverse. One he has been forced to struggle to overcome ever since.

Sections of the press thrive by feeding the public's appetite for scandal, gossip and salacious rumour and people in the public eye have to learn to deal with it or be destroyed. But for people like Mike Hatcher and Max de Rham, who were new to the experience, that kind of treatment was personally wounding. Hatcher took some of the sneers of his critics as low blows at his lack of education. Schooling was something he hardly had time for as a Barnardo's boy, yet he became a qualified engineer, a ship's captain and he is widely read in his subjects of shipwrecks and ceramics. In his chosen field of practical wreck recovery he is unsurpassed. Hatcher had no need to feel inferior. He was as good in his own way as his critics, and in some areas considerably better.

But the taunts still stung.

Especially those from the university cliques.

'Most of them never get their arses wet,' he said tersely. 'They wouldn't know what went on under the ocean. Put them down in a Kirby hat in 150 feet in nil-visibility where you can't see your hand in front of your face and they'd be crying like babies to be brought back to the top.'

Max de Rham's father was a Swiss diplomat, a member of a profession which avoided press exposure like the plague. The negative reports brought considerable pain to Max and the family. The suggestion that the *Geldermalsen* operation was 'uncultured' was especially unwelcome.

What then, was the real basis for the quarrel between the historians, archaeologists and academics and the commercial salvors?

Both have a common interest in locating wrecks. However the commercial salvor is usually interested in cargo (gold, silver, precious jewels, copper, tin, brass or bronze) rather than the wreck itself. His study of history is usually only undertaken to lead him to a site. Once there, his concern is to raise, undamaged, whatever may be valuable. What comes up is sold. If the return exceeds the high cost and high risk of wreck search and recovery, then there is a profit and that is why your salvor is in business.

In practice there are very few people who have been able to make a living, let alone a profit, out of salvage in recent times. It is a horrendously expensive and chancy business. Mike Hatcher and the legendary American, Mel Fisher, are two of the exceptions. On account of their success both have attracted sworn enemies in archaeological circles.

An archaeologist is almost always a scientist with a university or college background, the common qualification usually being a doctorate of philosophy. An archaeologist's search is for knowledge and an archaeological land site or shipwreck is a time capsule providing information about people who lived some time in the past. For this reason every small shard of pottery, each item on the site is of value. Coins are a prize, not for their collector worth, but because they carry dates, inscriptions and information. Clay writing tablets, hieroglyphics, friezes and statues all carry their own message from the past even if they were only the equivalent of shopping lists at the time.

The archaeologist measures, marks and records the site with

great care, once again hoping that the measurements may provide important information. Sometimes the technique may become an obsession, the method becoming more important than the objective. Ultimately what he or she discovers may end up in a museum. It may not be displayed unless it is exceptional, because most museum storeroom shelves are already crowded with items the public will never see. But the objects are there for future study should they ever be needed. It is also a professional requirement to publish the results of a 'dig', thereby adding to knowledge on the particular subject and the past in general.

Underwater archaeology is far more difficult than working land sites for obvious reasons. Scientists who would hire local labour to dig on land have to become divers themselves to literally immerse themselves in their subject in a 'hands on' fashion. Underwater sites are far harder to measure, excavate and protect than those on land. Work is ruled by seasons, weather, and above all by available finance.

There comes the rub.

Many archaeologists are attached to institutions, maritime museums or universities. Their personal incomes are usually secure and they have no need to profit financially from their work. But in their quest for notice and promotion within their profession they need to have projects which attract the attention of their peers. In that sense some marine archaeologists are highly competitive.

Searching for wrecks and working them is a very costly business and for that reason most marine archaeologists work wrecks found by other people. But they cannot avoid the costs of an actual excavation. So where does the money come from?

Institutions seldom have spare cash in their budgets for the costs of an excavation, where hundreds of thousands, if not millions of dollars may be involved. Grants may be available from governments, though there needs to be public pressure to support the project and it usually takes time to get an allocation.

So a successful archaeologist also needs to be good at arranging publicity, and getting the media interested. A skilful fundraiser as well as a scientist. It follows that there are many known targets which cannot be tackled simply because funds are not available. This is a frustration for the archaeologist. A frustration which turns to anger if looters destroy the site before it can be studied.

Is Hatcher a looter?

Many archaeologists would say so. But few are prepared to take an unprejudiced look at the other side of the picture.

Commercial salvors work only wrecks which can provide a return and incur enormous search and on-site costs. They also know that once they leave a site the looters will converge on it. In Cambodia, Sumatra, Thailand or the Philippines, a pot which can be sold for a few dollars to a tourist or Chinese middleman will keep a family for weeks. In the Third World dollars for food and sheer survival by far outweigh history.

Most salvors do not take measurements or survey in an archaeological sense, though on *Geldermalsen* Hatcher and Max de Rham insisted on a film and a photographic record and made a detailed plan of the wreck.

Generally speaking salvors are governed by the costs and the weather and in some instances (as Hatcher would find out) by politics. For these reasons there is always an air of urgency on a professional cargo recovery. The day starts at 4.30 am and the first divers hit the water at daylight. They are succeeded by others in shifts, taking their turns in the decompression chamber, the equipment working continuously. Work goes on seven days a week unless the weather makes it impossible. There is no home leave. The divers and crew stay on the vessel or salvage barge, on the job until it is done.

In contrast marine archaeological excavations move at a much more leisurely pace. There is an emphasis on measurement and grid photography. Work is seldom completed in a season and may go on for years. Many of the workers are students, volunteers or associates of the institution involved and they provide their labour and involvement on a holiday basis.

Archaeologists point to the speed of a commercial recovery and the information which is lost as a result as wanton destruction of 'heritage'. Commercial salvors reply that the length of time of an archaeological programme means that the sea itself destroys a lot of material once a wreck is opened up. In addition, looters in the off-season may rob the wreck of artefacts and treasure once the site is generally known. Wastage can occur both through working too fast or working too slowly.

In Western Australia, for example, a pile of silver coin on the seabed 'the size of a small car' at the wrecksite of the 1712 Dutch East Indiaman *Zuytdorp* disappeared when the site was left open without surveillance for several seasons. The coin may have been worth several million dollars if a commercial value were placed upon it.

'You cannot leave a known treasure on the seabed,' said *Zuytdorp's* prime researcher Dr Phillip Playford angrily, 'and expect that people with the means to get to it will ignore it. In the circumstances the dissipation of the coin hoard was inevitable. This should have been foreseen by the State and those responsible for protecting the wreck. The only way to have saved the coin was to make raising it a priority.'

Hatcher, for instance, was publicly criticised (despite their otherwise harmonious relationship) by Dr Christian Jorg of Groningen University, and Jorg's complaint was taken up by other academics intent on 'Hatcher-bashing'. In his book on *Geldermalsen* Jorg wrote, 'It is a pity therefore that Hatcher has paid little attention to a detailed registration of his finds. Where exactly was the ship's bell lying? Were the copper candlesticks and the wine glass lying close together? Every underwater archaeologist might ask numerous questions with regard to one small find, for it is precisely these kind of details that tell us more about life on board, the organisation and use of the object involved, the crew. In short it helps us gain more insight into matters about which so very little is known.

'...In the list of cabin goods such a candlestick is mentioned. But have Captain Morel and his passenger sipped their brandy by the light of this candle? We will never know because we have no information on the location of the find.'

The example of the candlestick was widely quoted in criticisms of Hatcher. In making it Dr Jorg made a number of errors in his eagerness to put forward the academic and anti-Hatcher view.

'Why didn't he ask me where the bloody candlestick was found?' an exasperated Hatcher demanded. 'I could have shown him within one metre on the plan of the wreck. The same goes for the other stuff. I knew where very piece was located!'

The candlestick may very well have been the one by whose light skipper Jan Morel and the English passenger Richard Bagge sipped their evening brandy. If only one were listed in the great cabin equipment that is the probability. But where it finished in the wreck, the position in which it was found in 1985, may not be of much help in the matter.

Let's say that at the time of *Geldermalsen's* striking the reef, the bronze candlestick (standard VOC issue) was on the captain's table in the great cabin at the stern ready for the evening meal. The ship was described as 'capsizing' immediately before she sank at midnight. It is more likely that she laid hard over on her side so that water gushed in through the companionways and hatches. In either event the candlestick falls, rolls and finishes in some corner of the cabin. The weighted ship falls faster and faster through 40 metres of water, striking the bottom with tremendous impact.

As in an automobile accident unsecured items are thrown about in total confusion. A child's toy in the back seat finishes up under the accelerator. A similar effect would have taken place in the dead ship, now a ghostly galleon 40 metres down. Everything loose has been shaken, rolled and thrown out of position. Then nature takes over. Teredo worms and myriad burrowing creatures attack the timber, the ship collapses into itself and eventually all that remains is a mound on the seabed. The candlestick which was once 12 metres above the keel now comes down to a position on top of the lowest cargo. The last fragment of deck on which it lay may have been washed by currents to another part of the wreck.

In short, while the candlestick should have been photographed and registered in situ, its location at the time of discovery may not have been a great deal of help in ascertaining its original starting point in the vessel. On the other hand there are many plans and some extremely detailed models of VOC ships of the period which show us the location of the cabin, and even the objects within. In some cases these are a more accurate source of information than the wreck itself.

While a candlestick might not have been the best example, other items in a shipwreck can add a good deal to our knowledge of life on board. On the 1629 *Batavia* shipwreck in Western Australia for example, a wide variety of interesting objects were found. There was a pair of leather shoes in a bleeding bowl probably belonging to the murdered barber – surgeon Frans Jansz; an apothecary's mortar with the words AMOR VINCIT OMNIA (Love Conquers All) may have been the property of former apothecary and under-merchant Jeronimus Cornelisz who led the bloody mutiny after the wreck. A pewter stand and inkpots were most likely the possessions of merchant Francisco Pelsart, who was commander of the vessel. Bronze mariner's astrolabes would certainly have been used by the skipper Ariaen Jacobsz, later thrown into gaol in Batavia.

Thanks to the records we can put names to objects and it certainly adds to the sense of history to be able to touch items handled by others three centuries previously.

On the *Batavia* wreck brass barber-surgeon's bleeding bowls used both for shaving and taking blood from ill persons were found. There were coins from the Netherlands, the German city states, Denmark, Burgundy, Spain and Mexico. There were pike butts, a suit of armour, pieces of lace, beardman jugs and a silver set of utensils intended for the Grand Mogul of India. Bronze cannon lay with the wreck, dappled gold in the sunlit waters. Ashore in shallow graves were the sword-hacked skeletons of victims of the mutiny grinning up out of the sand.

Such objects helped build the picture of the wreck and the tragedy which followed, but without the precisely detailed journal of Francisco Pelsart we would have only had a fragment of the story of the most dramatic shipwreck in Australian waters. The objects plus the records provide the complete picture.

In the same way Dr Jorg's own comprehensive research into the history of *Geldermalsen* provided a compelling picture of the ship and her tragic loss. The record complemented by the cargo. And the candlestick.

The porcelain recovered by Hatcher was an important contribution to history in its own right, offering Jorg a unique study opportunity in the weeks prior to the auction. In his book *The Geldermalsen – History & Porcelain*, written in 1986, he described his own wonder at his first sight of the cargo.

'We went to a shed in the Amsterdam dock area, and there on wooden racks I saw endless rows of porcelain. Cups, saucers, plates, bowls, stacks and stacks of them. I thought, This is how it must have looked in the days of the Dutch East India Company! Never before had such a complete cargo of porcelain been recovered from a VOC wreck. Here for the first time we would really get a complete picture. Which quality does the VOC purchase? What varieties and sizes were there? At last I would be able to fill in all the gaps which must remain in a story when one is studying only records.'

The small hiccup of the candlestick aside, Dr Jorg made a monumental contribution to the *Geldermalsen* story.

❀

Apart from the considerable ill-feeling and controversy surrounding *Geldermalsen's* salvage, there were several positive aspects. Even though Hatcher conducted the operation in a manner contrary to accepted archaeological principles, it still proved to be an important contribution to scientific knowledge.

Three books were written, including Jorg's *The Geldermalsen – History & Porcelain*; *The Hatcher Porcelain Cargoes* by Colin Sheaf and Richard Kilburn; and *The Nanking Cargo* by Anthony Thorncroft. Information on *Geldermalsen* appeared in many newspapers and periodicals ranging from dive magazines to scientific papers. The cargoes of the junk and *Geldermalsen* changed established thinking on the dates of some forms and styles of porcelain. The Groningen Museum got 50 valuable pieces of *Geldermalsen* material worth more than $100,000, donated by Hatcher and De Rham. Other pieces were donated to the Singapore Museum. The town of Middelburg got the ship's bell, a bell struck daily by the fo'castle on a journey which took the ship as far afield as India and China.

Of course it would have been nice if *Geldermalsen* material – a significant portion of it – could have been purchased and displayed in the Netherlands. This could have been done, as previously pointed out, with the government's 10 per cent share.

Surely, the reader might ask, there could be benefits for both Hatcher and the archaeologists for a scientist to accompany his expeditions, to use the opportunity and take advantage of the equipment and excavation techniques of the professionals?

'The offer is open and always has been,' Hatcher says.

Sadly, most senior marine archaeologists are not willing to risk their reputations accompanying him despite the possibility of a gain for science.

'I was portrayed as the bad guy,' said Hatcher ruefully after *Geldermalsen*. 'But maybe people should take a look at the governments whom they elect. If heritage belongs to everyone and everyone has a right to it, then governments should be doing far more in the way of preserving the past than they do. *Geldermalsen* was a good example of private enterprise doing the job for them, with no thanks in the end.

'People who feel keenly about the situation, especially the ones who criticised me savagely, should be writing to the papers and talking to their local member of parliament. Maybe one day things would change for the better if they were to put their energy into positives instead of knifing me in the back.' He adds, 'But I won't hold my breath waiting for the day!'

CHAPTER TWELVE

The Thai Incident

Life changed markedly for Mike Hatcher after the *Geldermalsen* auction. Having a healthy bank account certainly took some of the hard edges off everyday living. He bought an apartment in Singapore though he still often slept aboard *Restless M*, preferring the rocking of the boat, the water-lapping sounds of the harbour and the whistles of the tugs to suburbia.

There was another significant change. Hatcher had known a girl named Ghislaine Salter from the British Embassy in Singapore for some time. She had gone back to England and they met again at the time of the auction of the Nanking Cargo. This time a spark ignited. Mike Hatcher turned his back on bachelorhood after 45 single years (albeit with many girlfriends) and became a married man.

'It occasioned some changes in lifestyle,' he recalls with a grin. 'There were quite a few things about bachelorhood that didn't sit well with a new wife. I had to make a few alterations to suit.'

He discovered a new sport in windsurfing, which helped relieve the tensions of the *Geldermalsen* controversy. But there was still a lingering unhappiness. When he gave press conferences to try to put his point of view he was dismayed by the hostility of some sections of the media.

'I was very concerned about the situation in Indonesia,' he remembers. 'I knew I was in the right and the Dutch supported me even if only in a half-hearted way. But what if the Indonesians had applied for extradition and the Singaporeans had gone along with it? I didn't fancy my chances in an Indonesian court, let alone an Indonesian gaol.' He and Ghislaine discussed the matter quietly and decided it would be wise to put more distance between himself and Jakarta until the controversy died.

'Think of a place a long way away, where they've never heard of Mike Hatcher and *Geldermalsen*,' he said, 'somewhere where there's good windsurfing.'

The answer came in a moment.

'Hawaii! That's it!'

Hawaii had some of the best windsurfing in the world and it was sufficiently far away for Hatcher to disappear from the south-east Asian scene for as long as it took for people to forget. So Mr and Mrs Hatcher went to Hawaii, set up house on the island of Maui and began a new life. Their first daughter, Michelle, was born there and Hatcher was able to blast out on the surf on his sailboard any day that the breeze had the palms bending. Sun and salt water, and plenty of whitewater action made the days pass quickly.

'It was a great time,' he recalls. 'The conditions for sail boarding were just wonderful. I had several different boards and a garage full of sails, booms and gear. I sailed big waves off Hokipa. It was a whole new world.'

Then came a shock. After four years in Maui he received a letter from Canberra telling him he was no longer an Australian.

'I'd been out of the country so long that when I went to renew my passport they said, "Sorry, old son. You're not one of us any more". Hatcher was flabbergasted. 'I couldn't believe it. My father and sister were both Australian residents and citizens. I'd put in all those hard years with Barnardo's. While I'd kept the British passport as a convenience (and a right) I always thought of myself as an Aussie. To be told I wasn't wanted was like a hard right, coming in smack between the eyes. I queried it, naturally. Put on a show of great indignation. And indeed that I was the way I felt. But I was told that the only way I could get back into the country was by business immigration. I had to invest a heap of money in Australia and remain a minimum of 18 months. I said to Ghislaine I'd better do it. Get back in there quick before it becomes impossible. I don't want to live in England. It's too bloody cold.'

So the Hatchers moved back to New South Wales where his Australian story had begun in the 1950s. Ghislaine was pregnant with their second daughter Naomi, and Hatcher began the search for a property. Here his farm boy years stood him in good stead. With a shrewd eye for cattle country he found a beautiful property out of Grafton – Bardool Station in Kangaroo Creek. There were rivers running through it and it was flanked by timbered hills and looked like a scene in a Hans Heyson painting.

But there were days when his eyes strayed past the hills, his thoughts going to coconut palm islands, and the salty tang of the breeze off the South China Sea. The old restlessness, the itch, was still there. At night he read through Horsburgh's journals and other historic records of those waters he knew so well.

One warm January day in 1992 there was a phone call. David Doll, an American diving instructor working in Thailand, had some news he thought might interest Hatcher.

'There's a ceramics wreck,' he began. 'Out there in the Gulf. Some fishermen brought up vases in their nets.'

Hatcher felt a rising tide of excitement. 'How old is it?' he asked. 'How deep?'

'About 200 feet down,' said Doll. 'Not a casual dive, but workable.'

'Good. How old is the stuff? Has anyone dated it?'

'The fishermen took their finds to a dealer in Pattaya. He's identified it as Sawankhalok pottery from the Ayutthaya era. Very valuable.'

'Do you have a position on this wreck?'

'The fishermen know roughly. It's well out of sight of land.'

'International waters, then?'

'It's about 50 miles offshore. So I guess that's the case.'

'OK. Here's what you do. Buy the guy a GPS [Global Positioning System] and I'll send the money. Find out how much the fisherman wants and tell me what you're asking. I'll be up there as soon as I can to look at the stuff.'

'Great,' said Doll. 'So we're going to do it?'

'I'll tell you that when I've seen the pots and worked out the figures,' Hatcher said. He added, 'There's one other thing.'

'What's that?' asked Doll.

'Tell no-one else. No-one at all. That's very, very important.'

'You can trust me,' said Doll, sounding a little hurt.

'It's got to be better than trust,' Hatcher replied. 'Absolute secrecy. If any word gets out the deal is automatically off. I mean that. You understand?'

Doll said he understood.

In the background there was a slight sigh of resignation from Ghislaine. She had known that one day her husband would be off again into the blue, disappearing on one of his pet projects.

❁

Once again there were endless phone calls arranging the divers, the salvage vessel, a film photographer, the finance. When the deal was put together it seemed a neat package.

The charter vessel would be the 600-tonne *Australia Tide*, owned by Tidewater Port Jackson Marine, an Australian company. She was designed to be self-contained, with a decompression chamber and saturation dive system, and a four-anchor mooring capability. The divers were hired through Divcon International of Singapore. Nigel Oorloff, a Brisbane filmmaker, would make a pictorial record. This time, in view of past criticisms, Hatcher included an archaeologist, a young West

Australian named Michael Flecker. Ong Hoo Sin provided the financial backing through a wealthy Malaysian businessman, Jaya Tan and his brothers and father.

Hatcher was enthused and optimistic but might have been more concerned had he known that a boatload of Thai fishermen had been arrested in the Gulf of Thailand in December, 1991, by Thai authorities. They were charged with taking 500 pieces of ceramics from the very wreck he was seeking. Unfortunately that salient fact would not emerge until much later.

It was Hatcher's own firm belief, backed by legal opinion, that the wreck was in international waters and so he sailed with *Australia Tide*, still holding that conviction, on January 26, 1992, from Singapore, reaching the wrecksite three days later.

Australia Tide came with her own personnel. Captain Abraham de Vries from the Netherlands was in command, with Mark May, an Australian, as First Officer. The vessel had a crew of 14. John Allan from Britain was Chief Engineer, and together with the dive team there was a rich mix of races and religions. Of the 40 men, there were seven from Australia as well as others from Britain, the United States, Canada, New Zealand, the Philippines, Indonesia, Malaysia and Singapore.

'When I arrived in Singapore from Brisbane,' photographer Nigel Oorloff recalled, 'I found that the divers arriving at the same time had no idea what the project was. They thought it was a pipeline job. The people at Divcon asked me not to say anything to anyone until we were well out to sea.' Oorloff filmed the fitting of the hyperbaric chamber and the general mobilisation before *Australia Tide* left Singapore at 4 pm on Sunday, January 26. The weather was rough on departure. He kept to his cabin for most of the first two days, 'feeling seasick' and taking fright when salt water came in through the air-conditioner and wet his equipment.

'I jumped out of the bunk and grabbed the light switch, the cabin pitching and rocking. I heard the noise of water pouring through and moved the gear and cleaned it. Luckily the recorder was in a sealed carry pouch which stopped the water actually getting into the machine.'

On Wednesday, January 29, *Australia Tide* reached the wrecksite and some time was spent with a GPS in a speedboat pin-pointing the location of the wreck. In the evening Mike Hatcher called everyone together and briefed them on the specifics. The divers were in a state of eagerness and were thrilled to hear they would be working a wreck and not a 'boring old pipeline survey'.

On January 30 the ship moved into position and dropped four anchors which would keep her in position directly over the wreck. She could be moved precise metres or centimetres when necessary by winding in on one anchor line or the other, and releasing an equivalent amount of wire rope from the winch drums attached to the other bracket of anchors.

Mike Hatcher went down first on scuba tanks to confirm that this was indeed the right wreck. He surfaced with a wide grin and an armful of ceramic bottles – the wreck was beauty and seemed to contain plenty of vases, urns, porcelain and ceramic figures. The divers climbed into their gear and the diving bell went down to the seabed.

At 210 feet the depth was too great for working effectively with scuba gear. A 'bounce' dive like the one Mike Hatcher conducted was all right for reconnaissance, but working on the wreck for any length of time was a different matter. The time allowed on the bottom – a matter of a few minutes at that depth – was too limited and the risk of decompression sickness too high to be practical.

Instead the dive was based on the 'saturation' principle. The divers went down to the wreck in a bell which was always at equivalent pressure to 150 feet of water and came up the same way breathing a mixture of gasses which excluded nitrogen. On deck they lived, ate and slept in a hyperbaric chamber which was

Gaspar Island, a haunted place. The beach was thick with bodies in 1822 after the wreck of *Tek Sing*. (© Hugh Edwards)

Curious Indonesian fishermen check out *Restless M* at Gaspar Island.
(© Hugh Edwards)

Restless M mirrored on a tranquil sea. A fibreglass 85-footer, Mike Hatcher bought her with the name already on her stern. He thought it appropriate.

(© DIVE NEW ZEALAND)

Ready for the dive, Hatcher rinses his mask on the *Swissco Marie II* diving platform. *Restless M* is in the background. (© HUGH EDWARDS)

Barge *Swissco Marie II*, an island in the sea above *Tek Sing's* gravesite and home for 42 men. (© HUGH EDWARDS)

Divers ready to go down on the stage to the *Tek Sing* wreck 100 feet below. They would do a 90-minute shift before swapping. (© Hugh Edwards)

A huge mound of porcelain astounded the first divers. (© Hugh Edwards)

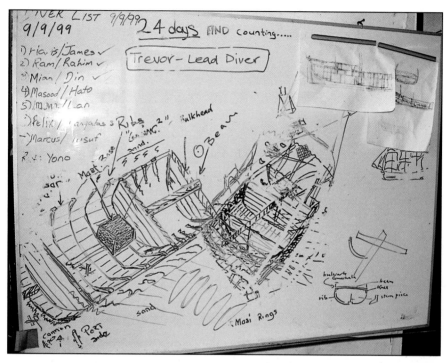

AW Rahim's sketch of the wreck of *Tek Sing*. (© HUGH EDWARDS)

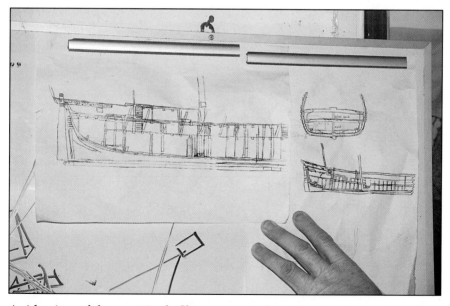

A side view of the great junk. She was more than 60 metres in length and carried some 2000 people, 1850 of whom drowned in the 1822 shipwreck. (© HUGH EDWARDS)

Rows and rows of porcelain far below the surface are checked out by Hatcher as the airlift fogs visibility. (© Hugh Edwards)

Pretty corals frame a porcelain dish and Mike Hatcher. (© Hugh Edwards)

A clam shell provides a contrasting image to the two exquisite porcelain bowls from *Tek Sing*. (© HUGH EDWARDS)

The virgin wreck; delicate porcelain bowls have become a part of the sea floor. (© HUGH EDWARDS)

The massive timbers of the junk and rope lashings remain intact.
(© DIVE NEW ZEALAND)

Mike Hatcher swims above enormous, perfectly preserved timbers in the cargo hold of the junk *Tek Sing*. (© HUGH EDWARDS)

Maan gets his Kirby suit
helmet ready to go below.

(© DIVE NEW ZEALAND)

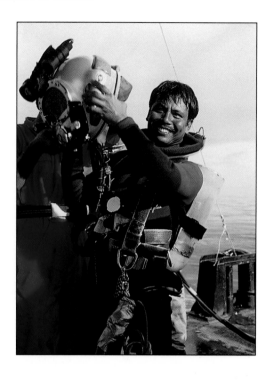

Visibility dropped dramatically when the airlift began spewing out huge
clouds of sand. (© HUGH EDWARDS)

The airlift worked as a giant suction dredge (or vacuum cleaner) removing the overburden. (© DIVE NEW ZEALAND)

Coral-encrusted vases, dishes and pillboxes recovered from the deep.

(© HUGH EDWARDS)

Artefacts from *Tek Sing* on Trevor McInery's table. They include bowls, tea and coffee cups and candlesticks. (© HUGH EDWARDS)

Cleaning and washing the treasures as they come aboard the salvage barge *Swissco Marie II*. (© HUGH EDWARDS)

Trevor's table weighed down by a fine display of blue-and-white porcelain. (© HUGH EDWARDS)

Little boys in blue with no pants proudly displaying themselves.
(© DIVE NEW ZEALAND)

Trevor McInery and a giant kettle
with a dragon on the side.

(© Hugh Edwards)

The king-size kettle dominates Trevor McInery's table collection of *Tek Sing*
artefacts. (© Hugh Edwards)

A Chinese 'chop' or merchant's stamp with ink pad and pestle. The chop still produced a legible signature. (© HUGH EDWARDS)

A pillar dollar of Charles III of Spain depicting the coat of arms of Leon and Castille and the Pillars of Hercules. (© HUGH EDWARDS)

Two pillar dollars minted in 1797 and 1804 in Spanish Peru. They were the preferred coins for Chinese merchants and were featured on the coat of arms of Charles III of Spain. (© HUGH EDWARDS)

Row upon row of delicate, handpainted bowls, washed and ready for packing. (© HUGH EDWARDS)

Bowls from *Tek Sing* look brand new in the morning sunshine on the salvage barge. (© HUGH EDWARDS)

Captain's table set for dinner with porcelain from the 1822 shipwreck and French wine of a more modern vintage! The chef excelled himself on this occasion. (© HUGH EDWARDS)

also permanently pressurised at 150 feet. The equipment was designed for oil rigs and was regularly in use on the offshore platforms.

Abdul Rahim, who had worked with Hatcher on the sunken U-boats and who made the big strike in 1999, was one of the diving team.

'The diving on *Australia Tide* consisted of 17 persons,' he said. 'Six of us did the actual diving, the others were technical and support staff. Bill Peni from New Zealand was the supervisor. When we weren't on the bottom we lived in the saturation chamber taking our meals in there and transferring from the chamber on deck to the diving bell by a transfer chamber. We worked 12-hour shifts. In each shift two divers would be in the water and one diver in the bell – the "bellman".

'Each diver would do four hours on the wreck with one diver changing with the bellman each two hours. The task of the bellman was to act as tender with equipment and for communications. He was also the safety diver in case one of the others got into trouble. This meant that for each 12-hour shift I was in the water on site for eight hours, and in the bell as bellman for four hours. It was pretty intensive down below. Off duty in the chamber on deck we read books and magazines, slept, and tried not to let the boredom get to us.

'In all we were in the chamber or the bell for eight days straight under pressure. That's a long time. But the work on the wreck was fascinating. First we cleared the surface debris to reach the cargo. There was a lot of coral, dead shells and weed which had to be shifted. We were using hot water suits because of the depth, with heated water flushing through to keep us warm. The difference was that we had a telephone system to speak to the deck and the bellman. The helmet also had a camera which carried a video-style picture of what was happening up to Bill Peni and the supervisory staff up above on a monitor. It was like watching the action on television. The helmets also had a strong light, both for the camera and because the work went on around the clock for 24 hours. It didn't matter whether it was night or day.

'We used an airlift to create a suction. We used this very carefully because we knew we were dealing with very valuable artefacts. The airlift sucked the sand away and left the objects exposed. At first the pottery was fairly rough and coarse. We figured that belonged to the crew. When we got deeper into the wreck the quality improved. There were some huge vases, maybe a metre high, and beautiful little statues and figurines and a fantastic elephant statue. We also recovered some small bronze cannon, about a metre long, with a bore of about five centimetres at the muzzle. The wreck appeared to be a one-masted Chinese junk, and we were told it was about 400 years old.'

The pottery and other objects were loaded into plastic containers below on the wrecksite, and those baskets placed in a much larger wire-mesh lifting basket on the end of a wire rope running down from a winch on *Australia Tide* above. Saniman, one of Mike Hatcher's 'family' of divers from the U-boat and *Geldermalsen* days, was one of the winch drivers. Usually he was bosun aboard *Restless M*, but he was a qualified winch driver, an excellent diver and integral on any of Mike Hatcher's expeditions. Usually known as 'Maan' he came from Binjai in Sumatra and was 28 years old at the time of the *Australia Tide* expedition in 1992.

For the first 24 hours the salvage operations ran like clockwork – pottery, vases, plates, and statues coming up in the buckets in the winch basket. On deck a team of workers cleaned the artefacts of sea growth, washed them and packed them carefully in cartons. Mike Hatcher, overseeing all phases of the operation, wore a pleased expression. Things were going as they should. In a few days, he anticipated, they would be homeward bound with the cargo.

The first cloud on the horizon appeared on January 31, the day after the commencement of work on the wreck. Saniman was on the night shift on the winch and when first sunlight came he saw a Thai fishing boat approaching. It anchored about 100 metres away and Saniman saw them begin scuba diving operations. He noticed baskets going down from the fishing vessel, and that the men on deck had rifles.

Mike Hatcher came on deck with a frown. Here was a problem he did not need. The fact that the Thais evidently knew of the wreck and would be returning to port before the salvage was complete meant that their position and purpose would become common knowledge. While he was confident that they were in the open sea and international waters the presence of the Thai boat made him distinctly uneasy.

Soon it was joined by a second boat.

'Go over and have a chat with them, David,' he said. 'And see what they're about.'

David Doll, the American dive instructor, spoke some Thai, and agreed to go across to the fishing boat. Because of fear of piracy in the Gulf guns were broken out on the bridge and made ready. Doll went across to the first fishing boat and soon returned with three of the divers. It turned out that they were not fishermen at all, but off-duty Royal Thai Navy personnel.

'They were angry,' Nigel Oorloff recalled, 'because they considered that this was their wreck and we were interlopers. They wanted us to go away.'

A dispute on national grounds was the last thing Hatcher needed. 'We've got to do a deal with these guys,' he said, 'otherwise they might scupper the whole project.' The Thais insisted that they were not on duty, but were diving on their own account to get some pieces to sell.

Mike Hatcher, Bill Peni and David Doll took them up onto the bridge. 'I understood that the deal that was offered them was US$5,000 plus some pottery pieces for them to go away and leave us alone,' Nigel Oorloff said. 'They seemed pleased with that.'

By the next day relations had improved to the stage where the Thais had set up camp astern of *Australia Tide*. They were taking down and bringing up baskets of their own. Soon, because of the 200-foot depth, one of their divers began experiencing symptoms of the bends. He was taken aboard *Australia Tide* and placed in the decompression chamber. 'The others watched enviously as crates and crates of ceramics came up from our divers below,' Oorloff recorded in his diary. The Thai diver was treated and recovered, and against all advice cheerfully stated that he would be diving next day.

However the fishing boat skipper indicated that he thought that the fine weather spell was about to finish and he was fearful of bad weather at that distance (55 miles) from shore.

The Thais asked for and received some more pots, saying that they had not been able to recover enough themselves. As their boat chugged away over the horizon followed by a black plume of diesel smoke Mike Hatcher watched it with narrowed eyes. 'I don't like it!' he said. 'I do *not* like it. I wouldn't trust those guys a solitary slippery centimetre!' Turning to Bill Peni he said, 'We'd better try and speed things up, Bill. I think we need to get it done and be out of here before anything goes wrong.'

Bill frowned. 'I hear what you're saying, Mike,' he replied. 'But to be honest I don't think we can go any faster. We're working 24 hours now.'

'See what you can do,' said Hatcher and walked to the side of the bridge, his eyes on the departing speck of the fishing boat. Instinct told him that the trouble would come from that direction. What sort of trouble was the question.

'I thought we had a right to be there. We'd had legal opinions before we left that these were international waters and that we had every right to salvage. But just the same I felt uneasy. A premonition of trouble, if you like. As it turned out I was right. I wish I'd been wrong.'

There was an ominous period of waiting. A deceptive calm.

But it was shortlived and soon the real drama began. The Thai fishing boat had been with *Australia Tide* for three days. On the evening of February 4 after it had returned to port, a Thai police patrol vessel suddenly appeared out of the darkness at 11 pm, showing a bright spotlight which swept the decks of *Australia Tide*. Armed police were standing on the foredeck and as the patrol boat came alongside they leaped aboard the salvage boat carrying rifles and revolvers.

'I was on the rear of the bridge,' Nigel Oorloff wrote in his diary, 'and saw them pushing the men doing the washing of the ceramics and shouting. It was apparent that they wanted our crew to stop the operation.' He began filming the confrontation from his high position.

'I then saw Mike Hatcher approach them and start talking. The commander of the patrol boat came aboard and went up onto the bridge with Hatcher to make a radio call to someone ashore. I kept filming while this was going on. Mike said that the call was to a lawyer in Thailand. After this the commander seemed pacified. He then returned to his patrol boat and sailed with a few salvaged pots which we had given them.'

The patrol boat left, throwing a wide white wake at 3.30 am on February 5. Mike Hatcher, Captain de Vries and the salvage team were left wondering what would happen next.

'It was clear that we had stirred up a hornet's nest,' Hatcher recalls. 'The question was whether we should abort the project at that point or stay and tough it out until all the cargo was up. My legal information was still that we were on the high seas and perfectly within our rights. There was also the point that with four anchors down and a diving bell on the bottom it would take some time before we could actually wind up the operation and depart.'

While Hatcher was pondering the question telephones were buzzing in Thai military and political circles and a major storm was brewing ashore.

On the evening of the day after the departure of the patrol boat a Royal Thai Navy vessel arrived out of the darkness at 2.30 am and anchored nearby. At 9 am the next day, February 6, the commander and several officers of the Navy ship came aboard for a meeting with Mike Hatcher and Captain de Vries.

'They were quite polite,' Oorloff recalled. 'They asked permission to come aboard and their behaviour was quite unlike that of the marine police. Several spoke good English. One of them, the Third Officer I think, said that the RTN [Royal Thai Navy] was about to commence submarine exercises in the area. He said that the RTN could not guarantee our safety and they suggested that we should leave. They then returned to their destroyer, and steamed off at high speed. Very impressive.'

However, far from being the end of the story it was just the beginning of a drama which was to make headlines around the world. At sunset the diving bell was brought up from the bottom with the divers still in a pressurised atmosphere and unaware of the dramas taking place on the surface. At 7.20 pm *Australia Tide* began retrieving her anchors. But before this operation could be completed those on deck were startled to see no less than six Royal Thai Navy warships approaching out of the darkness at high speed.

Nigel Oorloff ran for his camera and later wrote in his diary that the Thai Navy vessels circled *Australia Tide* in a most aggressive manner before demanding that they be allowed to come on board. In response to their belligerent attitude de Vries and Hatcher refused permission in spite of the fact that most of the RTN vessels had guns and missiles. Ten minutes later *Australia Tide* was forcibly boarded by around 10 armed commandoes who pointed their weapons at Hatcher and his crew, threatening them. During the confrontation Sanimon was hit with a rifle butt and had the weapon pointed at him in a menacing manner [he claimed this under a statutory declaration].

'On the bridge!' Oorloff recalled they said in English and they demanded that *Australia Tide* accompany them to Sattahip, the Royal Thai Navy base. De Vries was understandably very angry, refused their demands and accused them of piracy on the high seas.

For the next three days *Australia Tide* remained on the wrecksite surrounded by six Thai Naval craft in a stalemate situation. Captain de Vries meanwhile had sent out a distress signal to the Maritime Safety Centre in Canberra and news bureaus around the world were alerted to the confrontation in the Gulf of Thailand. It made the papers in Australia, Britain and the United States, and of course in Thailand, Malaysia and Singapore.

The basis of the argument was that while *Australia Tide* was undoubtedly in international waters 55 miles from the Thai coast, Thailand claimed an 'exclusive economic zone or EEZ' extending 200 miles from its shores. The ship had 'right of passage' they said but no right to take antiques from the sea floor within the zone. Legal advice to the Australian Embassy in Bangkok suggested that the Thai antiquity rights in the exclusive economic zone were questionable to say the least.

David Lyman, senior partner in the law firm of Tilleke & Gibbins in Bangkok, acting on behalf of Hatcher and the salvors, said that his firm had examined the validity of the so-called EEZ prior to the *Australia Tide* incident. It was their opinion that the Thai government had no legal right to seize the cargo.

'The Thai Government seem to be relying solely,' Lyman said, 'upon several clauses of the 1982 *Convention of the Law of the Sea* as their legal justification for boarding the vessel ... Attached are the copies of the pertinent portions. Sections 303 and 33 don't apply when considering the location of the vessel as being 55 miles or more from the Thai coast. That location is outside Thailand's internal waters, territorial sea and contiguous zone, though it is within the declared EEZ.

'Section 149 might apply, but "The Area" mentioned in that provision has never been defined by Thailand. The waters of an

EEZ are still international under the 1958 Geneva Convention, though under the 1982 Convention they are not "high seas". In EEZs coastal states assert their sovereignty for specialised economic purposes as to their natural resources such as fishing and mineral exploitation. It is widely accepted that antique wrecks and their cargo are not "natural resources".' David Lyman added that while Thailand had signed the 1982 Convention, 'The Thai Government never ratified nor acceded to it and never adopted it as part of Thai domestic law'.

Out on the ocean the war games continued. Thai naval vessels periodically 'buzzed' *Australia Tide* in a show of strength. While the stand-off continued messages were passing rapidly between Canberra and the Australian Embassy in Bangkok and the Thai Government. Hatcher and the salvors had hoped for a strong stand by the Australian Government. Perhaps even an appearance by the Royal Australian Navy vessel HMAS *Perth* which was in south-east Asian waters.

However, they were to be disappointed. Copies of cable correspondence between Canberra and Bangkok obtained later under the Freedom of Information Act show that the Australian Foreign Affairs Department took a weak stance in protecting its nationals. Rather than questioning the legality of the Thai confrontation the Department instead searched for ways of minimising their responsibility.

For example, the ship *Australia Tide* was being purchased by an Australian company, Tidewater Port Jackson (TPS) in Melbourne. A confidential outward cable from Canberra to the Australian Embassy in Bangkok noted, 'Tidewater Port Jackson are currently the operators of the vessel which has been under charter to them for some time. TPS are currently in the process of buying the ship and expect the transaction to be completed within the next week.'

However, because the purchase was still in process the vessel was still registered under a Panamanian 'flag of convenience'.

With this technicality the Foreign Affairs Department concluded that the vessel was not Australian-owned or registered.

Divcon, the company who contracted the divers, was run by Australians and Anthony Ruedavey, brother of the general manager Geoffrey Ruedavey, was on board *Australia Tide* as a diver. Mike Hatcher, the charterer and salvor, at this point had not been reissued with an Australian passport and was using his British passport, so the Foreign Affairs Department chose to regard him as British.

In short, although the vessel was (apart from the technicality of the process) Australian owned, the dive company was Australians, Hatcher was British and there were seven Australians on board, the Foreign Affairs Department minimised their responsibility to 'concern for the welfare' of its nationals. An outward cablegram from the Department of Foreign Affairs to the Ambassador Richard Butler in Bangkok on February the 8, 1992, contained the following advice for Ambassador Butler and Embassy staff under the heading:

CONFIDENTIAL
In going back to the Thai Foreign Ministry and in any further discussions with the commercial parties involved, you should speak in the following lines:

Welcome the assurances of Thai restraint offered but state that we are concerned about the potential for aggravation by the sizeable Thai Naval presence. Reiterate that our immediate concern is the welfare of the seven Australian nationals on board the *Australia Tide* in what seems to be a sensitive and tense situation. We look to the Thai authorities to ensure their safety.

State that the Australian Government position is that the matter is at present one between the commercial interests involved and their legal representatives on the one hand and the Thai authorities on the other.

Emphasise that the national and commercial interests of a number of countries other than Australia are involved and reiterate our legal view that the action is taking place in what Australia and others clearly regard as international waters.

Senator Evans has been consulted through his private staff and agrees with the above approach.

Please keep other Embassies in Bangkok whose commercial interests and nationals are involved fully informed of developments. Particularly Singapore.

In short the Australian Government, though it had been advised through its own departmental inquiries that *Australia Tide* was in international waters and acting legally, was not prepared to support its nationals on the question of ownership of the shipwreck artefacts. (The matter is one between the commercial interests involved and their legal representatives on the one hand and the Thai authorities on the other).

Newspaper reports on the confrontation took different angles depending on where the papers were published. Thai reports with information given them by government sources were naturally strongly anti-Hatcher.

On February 8, 1992, the *Nation* ran the following story:

THAILAND NAVY MOUNTS SEARCH ON AUST VESSEL

MINISTRY DENIES PIRACY CHARGES

The Thai Government defended itself yesterday against charges of piracy after armed marine police boarded an Australian ship said to be hunting for treasure in the Gulf of Thailand. The Thai Foreign Ministry said its naval forces were within their rights to board the 600-tonne *Australia Tide* because the ship was in Thai territorial waters.

'Senior Thai Government officials do not like the word "piracy",' Thai Foreign Ministry spokesman Sakthip Krairiksh told a news conference. 'The vessel violated the economic zone of Thailand with an intention to bring undersea artefacts out of the country.'

Australian Embassy officials in contact with the ship said Thai marine police assaulted crewmembers, threatened to arrest the captain and took items away after they boarded the vessel on Thursday about 65 miles south of Sattahip.

They said the vessel appeared to be involved in diving operations for ceramics from an old wreck in the Gulf.

'This is an act of piracy,' the ship said in a message sent to Australia's Maritime Safety Centre in Canberra.

An Embassy official said three Thai navy and marine police vessels had surrounded the *Australia Tide* after its Dutch captain refused to pull up anchor and head to Sattahip naval base.

'It's a stand-off,' he said, adding that Canberra was alarmed by the incident and considering an official protest. Sakthip said the Thais would ask the ship owner to return what the crew had found to the Thai Government. Thai officials asked to go on board but the captain would not let them search the ship and would not talk to them, he added.

The Melbourne-based ship owner, Tidewater Port Jackson Marine, said the vessel was leased as a supply ship for the oil and gas industry in the Gulf of Thailand.

Thailand declared a 200-nautical mile economic zone in the Gulf in 1981 but its status under international law is unclear. It overlaps with similar claims by Malaysia and Vietnam.

The *Australia Tide* is registered in Panama. The crew of between 40 and 50 includes Australians, New Zealanders and an American, the Australian official said.

'We believe it's purely a technical misunderstanding,' Jim Collard, company secretary of Tidewater Port Jackson Marine said in Australia. But western diplomats said they suspected corrupt Thai officers deliberately raided the ship to get their hands on any treasure and to extract a large fine from the captain.

Sakthip said Thai Navy and Foreign Ministry officials and Australian diplomats would visit the ship to assess the situation.

On February 9 the *Nation* followed up with a further report:

NAVY THREATENS TO BOARD TREASURE SHIP, ARREST CREW

Thai Government officials insisted on Saturday that an Australian-owned ship, suspected of hunting for sunken treasure in Thai waters, would not be allowed to leave until it is thoroughly searched.

'By law we have the right to search the ship and retrieve any artefacts found on board,' said a Foreign Ministry official who declined to be named. A senior Thai Navy officer said that if the problem could not be settled by negotiations, then the Navy would board the ship, the *Australia Tide*.

'At present the naval authorities have not arrested any crewmembers. We have asked permission to board the ship and search it, and if the captain continues to refuse our request we might be forced to board it and arrest the crewmembers,' said Navy Chief of Staff Admiral Suravuth Maharom.

A spokesman of Singapore-based Divcon diving company admitted yesterday that the company which operated the *Australia Tide* had been contracted to retrieve porcelain artefacts from the Gulf of Thailand's seabed.

In Bangkok, Australian Embassy officials attempted to play down the incident, insisting that it was a legal problem between the *Australia Tide's* owners and Thai authorities.

'We have no plans to visit the ship and crew. We have spoken with the Foreign Ministry and made known our concern for the safety of the crew, but for the time being it is not a consulate matter but a legal one. We will simply observe,' an Embassy official told AFP.

The official added that the Embassy had been in contact with the ship and was assured there was no risk to three divers, one Australian and two New Zealanders, undergoing decompression on board.

'This is a normal on-ship procedure and nothing out of the ordinary,' he added. The 40-man crew is believed to be made up of Australians, Americans, Canadians, Japanese, New Zealanders, Filipinos and Singaporeans.

At present the *Australia Tide* is about 55 nautical miles south of Chuang Island in the Gulf of Thailand, surrounded by several Thai navy vessels.

Thai officials say the ship was spotted on Thursday and after the captain refused to weigh anchor and sail to Sattahip naval base, she was boarded by Thai sailors. They later returned to their ships after the captain refused to allow a search to be carried out, the officials added. A radio message from the ship said several crewmembers had been assaulted by the boarding crew, but Thai officials denied the claim.

Officials say the *Australia Tide* was in the area in December and although no action was taken at the time, it was suspected of illegal treasure hunting. The region was a traditional route for ancient Thai and Chinese junks carrying valuable Sawankhalok pottery.

The Associated Press, reporting from Melbourne, quoted Matt Harsley, the Singapore-based managing director of Divcon, as saying that the 87-metre *Australia Tide* was on an assignment to retrieve porcelain artefacts from a 12th century Chinese vessel in the Gulf of Thailand. He said the crew was still involved in negotiations with the Thai Government to return to Singapore, but the situation was a 'Mexican stand-off'.

'They're surrounded by six navy vessels at the moment,' said Harsley. 'They've got a destroyer, frigates and police boats – it's bigger than the Spanish Armada.'

The *Bangkok Post* of February 11 not unexpectedly came out with a hostile editorial putting a strongly pro-Thai point of view:

TREASURE HUNTERS OR COMMON THIEVES?

Treasure hunts usually bring to mind visions of Indiana Jones-type figures striding through jungles or deserts clutching mysterious maps and overcoming a variety of physical perils to find unimaginable wealth and glory in long-lost tombs or equally exotic locations. But this is the romantic stuff of which Hollywood dreams are made. Present-day reality is quite different.

Today's treasure hunters usually operate under licences issued by the country in whose territory artefacts are being sought and work under strict supervision. Penalties for those trying to smuggle out historical relics or mount unauthorised expeditions are severe and frequently involve heavy fines and/or jail terms. The South American nations are particularly strict in this regard and within the past decade Britain, the United States and Europe have tightened regulations governing the salvage of national treasures. No longer does the ancient 'finders keepers' rule of thumb apply. Buried treasure is owned by the country in whose territory it is found or, to be more precise, by the citizens of that country. The Government has the responsibility to protect and administer it on their behalf.

The affair of the *Australia Tide*, apprehended in Thai waters with a consignment of porcelain artefacts plundered from a centuries-old Chinese junk, is a classic illustration of this principle in action. As Navy Chief of Staff Admiral Suravuth Maharom put it 'this ship has stolen our resources, so what else could we do. We have the legal right to board it and seize any antiques found on board. If we did nothing, other ships would come and take away other resources'.

He theorised that some Thai fishermen had first discovered the sunken Chinese vessel and sold the secret of its location to the treasure hunters. Later reports pointed an accusing finger at an unprincipled antique dealer in Pattaya as the mastermind behind the operation to salvage porcelain pots and other artefacts believed to have been produced 400 to 500 years ago during the Ayutthaya Era and sell them abroad. Whatever the background, it is significant that the affair ended peaceably and that the plundered antiques are now safely in responsible Thai hands. Had a similar situation occur along the coastline of another country the confrontation could have been resolved not by polite negotiations, but by gunfire.

The Fine Arts Department has described the recovered jade-green Sawankhalok porcelain as of an extremely rare type worth a fortune on international antique markets with only a few examples held by the Thai National Museum. Their theft from our shores would deprive us of the opportunity to put together an accurate picture of the Thai way of life during the Ayutthaya period, an era known to be rich in arts and crafts. As such their value cannot be assess in purely monetary terms.

Now that artefacts of such immense archaeological value have been recovered we must ensure that they are properly cared for and placed on public view in the National Museum so that we can see our heritage. It goes without saying that a careful inventory must be taken to ensure that no-one makes any future claim of lost or switched valuables and the Fine Arts Department is best suited for this, and indeed appears to have the task well in hand. The next priority is to comb known trading routes ourselves to recover priceless antiques which could lie a mere 60 metres below the surface. We have the knowledge and surely the will to recover our artefacts ourselves. If we do not, we stand to lose them to mercenary adventurers.

It took many painful years to recover a priceless lintel from a museum in Chicago. Ban Chiang pottery is hardly rare in the western art world. Nor are desecrated Buddha heads. Had the Navy not been vigilant enough to intercept the *Australia Tide* we would have lost another little piece of our history to unscrupulous black marketeers. It is time to re-examine the laws protecting our national treasures and tighten them if necessary. Accompanying this must be a review of all procedures governing the export of antiquities and the stiffest of penalties for smugglers. No price is too great to pay to prevent further losses.

Out on the waters of the Gulf the stand-off continued with the Royal Thai Navy insisting that Australia Tide take the cargo of artefacts in to their Sattahip base. Captain de Vries and Mike Hatcher refused to budge from their stance.

'They played it rough,' says Hatcher. 'Their marines placed limpet mines on our anchor chains. They placed a secret briefcase bomb among the artefacts, and they continually kept their guns pointed at us. They made no bones about the fact that they would open fire if we attempted to run for Singapore. Though they put it a little more delicately than that. The phrase they used was that they "Could not guarantee our safety" if we attempted to move. But we knew what they meant.'

As the first deadline for *Australia Tide* to sail for Sattahip came and went Captain de Vries and Mike Hatcher were invited over for a meal with the Commander of the Royal Thai Navy. Hatcher believed that they had struck a deal whereby the cargo could be taken to Singapore and held in trust while the lawyers worked out a count settlement.

'It was suggested that if the Thais won custody of the artefacts we would be offered compensation,' Hatcher recalls. 'It wasn't what we wanted. But it seemed to be the best deal we could hope for in the circumstances. We had the goods but they had the guns.'

However when the proposal was relayed to the shore it was given short shrift by the Thai administration. As the days passed and the Australian Government failed to take a strong stance the Thais became more determined and more resolute in their attitude.

There was one last slim chance. A drama within the major drama.

Geoff Ruedavey, one of the divers in the saturation chamber, still undergoing depressurising, developed some symptoms of the bends. He was moved into the transfer chamber and re-pressurised to greater 'depth', but there was concern for his safety and a belief that he needed to see a specialist diving doctor for medical treatment as soon as possible.

Captain de Vries notified the Thais who said that Ruedavey could be examined by one of their own doctors. Hatcher and de Vries said that this was unsatisfactory and that they were taking the sick diver to Singapore. De Vries actually had *Australia Tide's* engines started, but he was warned in unmistakable tones by the Thais not to raise anchor.

Finally, a meeting was arranged on board *Australia Tide*. The confrontation had dragged on for 10 days and everyone was weary of it.

'In the end we had no option,' Mike Hatcher recalls. 'If they had forced us into a Thai port the ship and gear might have been confiscated. We might have ended up in a Thai gaol and still lost the cargo. Their final offer to us, which we accepted, was that we transfer the cargo to their tug. After that we would all be free to sail for Singapore. We didn't really have a choice. I was very concerned for the safety of my divers and crew. We seemed to be getting no help at all from our own government. We felt very much on our own out there. The fact that the Thais seemed to be becoming more determined every day indicated to us that things were probably only going to get worse.

'We did get an agreement that the cargo would be "held in trust" and that there would be fair legal examination of our rights. Also that at the very least some compensation would be offered, for the $600,000 to $700,000 we had spent raising the ceramics. That seems a bit of a laugh now. Looking back it seems quite plain that there was never any intention of letting us have any of it back or offering compensation. It was a hijack. We just had to cut our losses and run.'

The *Nation* noted the end of the Thai incident on February 10, 1992:

AUST VESSEL FREED IN GULF, ANTIQUES SEIZED

The Royal Thai Navy yesterday released an Australian-owned ship after seizing antiques said to be worth millions of dollars, naval officers said.

The 87-metre *Australia Tide* had been surrounded since Thursday by Navy vessels in the Gulf of Thailand, about 65 nautical miles south of here, on suspicion of hunting for sunken treasure in Thai waters. The ship, with a crew of 40 to 50 believed to be made up of Australians, Americans, Canadians, Japanese, New Zealanders, Filipinos and Singaporeans, was allowed to leave after Thai Navy officers went on board and confiscated porcelain artefacts salvaged from a Chinese junk on the seabed.

A navy ship, HTMS *Rin*, had arrived here with hundreds of confiscated jars and vases, naval officers said. One officer said the antiques were 'in spotless condition' and were worth millions of dollars.

In Singapore, Matt Harsley, the Managing Director of Divcon International, which was in charge of conducting the operation, confirmed that his diving company had received clearance for the *Australia Tide* to return to Singapore.

Harsley also confirmed that all artefacts salvaged from the *Australia Tide*, which was chartered from the Melbourne-based company Tidewater Port Jackson Marine, had been 'transferred to the Thai authorities in return for free passage'.

Navy Chief-of-Staff Admiral Suravudh Maharom said the seized antiques were moved to the naval base here en route to Bangkok to be examined by officials of the Fine Arts Department. He said the Australian ship clearly demonstrated an intention to hunt for treasure in an area where a Thai trawler was recently seized on the same charges. He said he had reported the incident to Supreme Commander Gen Suchinda Kraprayoon.

Prime Minister Anand Panyarachun yesterday defended the boarding of the Australian ship by the Navy, saying Thailand had acted within its rights.

The Premier, who was visiting the northern province of Chiang Rai, said he had already ordered officials involved to contact the embassies of the vessel's owner and of the crewmembers and explain the actions of the Navy.

'The Thai Navy acted within its rights. We did not commit piracy. The ship was seized within our economic zone,' he said.

Thailand declared a 200-nautical mile economic zone in the Gulf in 1981, although the status of the zone, which overlaps similar claims by Malaysia and Vietnam, is unclear under international law.

Thai officials say the *Australia Tide* was in the area in December. Although no action was taken at the time, it was suspected of illegal treasure hunting, they said. The area was a traditional route for ancient Thai and Chinese junks carrying valuable pottery.

Officials said the two Thai Navy ships which arrived here earlier yesterday had more than 2000 confiscated jars, vases and jade-coloured porcelain pieces which were packed in 130 cardboard boxes by the *Australia Tide* crew.

Navy officials said negotiations were held with the crew before the ship was released and denied reports in newspapers yesterday that some crewmembers were assaulted after officials boarded the ship.

Mike Hatcher was seething when *Australia Tide* returned to Singapore. He was not a man who gave up easily and in the months and years which followed he made continued submissions to the Australian and Thai Governments seeking what he considered to be 'justice'. He received some sympathy in Australian governmental circles and the issue continued to be raised through the Australian Embassy in Bangkok for some years after the forced handing over of the cargo. But with no success.

Hatcher grudgingly acknowledged that, though he was disappointed that the Australian Government did not intercede on his behalf in the property claim at the time of the incident, the constant official concerns experienced for the welfare of the Australians aboard and representations by Embassy staff probably kept RTN fingers off their triggers at a crucial time.

The Thai Navy's chief of staff, Surravuth Maharom, told the *Bangkok Post* at the time that special consideration had been given to the fact that the ship was Australian.

'If this had involved other countries,' he said frankly, 'the vessel might have been fired at.'

Hatcher engaged lawyers upon his return, but in the end it became clear that he had no chance of swaying the Thais on the matter of the cargo. Whatever the shadowy legal interpretations which might be placed on exclusive economic zones or freedom of the seas, there was one unrelenting law. Possession was the key, and as Hatcher said, 'They had the guns and they got our goods. End of story'.

Perhaps David Lyman, for a time Hatcher's Bangkok lawyer, summed it all up best in his letter to the Australian Embassy in Bangkok on February 14, 1992.

The bottom line is, in my opinion, that the salvors were entirely within their rights to dive the wreck and collect its cargo of antiques, while the Thai Government through the Royal Thai Navy in seizing the cargo from the *Australia Tide* where it was anchored acted without legal right or even the colour of legal right. In any event the Thai Government now has possession of the cargo ...

This case evokes all the romance, danger, courage and tragedy of iron men sailing the high seas in wooden ships combatting the elements and the desires of other men. Because of the Thai nationalistic fervour which this case has attracted, my partners are very reluctant to take the claim much further than advice and perhaps assistance in negotiations with the Thai Government. In this atmosphere the legality of the actions of the salvors and the illegality of the Royal Thai Navy and Thai Government are almost immaterial. Emotion rules over rationality. So much for 'The Rule of Law'.

Very truly yours,
Tilleke & Gibbins
David Lyman
Senior Partner

There was one bright note in the *Australia Tide's* sombre return to Singapore. Geoff Ruedavey, the diver who had suffered the symptoms of the bends, made a full recovery and was given a clean bill of health after a medical check-up on arrival in Singapore.

As for the cargo, Mike Hatcher's old slogan 'finders keepers' suffered a severe reverse, though the second part of the old adage which may date back to buccaneering days, 'losers weepers', remained true.

CHAPTER THIRTEEN

The Killing Fields of Cambodia

My first contact with Michael Hatcher came about in an oblique sort of way. In fact what became known as the Condor Reef adventure began with a discordant fanfare ... the unwelcome jangle of my bedside telephone at first light one grey September morning. It was my publisher, and she wanted me to write a book about the controversial master salvor who was planning a major recovery in Cambodia.

She had called me because of my own association with East Indiamen wrecks. In 1966 I had written a book called *Islands of Angry Ghosts* about our diving discovery of the 1629 treasure ship *Batavia*. It was a wonderful experience and as I lay back on the pillow all the old memories came flooding back. My wreck-diving days had been great – weed-grown cannon, sun-dappled below the waves ... the glint of silver ducatons and crowns with embossed dates going back to 1544, those wonderfully irregular pieces-of-eight from Mexico and Peru beloved by the buccaneers. *Cabo de barra*. When they were spun on a wooden counter, the old coins rang like bells ... they had come all the way from the Spanish Main.

Ashore in shallow graves there had been the sword-hacked skeletons of victims of the *Batavia* mutineers. It was the fantasy of 'Treasure Island' encountered unexpectedly in real life. I literally had to rub my eyes at times to make sure I wasn't dreaming. The names of the famous ships were engraved forever on my frontal lobes … *Tryal* 1622; *Batavia* 1629; *Vergulde Draeck* 1656; *Zuytdorp* 1712; *Zeewyk* 1729 …

Our Dutch ships had shared three famous initials in common with Hatcher's *Geldermalsen*. VOC represented the seven provinces of the Netherlands and was stamped into cannon breeches, sword hilts, candlesticks and castle gates. It was on all manner of weapons, badges and company insignia. The letters flew on pennants from the masts of ships sailing from the Lowland Seas around the Cape of Good Hope and as far afield as Japan.

'Jesus Christ is good!' the Dutch had said, 'but trade is better!' In its day the VOC was probably the most powerful trading company the world had ever known.

On their unfinished voyages our West Australian ships had been outward bound on their way to the East Indies. All of them were treasure ships, carrying tonnes of silver coin in iron-bound chests – money to pay their way and purchase cargoes. Money to attract divers and treasure hunters in our own time.

Mike Hatcher's *Geldermalsen* had been sailing in the reverse direction, on a return voyage to Holland, laden with tea and porcelain. A different kind of treasure, but just as valuable, it seemed, to modern-day collectors. I reflected how lucky we were to have been on the diving scene at the time the wrecks were found. I had believed those days were past.

Were there new wrecks to be found? That sudden thought made my heart beat a little faster. Why hadn't I thought of it before? After all, how could one reasonably write a book without some actual participation in the adventure?

❁

I was sent some material to refresh my memory about Michael Hatcher. The pictures showed a powerfully-built man of middle height, slightly balding with direct eyes and a trademark cocky grin. 'Up yours!' the expression seemed to say. You could like it or lump it, and it didn't matter a rat's end either way to him. In the pictures Mike Hatcher looked just as he had been portrayed, a latter-day pirate. The only law he respected, it was suggested in the descriptions, was survival. He had the usual seaman's contempt for bureaucracy and red tape and would short-cut any regulation if he could get away with it . . . so long as it didn't involve getting arrested and tied up in port.

Where wrecks were concerned he was smart enough to have thoroughly acquainted himself with international law. But he didn't feel particularly bound by it. Unless a gunboat came over the horizon. Hatcher knew all about gunboats, I discovered, from an unfortunate incident in the Gulf of Thailand. Tough luck, I said to myself.

And cargoes?

'If I take the risks and I'm good enough to find a wreck and raise the cargo then I reckon it's mine. The archaeologists don't like me, but that's their bad luck.'

He had invited archaeologists to join him on the wrecks, but no senior marine archaeologist had been prepared to risk the stain on his reputation which might have resulted from rubbing shoulders with 'the Hatch'. The academic union had shut him out. In his own terms that was a recommendation. 'The buggers are jealous.'

By the time I met the man I already knew a great deal about him. Or at least I thought I did. The meeting was at the Tradewinds Hotel in Fremantle in November, 1996. 'Mike Hatcher,' he said, after I'd knocked on his door. The handshake was firm and strong. 'Good to meet you. Coffee?' There was a moment or two while he messed with the hotel coffee jug and we appraised each other. We were similarly dressed in blue shirts and jeans with boat shoes. The casual uniform of boating people the world around.

'So you're going to do the book?' he said. I gathered he had decided I was OK. I nodded, having just made my own decision.

'Here then,' he said. 'Have a look at this.' He fished a file from his briefcase and tossed it over to me. It was titled LOSS OF THE SHIP OF MR RALPH LAMBTON and consisted of research by the English author and wreck researcher Nigel Pickford. It was an impressive piece of work and included photocopies of charts, and there for the first time I saw the name CONDOR REEF.

Even on paper you could see that it was a ship trap. It lay waist-deep below the surface and twenty miles from shore in the Gulf of Siam, better known today as the Gulf of Thailand. A lone spire of granite rock rose like a pyramid from 15 fathoms, or 100 feet of water, to lip the surface. It lay in the regular path of southbound sailing ships seeking the land breeze down the Gulf of Siam. It must have been murdering vessels for centuries. It was named after a German ship, *Condor*, wrecked there in 1861. The ship was lost but the crew was saved.

'A nasty brute,' I commented.

Hatch nodded. 'An evil mother. It should have been called Killer Reef.' The description reminded me of the 'Killing Fields' of Cambodia's recent and notorious history. Two Australians who sailed that coast in a yacht in the 1970s seeking adventure were captured by the Khmer Rouge. They were accused of spying for the CIA, tortured and murdered in Phnom Penh's infamous Tuol Sleng interrogation centre. Their photographs are on the wall there today with hundreds of other victims of a barbarous regime.

Hatcher had known both men personally. 'When I saw the photographs I felt like vomiting,' he said. It was a moment or two before we got back to the reason for our meeting.

In November 1679 the reef had claimed the vessel of Ralph Lambton, or rather the ship of the King of Siam which Lambton was skippering on a voyage to Surat in India. She went down so quickly that they were unable to save even the King's letters of credit. She took with her a mixed cargo, including 10,000 Rix dollars in silver. But what particularly interested Hatcher and his consortium, United Sub Sea Services, was a consignment of porcelain which may have numbered 100,000 pieces. They were from the Ming period in China, the era of manufacture considered most valuable by collectors.

'It seems not at all improbable that such pieces could fetch between one hundred and one thousand English pounds each,' Nigel Pickford had written.

My mind was already working ahead. With a limited area of reef and the fact that Hatcher had already made a preliminary visit, the question arose whether he might have already found the wreck and was raising money on a certainty. Was he simply being cautious for reasons of security? When I asked him this he nodded briefly and changed the subject. When I changed tack and asked about the appearance of the wreck I discovered that he did not care for close questioning. The eyes flashed.

'Hugh, I *have* found the wreck! Let's leave it at that. Huh?'

We parted on good terms and Hatcher flew off to his property in Grafton, New South Wales. After that he was due to fly back to Cambodia. I went home to Swanbourne to think long and hard about our interview. Then I took up the offer to write the book.

Soon after Hatcher and I met with the publishers – a meeting at which Hatcher was at his sparkling best, relishing the opportunity to bring a whiff of gunpowder and buccaneering days into the boardroom. We departed with a contract for a book on Hatcher's life with the proviso, of course, that the wreck on Condor Reef, 'Ralph Lambton's Ship', turned out to be as rich as the records indicated. At the time it seemed a mere matter of course.

❀

Early in March, 1997, I bought an air ticket to Cambodia. In the weeks after the initial meetings with Hatcher and the publishers I had done some research and had read as much as I could about that most unfortunate of countries. The titles included *Highway To A War* by Christopher Koch; *Brother Number One, A Biography of Pol Pot*, and *A History of Cambodia* by David P. Chandler; *Cambodia* by David Bowden; and Lonely Planet's informative *Vietnam, Laos, and Cambodia. The Gates of Ivory* by Margaret Drabble and *Bali & Angker, A 1930s Pleasure Trip Looking at Life & Death* by Geoffrey Gover painted a picture of Cambodia in French colonial days that completed the list.

I admit to being troubled by the books and from seeing for a second time the history-making film *The Killing Fields*. But perhaps it was the reaction of more widely-travelled friends, frequent visitors to south-east Asia, which affected me the most. Without exception and without hesitation they all said the same thing: 'Cambodia? You'd need a really good reason to go there.' 'A dangerous and unpleasant place. Don't go there. That's my advice. Don't go.'

It was true that the country had only been open to westerners for four years following the infamous Pol Pot regime and the Vietnamese occupation which had followed it. There had been some murders of Europeans, including Australians, in circumstances which resulted in wide newspaper publicity and hardly helped change an unfavourable outside impression.

The most notorious incident was what came to be known as 'the Backpacker murders'. They followed the abduction and murder of Queensland model Kellie-Anne Wilkinson in April 1994.

On July 26, 1994, 29-year-old Australian David Wilson, 27-year-old Frenchman Jean-Michel Braquet and 26-year-old Briton Mark Slater took an ill-fated train ride from Phnom Penh the capital, in central Cambodia, intending to go to Sihanoukville on the south coast. They were seasoned backpackers accustomed to travelling in remote and often dangerous parts of Asia and they laughed when warned of the possible risks of the train journey which passed through territory still held by Khmer Rouge splinter groups. But the train was ambushed and the three marched off at gun-point. Demands for a ransom were sent to Phnom Penh.

The attack was organised by a Khmer Rouge rebel leader, Chouk Rin, and carried out by his senior officers Sam Bith and Nuon Paet. Pathetic pictures and film of the hostages pleading for the ransom to be paid were shown in newspapers and on television around the world.

It should have been a straightforward hostage situation – demands would be made, money paid and the hostages eventually released – but crucial negotiations were botched and the families blamed the Australian Government for allegedly mishandling the case. The Cambodian Government in Phnom Penh was furious at their loss of face in the eyes of the world and decided to make an example of this particular rebel group. They responded to the Khmer Rouge demands with an artillery bombardment of the Phnom Vour (Vine Mountain) base of Nuon Paet where the captives were being held.

Chouk Rin defected to the government, giving information which led to a military encirclement of the rebel position. In the ensuing gunfight the three captives became the first casualties. Nuon Paet had them shot and buried in shallow graves and then fled, escaping the net.

It was a catastrophe and one not soon forgotten. There were echoes in March 1998 when the former Australian diplomat in Cambodia, Alastair Gaisford, told a Melbourne Coroners Court inquiry into David Wilson's death that the Australian Foreign Minister's office had ignored pleas from Phnom Penh Embassy staff to prevent the Cambodian military going in hard, thereby negating the chances of the hostages being released alive. The Commonwealth reply was that all that could have been done was done.

When I flew to Cambodia in March 1997 I had the deaths of David Wilson and his friends and Kellie-Anne Wilkinson weighing heavily on my mind. There were also quite a number of other deaths which did not receive the same publicity.

'Whatever you do,' Mike Hatcher had warned me, 'do not photograph anyone who's carrying a gun. That especially includes police and army personnel.' He told me of the recent case of Highway 4 (on which I would have to travel) where some Australian tourists driving back to Phnom Penh from the coast stopped to observe Cambodian Army personnel forcibly and roughly searching people dragged out of a vehicle.

The cameras clicked. The soldiers turned and shot the tourists dead at point blank range with machine pistols, riddling their bodies with bullets. The glint of the lenses, they explained later, had been mistaken for weapons.

❋

The flight from Perth to Kuala Lumpur was unremarkable except for the skull and crossbones 'Death Penalty for Drugs' notices at the airport. Like everyone else, I had a cold moment and hoped my luggage had not been tampered with. On the second leg of the journey, Kuala Lumpur to Phnom Penh, the plane was almost empty. Clearly Cambodia was not a popular destination.

During Pol Pot's regime (between 1975 and 1978) one to two million (the correct figure may never be known) people of a country of only 14 million died in a bizarre social experiment. Many of them were executed or murdered in a grotesque attempt to 'de-westernise' the nation and remove all traces of European influence. Even the calender was changed, and 1975 become the 'Year Zero'.

Pol Pot (real name Saloth Sar), the revolutionary leader who overthrew the US-backed Lon Nal regime in 1975, closed the country to the outside world. His philosophy espoused a return to what was perceived as the good and wholesome peasant culture of the countryside. Country people were 'base people' while townsfolk were 'new people' corrupted by outside influences.

The capital Phnom Penh and the provincial towns were emptied and the 'new people' were marched out at gunpoint to labour in the rice fields and on social projects. Given minimum food, quite unused to manual labour, thousands were taken away into the forest and killed 'with sticks and knives' as useless encumbrances on the programme. The drive to stamp out western influences was taken to extraordinary lengths. Men were shot for wearing glasses ('intellectuals') or for speaking French or English ('traitors') or simply for being educated ('corrupted'). Of the 6000 doctors in Cambodia at the fall of Phnom Penh in 1975, only 57 survived the regime.

Yet Pol Pot was born into a well-to-do farming family, and his cohorts had learnt their Marxist philosophies in the universities and cafés of Paris. Surely they were the prime example of Cambodians educated elsewhere, their ideologies derived from largely French revolutionary sources? Why were learning and western influences acceptable for them, yet fatal for others?

When the Vietnamese invaded Cambodia under provocation in 1978, their soldiers were horrified to find thousands of human skeletons piled together at various points in the countryside. 'The killing fields', so infamous today, were revealed to the world. The Vietnamese left the bones unburied as a tribute to the victims and a permanent reproach to Pol Pot's murderous regime. As I flew towards Phnom Penh these bleached and tragic relics of man's inhumanity to man were still visible in some places.

The Khmer Rouge were still active according to a news release from the Department of Foreign Affairs. 'Australian visitors and residents should be warned,' the release spelled out, 'that a high level of danger exists from banditry against foreign nationals, both in the countryside and in Phnom Penh itself.' I was startled to see a paragraph which stated that travel by road to Sihanoukville should not be regarded as safe ... it was the very road on which we intended travelling!

Looking down I saw reefs, islands, some wide and generous bays with fishing villages and finally an unmistakable mainland. Strange to think that a European landing on these shores would have met with certain death until quite recently. In fact it had only been possible for westerners to visit the country, without special arrangements, since the Hun Sen–Prince Norodom Ranariddh Coalition Government took control in 1994. The Khmer Rouge had melted back into the forest rather than fight the election but had remained a force, a literal poisonous snake in the grass, fighting a lost guerilla cause until 1999.

In 1997 we wondered what we were likely to find. Previously all my own interest had been directed towards the excitement of discovering Captain Lambton's lost treasure ship, but now, with Cambodia before my eyes, a dark and ominous land mass, my thoughts were otherwise occupied.

Aside from all those other ghosts, another spirit rode in the aircraft with me. My father (who had died in 1995) had been a compulsive traveller, fascinated by art and architecture. In the 1970s he had visited Cambodia and the temples at Angkor Wat and counted it as one of the greatest experiences of his life. If there was an art gallery, a cathedral, a temple or set of ruins from South America to Vietnam worth a visit he had probably been there at some time.

I also recalled, as a point of trivia, that scenes from the film *Lord Jim*, starring Peter O'Toole, were shot at Angkor Wat in the 1970s. At the time Cambodia was a French province and gracious living was the order of the day among the Europeans. The Cambodians, it was universally acknowledged, were among the kindest, gentlest, most naturally artistic people on earth. They were Bhuddists, it was explained. Incapable of violence.

What happened to turn this fairytale into the nightmare horror of the brutal days of Pol Pot? Cambodia's tragedy is too complex for the scope of this book, though readers may care to seek other sources. Briefly, the country was a victim of clumsy and indifferent de-colonisation by Europeans and a serious casualty of the Vietnam War. Cambodia was a neutral country in that conflict, but because the Americans were aware that the North Vietnamese were moving troops south across the border they included eastern Cambodia in their B-52 bomber raids without any serious consideration of the consequences.

They also bombed around Phnom Penh in a fruitless effort to prop up the doomed Lon Nol regime, playing further into the hands of the Marxists. A total of 257,465 tons of bombs – no casual amount – was dropped on the Cambodian countryside. This amounted to about 76,780 individual bombs because the weight of these fearsome weapons of destruction was around seven tons per missile.

When a B-52 bomb fell the blast was incredible. A description of the bombing from *Highway To A War* by Christopher Koch tells something of the effect. People on the ground could neither see nor hear the bombers because the B-52s flew too high and the men in the aircraft which flew from Guam and back again saw only a landscape so far below that it all seemed quite impersonal to them. On the ground it was different. Some of the bomb craters were more than 10 metres wide.

'The earth heaved in a huge spasm and I found myself hugging it as though I were clinging to an upturned boat. Then a roar engulfed us unlike anything I'd ever known. It was not a sound, it was something beyond sound; it opened up a gaping hole in my head making my mind cry out in terror, making the whole world rock and sway. The palms and bigger trees were bending like grass. This is not right, this is not war, nobody should be doing a thing like this, I said and I pissed my pants ... I was very ashamed. In all my years of covering action I'd never done such a thing. So I felt better when I learnt that many of the NVA soldiers did the same, in their first B-52 raid.

'...I found that I was shaking uncontrollably and saw that Mike and Dimitri were shaking in the same way. Captain Danh lying close by was looking across at us with an expression of cheerful sympathy. He pushed back his old-fashioned sun helmet with its red star. Then he smiled and sat up.

"'We are lucky, Mr Jim," he said. "That was not really very close. One kilometre nearer and maybe we would have no eardrums.'"

The effect on the Cambodian rural economy was understandably catastrophic. People fled the areas where the bombs were falling and resentment against westerners, and particularly Americans, peaked at an all-time high. The social upheaval and economic chaos caused by the bombing delivered the country into the hands of a communist guerilla leader – a mysterious, shadowy figure and former schoolteacher who would become known as Pol Pot, 'Brother Number One', and who would eventually be ranked in infamy with Adolf Hitler and Joseph Stalin as one of the century's most evil men.

That was the perception of outsiders. Ironically, he had wanted nothing but good for his people, but the interpretation of his ultra-Marxist philosophies by cadres down the line was brutal in the extreme. In 1975 his message seemed sweetness and light. He promised a better world for Cambodians. They believed him and the puppet regime of Lon Nol, the choice of the America CIA Department and the western powers, was rolled over with ridiculous ease. After the disaster of Vietnam, Americans wanted no more of doomed far-eastern adventures and eventually washed their hands of the area.

The Cambodian royal personage, King Sihanouk, whose hobby was making films, survived the French, the west and the Khmer Rouge, making ineffectual peace with all of them. He was too important for any of the regimes to dispense with. It was entrenched in Cambodian folklore going back thousands of years that the king brought the rains twice a year, the rains which filled the great Mekong River, Cambodia's main artery, Lake Tongle Sap and the other water systems, which were essential for the rice crop that fed the nation.

No king, no rain, was the belief.

On the basis of that equation, the king remained, a golden figure above all the various crises, too elevated and other-worldly to smell the blood or hear the cries. He was still there for the same reasons when my aircraft, MAS Flight 758, came in to land at Phnom Penh airport on February 19.

The expedition had arisen out of a meeting between Hatcher, John Wade (an Australian former oil company executive in north Queensland and the Northern Territory) and the French firm Friedlander who were carrying out engineering projects in Cambodia and were represented by Max Couteau. Together the three men formed a group to look for shipwrecks along the coast of Cambodia, an area which had been closed to outsiders since the early 1970s. No serious wreck searches with modern equipment had ever been carried out. Who could guess what might be there on an ancient trade route?

The initiative had come from John Wade who was operating agencies in Ho Chi Minh City, the former Saigon. He had met Couteau, whose firm Friedlander was engaged in various harbour and engineering works. Wade had read two articles about Mike Hatcher in the Australian press (*Business Review Weekly*, 10/11/1995; and *The Bulletin*, 28/11/1995) and had sent a fax arranging a meeting. The result was a three-way project under Hatcher's masthead United Sub Sea Services. Friedlander had obtained an exclusive licence from the Cambodian Government to look for shipwrecks on the virgin coast and Hatcher's research, through Nigel Pickford in England, had turned up the intriguing story of Captain Lambton's shipwreck.

An examination of charts old and new indicated that there was only one point where Lambton's vessel could have struck. It was labelled Condor Reef.

'Bingo! We're in business!' declared an exultant Hatcher with muted applause from John Wade and Max Couteau ('*Not* Jacques Cousteau,' he would say. 'No *ess*!')

And what sort of vessel would venture out to Condor Reef across the Gulf to raise the Ming porcelain and whatever trinkets of the King of Siam might also be there?

The junk *Song Saigon* of course.

At the time of my arrival it had been billed as a master-stroke, the inspiration of John Wade and Max Couteau. Both would seek to shed the blame later.

Song Saigon was a replica of a 17th century Chinese junk and had been built in Saigon for tourism purposes by a French entrepreneur. She was built to sail the Mekong River and was a vessel of considerable size – 30 metres in length, 180 tons burthen. Described as the 'ultimate in luxury' she had been constructed from teak and mahogany and had once taken the American president Gerald Ford on a Mekong cruise.

Since a film was to be made of the diving and recovery, it was suggested she would provide a romantic and inspirational backdrop. John Wade thought she could later be sailed to Sydney, Australia, for the convening of the World's Tall Ships in 1998 and thereafter sold as a tourist vessel, floating restaurant or whatever, at considerable profit. *Song Saigon* would be one of the main characters in our Condor Reef campaign. But for all the wrong reasons.

❁

On arrival in Cambodia, I was met by the French Friedlander business manager who ferried us out of the capital along the infamous Highway 4. A thought-provoking trip, to put it mildly.

My diary records:

We are in an old Mazda. The driver belts along at 120 to 140 k's where he can find space, one hand pressing urgently and permanently on the horn. 'Fast is safe,' he assures us. That's not the principle we have at home. I wonder what he means with a certain disquiet. Initially we pass dried rice fields with dykes separating them. The terrain is familiar from news clips of the Vietnam War. There is stubble and cracked brown earth reminding us that it is near the end of the dry season, and water palms stand tall on the flat plains like giant cotton palms. There isn't much shelter in a rice field if some one is shooting at you with serious intent. Later we go through hilly country with the little wooden huts of timber cutters and charcoal burners lining the road. The country is stripped of timber to the horizon. No-one seems to be planting more trees. Obviously and of dire necessity the charcoal burners live for today and tomorrow can take care of itself. But what will they do when the last twig is burnt?

Periodically there are police and soldiers with steel helmets and automatic weapons. Usually AK-47s. Most weapons are carried in the 'ready' position as though the owners expect to use them. There are a lot of customs stops with red-and-white segmented barricade poles that can be lowered to block the road. The military and police are armed to the teeth, and backed up by utilities with enormous 50-calibre (AK-60) machine guns mounted in the rear. The weapons are so over-sized that you would expect the recoil to roll the vehicle over. But they earn respect from the locals. Me too!

No-one of European origin travels this road at night. Nor do they begin a journey after midday in case of breakdowns, which is why my party were anxious to get away. Are the villains the bandits or Khmer remnants? There is some suggestion that Army troops do a little 'moonlighting' to supplement their inadequate pay, which is often weeks behind. All parties have guns, and (so it is said) little scruple about the lives of foreigners or their own people. Civilians in the country are often dressed like the Viet Cong in Vietnam, wide straw hats and black pyjamas made soldiers indistinguishable from ordinary farmers.

When the sun goes down and the moon comes up behind the palms the road becomes no man's land. I cross my fingers and hope there are no mechanical problems! I find myself listening attentively to the Mazda's engine beat and chassis rattles.

In the car is Max Couteau, ('No *ess*!') the manager of Friedlander, and Saro Tan, a svelte and influential Cambodian gentleman who apparently smooths the passage for Friedlander's needs in the intrigue-riddled Cambodian government circles. Max and Saro Tan chat in French (courteously apologising to me for lack of English) all the way south. The significant word 'Khmer Rouge' crops up a lot. I find myself hoping there aren't any of the red-and-white checked turbans notorious from 'The Killing Fields' along the road today. And then find that most of the locals wear them anyway! They are called 'Kramas' and double as sarongs. Some are blue-and-white checks.

Eventually, after a journey of four hours, we reach Campong Som (Sihanoukville). It is a ramshackle town and port on the Gulf of Thailand and Cambodia's only maritime entry. The Vietnam border is a short distance to the south east, maybe 50 kilometres, and in between is bandit country. Recently a Khmer Rouge chief, piqued by his apparently waning influence, stopped several taxis of Asian tourists and sent 17 heads in to town. Just to let them know that he was still around.

We booked in at the Seaside Hotel some distance out of town, where the film crew were staying, and retired after an excellent seafood dinner with French wine ('92 Bordeaux), to sleep like the dead. The Seaside is a pleasant surprise. An excellent hotel with air-conditioning and good plumbing – both essential in the tropics. Prices were reasonable. I would recommend it to anyone.

❁

At length the eagerly awaited junk *Song Saigon* was seen entering the harbour. We went down to the wharf to greet her and were dismayed by what we found. It was immediately obvious that *Song Saigon* was not going to sea (or anywhere) for she was in appalling condition. The crew who brought her from Ho Chi Minh City, including John Wade, had a nightmare trip, with engines and pumps failing. The junk leaked so badly that she had to have the pumps running continuously. When the mechanical pumps failed they had to pump by hand, between bouts of seasickness, and also cope with the diesel fumes and rank stench of the bilges.

'It wasn't exactly a fun trip.' A pasty-faced John Wade, normally a pleasant and cheerful fellow, shuddered at the recollection. A spot-check of the junk brought grim news – the main generator was burnt out, the refrigeration unserviceable and the insulation so rotten that the only solution was to rip it out and throw it on the wharf. There was one French engine and one Russian motor, both surly, unresponsive and unreliable lumps of metal. The batteries wouldn't charge. The pumps wouldn't work. Something was wrong with the steering. But beside the wharf *Song Saigon*, with her gaudily-painted decorations and dragon bow, *looked* fantastic.

I noted in my diary that the equipment [was] 'a curious mixture. The bilge pumps have been scavenged from GM truck parts from the Vietnam War. The wiring, like the New Zealand rugby team, is "all black", especially where little fires have burnt through the insulation. Heaven knows where the switchboards and regulators came from. We suspect that they are Russian or Chinese. They have been chewed at some time by rats.'

'Any self-respecting rat,' John Dyson remarked, 'would have jumped ship the moment she touched the wharf!'

Indeed, now that the indelicate subject had been broached, we noticed that there were quite a number of rats running about brazenly in the wharf environs. Did they speak Cambodian or

Vietnamese? A Cambodian-speaking dog made some short dashes in a vain attempt to catch one of them but the rats were too spry. The dog soon gave up and lay down to sleep in the dust, twitching his skin from time to time to keep the flies away. The rats ignored him and continued about their business.

Hatcher was unimpressed. 'How could they charter a boat in that condition?' he asked in disgust. John Wade kept wisely in the background, pleading ignorance of all things nautical. 'I get seasick simply reading the shipping news,' he explained. 'I really don't know about boats.'

While we were standing about surveying the debacle like a group of stunned mullets, Wade apprised me of an extraordinary coincidence. The list of wrecks on Condor Reef which Nigel Pickford had provided included an American clipper ship called *John Wade*.

'Is that an omen, or is it not?' he asked me.

I wasn't sure of the answer to that, but I did note that *John Wade*, built in Massachusetts in 1851 was a 152-foot, 638-ton clipper ship, designed for fast far-eastern voyages, usually with China as a destination. In March 1859, under Captain King, she struck and was wrecked on the uncharted Condor Reef. All hands were saved. Her figurehead was a bust of Captain John Wade after whom the ship was named.

How many other victims had Condor Reef claimed? Were there 1000-year-old Chinese junks beneath the shining surface? Perhaps there were Portuguese carracks, or an Indiaman or two? Information was sparse, for this was an out-of-the-way part of the world, but we were impatient to find out what really was down there on the seabed.

❈

Much to everyone's chagrin, repairs and alterations to the junk dragged on for days. She had sails but they hadn't been used in years so they were spread out on the wharf where a team of 20

Khmers recruited for the purpose sat patiently cross-legged fitting new bamboo battens.

Hatcher was angry and wanted to know who was going to pay for bringing the junk up to scratch. His investors? ('No bloody way!') The French who were responsible for the charter? Or the owner?

Every day we went to the harbour and every evening we went back to the hotel depressed, though we were somewhat revived by the magnificent seafood meals at the Sea View restaurant. Here there occurred the bizarre incident of the one-legged man. He was a beggar, a former soldier still in the tattered remnants of his uniform. One leg had been blown off by a landmine and in a country where there was no welfare or pension begging was the only recourse for a man so broken in body. Each morning we gave him whatever small change was left over from the previous night and he thanked us deferentially. One day we had to come and go a number of times. Each time we passed the beggar would raise himself on his crutches, skip in a fast but crabbed gait towards us and thrust out his cap.

It had been agreed that, on general principle, we would not contribute *every* time we went through the gate. Now the beggar turned on an extraordinary fit of rage at our refusal. He cursed and screamed and threatened us with his crutch until one of the armed guards at the gate stepped forward and worked the bolt of his rifle. The snickety-snick sound of cold steel, a sound he doubtless knew well, cut him short and he crabbed away still mouthing curses. I found the incident very upsetting. We had been generous during our stay. Why the anger? Did he hate us because he had come to rely on us? Did we represent all the reasons for the loss of his leg?

I felt a deep sadness for him and a sense of helplessness over what was a disaster on a national scale. David Bowden records in his book *Cambodia* that Cambodia has the highest proportion of disabled people of any country in the world. The 8 to 10 million mines laid meant that 1 in every 263 people had an amputation which translates to 30,000 to 40,000 amputees, with 300 more victims maimed every month. A high proportion of victims are innocent women and children. You see them everywhere in Cambodia, some with rudely-made wooden pegs, others on crutches. The worst cases – double amputees – are on ground-level trolleys like skateboards, pushing themselves painfully and patiently along.

'A bullet is better,' a doctor told me. 'You can make a full recovery from a bullet wound. But with a landmine you are a cripple for the rest of your life.'

The next day the beggar was back at the gate, accepting our small crumpled notes with a nod. Avoiding eye contact, under control, the anger contained somewhere within.

'It's a cruel world,' said Mike Hatcher waving me past him. 'A cruel, cruel world. But we can't help them. Don't let it get to you.'

That night I dreamt I stepped on a mine, and woke up shouting and drenched in sweat. In my sleep I had kicked the metal underwater camera at my bed end. Sitting up, heart beating wildly, I clutched the sheet around me and felt flooded and flushed through with gratitude that it was only a dream. I felt my legs to be sure.

Tragedy dogged all our work with wrecks, I told myself sternly. Most shipwrecks took people down with them, choking to death on salt water. Would they have exchanged their unexpected and untimely fate with that of the beggar? Logic does not apply itself well to the ruins of a human life. I could find no answer that pleased me.

I wondered too whether the beggar ever dreamt he had legs. Whether he ran and walked again in his sleep. What he felt when he awoke.

❁

Back at the dock, the junk was finally ready to sail and the prospect of diving in clear green water came as a relief. The secrets of Condor Reef were about to be revealed. I packed my landmine-underwater camera and made ready for sea, but somewhere in the back of my mind I could still hear that tap-tapping of a crutch.

CHAPTER FOURTEEN

The Secrets of Condor Reef

Song Saigon looked magnificent with her distinctive bamboo ribbed sails raised. They glowed red-gold in the sunshine and the high-pooped hull with its low bow, so much on the lines of the 17th century Portuguese caravels and Dutch East Indiamen, was a picture from another time. Under sail she slipped along at six knots, far faster than she could manage with her bastardised French-Russian motors.

Mike Hatcher was all smiles.

The film crew spent the afternoon getting shots from another boat, taking the usual variety of angles before the sails came down and *Song Saigon* returned from the cool breezes of the sound to the dusty wharf haunted by rats and lizards. That was the first and last time her sails went up. It had taken two hours to raise the mainsail for that one theatrical effect.

'Pretty as a picture,' said Mike Hatcher admiringly. 'She'd look magnificent on Sydney Harbour.'

I would have liked to have gone out to Condor Reef under sail and sensed that *Song Saigon* would have preferred it too. But Rahim, who had sailed in working junks as a boy, gave an expressive shrug and pointed to the main mast rigging. It was bound with electrical tape. In places the tape had peeled away to reveal rusted once-galvanised wire with broken strands. Clearly it was his opinion that the masts and rigging would not survive any serious squall of wind. As it turned out he was right. Though it had been agreed that we would all maintain tight secrecy about our objective – the official story was to be that we were making a film about the junk – some journalists managed to find their way on board via *Condor*, our tender craft. It appeared they were friends of our French partners in Phnom Penh. Mike Hatcher scowled darkly when they came on board. 'Tell them nothing!' he commanded.

Having achieved the most difficult part of the exercise – actually getting aboard the junk, apparently with the blessing of Max Couteau – the journalists took the next step with polished professionalism. One of them managed to make Mike Hatcher sufficiently angry that, losing his cool, he told them far more than he had intended. An old newspaper ploy.

Imran Vittachi of the *Phnom Penh Post* had obviously done his homework on Hatcher's history. He produced a very creditable piece taking up the full back page of his newspaper under the heading TREASURE HUNTERS TEST CAMBODIAN WATERS. There was a large picture of the junk under sail. The article quoted Max Couteau as saying 'The chances that we come across a junk full of porcelain are as high as 80 per cent'. It also said that we were 'In search of wrecks containing porcelain, gold, and other riches'.

GOLD?

'There was gold on all the ships,' Couteau added. 'What did the captain of a merchant ship that sailed from England or France take with him as money when he sailed to the other ends of the earth? He could only pay in gold. So there are strong chances we could find gold.' Max's logic was correct. But in fact the ships carried silver for the reason that silver coin was worth more in the Far East than in Europe.

Regardless, the tenor of the article was exactly what Mike Hatcher did *not* want. 'Bloody hell!' he roared. 'We're sailing in pirate waters with two pop guns as our only protection. What does Max think he's doing? Inviting the pirates to the party? They cut throats for gold!' He was still fuming as we packed our gear in preparation for departure. A departure which would see a series of frustrating delays due more to local politics rather than the practical problems with the junk. We were assured that those had been largely overcome. The deficiencies would only be exposed when we were on the open sea.

The current problems centred around Captain Alaine Dumesmic, a French tramp steamer captain who had been recruited off the beach in Saigon to skipper *Song Saigon*. It seemed that when the junk first arrived from Vietnam the harbour master had instructed the captain to anchor out in the Roads pending berthing instructions. Alaine considered this unreasonable. Having no confidence in *Song Saigon's* anchoring system, or the harbour authorities for that matter, he took her in and laid her against the wharf, cutting the engines with a Gallic shrug and a puff of smoke from the cigarette which always seemed to be drooping from his whiskery face.

'Eet was not necessary to anchor,' he explained with another exaggerated hunch of the shoulders. 'Iss not eemportant!' He was wrong, of course. Things had been going wrong for Alaine for some time, and this was just another instance.

It may not have been Alaine's fault that the rusty tramp steamer he had skippered from Marseilles had engine trouble in Saigon. Or that the owners seemed disinclined to pay the costs of repairs and his ship was rapidly becoming an abandoned hulk. Or that Alaine seemed to have become an out-of-work beachcomber far from home. The *Song Saigon* charter was a godsend for him in that regard.

But he should, in his years at sea, have learnt something about harbour masters. In their own area – the port and its precinct – they reign supreme. Cross them at your peril. They have a thousand ways to avenge acts of disobedience or disrespect. In this case Alaine had been given a specific instruction and he had disobeyed it. In doing so he had caused the harbour master to lose face, a very serious business in the Far East. Where the master in a western port might have angrily demanded Alaine's presence and an apology, the harbour master at Sihanoukville silently bided his time. Alaine and all the other westerners fussing about that ridiculous vessel would keep.

No vessel could sail without a clearance. The harbour master's office held our personal passports. No-one was going anywhere until he said so, and he was obviously going to remain silently offended until he had punished us sufficiently.

No-one could tell how long this might take.

The French tried diplomacy. Mike Hatcher made a personal appearance and apologised for the captain's lack of courtesy. It made no difference. A hint, a suggestion of a discreet payment was contemptuously refused.

The harbour master had us over a barrel and he knew it.

Friedlander in Phnom Penh went directly to the Minister for Transport. A fax was sent to Sihanoukville authorising departure. The harbour master raised his eyebrows, said something in Cambodian to his secretary and tossed the fax into a crowded basket.

'A fax is a copy,' he said. 'Anyone can make a copy. I can only act on a signed original.'

Touché.

Eventually it was decided to do what probably should have been done in the first place.

Alaine was a small gruff man with oil-stained clothes and a beard of permanent seven-day whiskers. He usually had one end of an oily rag tucked in his trouser pocket. His large, sad eyes were a reminder of a down-at-heel version of Peter Lorre from the film *Casablanca*. A bent cigarette was always in one corner of his mouth. He sighed frequently giving the impression that he regarded defeat as his natural lot in life. The harbour officials were all smartly dressed. His sloppy appearance, his slouch, and the Gallic vehemence of his manner may have been taken for rudeness. Though when you got to know him he was a gentle and pleasant fellow. Inoffensive to a degree.

In a last-ditch effort Alaine was taken in hand. He was scrubbed and shaved, made to wear a brand new white shirt, and sent along to the harbour master to grovel and apologise like a naughty schoolboy before the headmaster. No doubt the harbour master enjoyed the moment.

In spite of these efforts, there was still no permission to clear port, but slowly things at last began to happen. During the afternoon a high-ranking Army official and his bodyguards came to the wharf escorted by a truck with a cannon mounted on the back and assigned us two soldiers in very smart uniforms and steel helmets. One had an AK-47, the other a rather rusty looking sub-machine gun of Chinese or Russian manufacture. They were to be our defence.

Defence against what, we wondered? Viets, Thais, Khmer Rouge, pirates . . . ?

One of the general's own bodyguards, we noticed, had a stun-gun. This is an anti-personal device which looks like a mobile phone, but has two prongs and is capable of giving a violent electric shock to anyone unwise or unlucky enough to be on the receiving end of it.

The general departed with an air of great aplomb, giving us a wave in the manner of General Macarthur farewelling his troops. The difference being that we had a military force of two.

The diving gear was brought on board and I registered dismay at the sight of the tanks and equipment. There were three good scuba sets which belonged to Mike Hatcher, Rahim and Maan. The rest had been supplied by the French and were steel tanks with bubbles of rust coming through the paint. There were no identifying marks or signs that they had ever been tested. They were old J-valves, and in my opinion, dead dangerous. In Australia we had been using aluminium tanks for 20 years which were required to be tested annually. No scuba filling station at home would have filled these. They would have been condemned on sight. There were only four weight belts for the 10 people who would be diving. Looking at the rag-tag collection I lost my composure for a moment.

'This is very unprofessional,' I told Hatcher. I felt like an alpinist who has been thrown a coil of frayed cotton clothes line from someone's backyard and told that this is the rope for the ascent, or a parachutist who finds his canopy chewed by rats.

'I've got troubles enough at the moment,' Hatch replied tersely. 'Some other time, huh?'

I understood what he was saying and so far he had been very restrained. He had had his moments, flashes of anger at the state of the junk, the poverty-stricken equipment, the enforced delays. But he had managed to keep his emotions in check. I think he sensed that the whole adventure was at risk of unravelling. One explosion of temper, however justified, could see the French pack up and retire to Phnom Penh in a huff. Our expedition would be over before it had begun. He had his own investors to answer to and after the Gulf of Thailand disaster he was very anxious to avoid another failure.

If it had not been for his crew of John Dyson, Rahim and Maan there was serious doubt whether *Song Saigon* would ever have left the wharf.

John was a skipper of one of the big north Queensland tourist catamarans and an excellent seaman and practical engineer. He had come for a holiday, but instead had spent his time covered in oil crawling about the junk's bilges trying to find out which defective wire went where. Rahim and Maan similarly had spent their time wielding spanners and screwdrivers, trying to coax worn-out machinery back to life. They had ready smiles and seemingly endless patience.

Every day we would go to the junk confident that *this* would be the day and every night we returned defeated to the Seaside Hotel to gales of laughter from the staff.

During our period of enforced penance there was a local sensation. Two containers on the wharf, allegedly containing rubber from the north of Cambodia, were found instead to contain hashish. Seven tons in each container ... enough to keep North America going for a week. The intended destination, presumably for breaking down into smaller quantities and re-shipping, was Sri Lanka. The consignee was one of Cambodia's richest and most influential businessmen, a man with a great deal of political pull. The embarrassment was the last thing the harbour master wanted on his patch. He and his co-officers were in a state of agitation, and *Song Saigon* and her be-whiskered captain were understandably low on their list of priorities.

While waiting for the mess to be sorted, we spent a bit of time exploring Sihanoukville, a pretty little town that had been a bright French coastal holiday resort in the days before Pol Pot. Near our hotel a row of fire-blackened, burnt-out two-storey villas told the story of what happened when the Khmer Rouge came to town. Reminders of French influence were put to the torch, along with some of the people considered too westernised.

Religion was also banned and the temples (Cambodians are Buddhists) burnt. They had been restored not long before our arrival and were resplendent in white, chocolate, and gold paint. That sounds an unlikely combination, but it looked very effective in the tropical surrounds.

The most common tree was that most useful of plants, the coconut palm. Sihanoukville was built around hills and there were patches of remnant jungle inviting a bush hike.

'On no account,' said Hatcher forcefully, 'go off the beaten path. Stick to tracks where everyone walks. Otherwise you might put your foot on one of those little green things. There are still plenty of 'em about.'

Flanking our Seaside Hotel was a cat-house, a bordello with the name COBRA in flashing lights. The girls used to sit outside in the afternoons, some of them were very pretty and would wave enthusiastically to us as we went past. Karaoke was advertised as the other speciality of the house. Most of the clientele, we noticed, seemed to be high-ranking Army officials. Cars with bored drivers waiting for pleasuring bosses were often outside the Cobra.

Down the road were two magnificent lion statues, one male and one female. The Khmer Rouge had destroyed the originals as being 'decadent'. Re-built by the new government, they looked from some angles as though they were *in flagrante delicto*. However a walk around them showed that they were simply being friendly. We were told that when the restored statues were first installed on their pedestal the local people had a complaint. Mr Lion's testicles, they said, were too small. On their petition he was given a larger pair. The smile on Mrs Lion's face seemed to indicate an approval of the alteration.

Finally, after 14 days of waiting, at 4.30 in the afternoon on Friday, February 28, 1997, the word suddenly came from the harbour master's office. 'You can go now!'

The dead freezer had been replaced by two upright refrigerators. An ugly yellow commercial generator was lifted by crane on to the junk's foredeck, all attempts to bring the junk's own generator back to life having failed.

Two female cooks came aboard smiling, with pots and pans, and the last of the food was loaded. The clearance papers arrived by motorcycle messenger from the harbour master's office, *Song Saigon's* bows were pulled away from the wharf by our tender craft, the appropriately named *Condor*, and we were on our way.

'Condor Reef here we come!'

The ship's company consisted of Mike Hatcher, expedition leader, Alaine Dumesmic, skipper, Rahim and Maan as crew, and divers and technicians. Friedlander had supplied Olivier Toupin and Didier Faraud as divers and electrical engineers. The cooks were Mahli and Mohm, the film crew Steve Standen, camera, Ian MacLagan, sound, and Jeremy Taylor. The two Cambodian soldiers were Leng and Tin. Officially they had no English but the taller one was reading a book written in English. We suspected that they knew more of the language than they admitted and that they had been installed by the government to keep an eye on us.

Song Saigon dipped her bows through Compong Som Bay, threading between lines of fishing boats with nets over the side. The sun went down in crimson glory, the wake bubbling behind us. Behind us also, a puppet on a string, was *Condor*, an extraordinary craft which needs some introduction. She was 27 feet long, a steel box, built on landing barge lines with a loading ramp at the bow that lowered level with the water. She was built for ferrying vehicles across rivers and estuaries and probably performed that role very well. But her choice as a dive boat seemed questionable. She was equipped with a Nissan truck engine and a jet propulsion unit of doubtful parentage. Like so many other things in Cambodia she had been cobbled together from re-cycled scrap. Colourful flags completed her bizarre appearance.

No wonder the crews of the fishing boats we passed gazed in open-mouthed wonderment. A Chinese junk towing a landing barge would probably make people stare on any waterway anywhere in the world.

❀

Into the night *Song Saigon*, 'Saigon Suzie', lifted her bow to the swell of the open sea as we passed through the headlands of Compong Som Bay. Finally, in the light of a perfect morning, Condor Reef lay before our bows, the mainland now out of sight. The reef showed first as a bright green luminous patch. We could see it clearly in the morning light, but at night, or in rough weather, it would be invisible. It was the worst kind of hazard for shipping, but it still had no warning light. Not even a buoy bobbed to mark the danger.

There was high excitement on board.

Was this the spot where John Lambton's ship had lain since 1672 with its 10,000 Rix dollars and the Ming porcelain treasure? Would we find it on the first day?

Hatcher was confident. 'It can't be anywhere else,' he said. 'I think you'll find that we locate it very quickly.' We piled into *Condor* and steamed over to investigate while the junk drifted on a mirror-calm sea. The top of the reef was so shallow that (to general cries of alarm) *Condor* grounded on one point of granite with a nasty scrunching sound. Fortunately the hull wasn't pierced, and we avoided joining the original *Condor* on the bottom. But it was a lucky escape.

We dropped the loading ramp and plunged in for a snorkel swim. The reef was unlike anything I had ever seen before. Granite slopes fell away into deep water with great cracks, splits, ledges, and boulders. The visibility was excellent, perhaps 100 feet or more. There was little coral, despite the tropic latitude. This was probably because the local fishermen had been using explosives to fish. A wasteful and destructive method. Risky too. They dismantled old artillery shells and packed the explosive in brown earthenware pots. There were bits of broken pot all over the reef, and a few one-armed fishermen.

Usually when searching for a shipwreck a diver looks for straight lines or circles indicating something foreign or manmade on the bottom. But this reef, with the granite splitting in straight cracks and wedges, made things very difficult. Everywhere there were fishing nets snagged on ledges and recent score marks on the granite showed that fishing vessels frequently ran foul of the reef. In addition, heavy twin wire strops on the bottom and big tractor tyres of the kind used as fenders by tugs showed that there had been a major salvage not long before. And that perhaps it had not gone smoothly.

But what of older ships?

Mike Hatcher's hopes of quickly discovering something significant did not materialise. On that first swim we found some very old anchors, bearers from a composite (wooden planking, iron frames) 19th century ship (perhaps *John Wade*), and a trail of small wreckage, copper sheeting, shards of broken pottery, some brass and a large lead ingot. Hatcher reported two iron cannon stuck in the reef. The others, inexperienced in searching for wrecks, passed over the items which were disguised by sea growth until they were pointed out to them. Rahim and Maan, who were very experienced with wrecks, were busy setting up the side-scan sonar and did not participate on the first snorkel swim.

Condor carried both the sonar and the magnetometer. A sortie with the magnetometer ended disastrously in the first few minutes. It snagged on a rock and broke the line and although it was repaired, it was never the same again.

Despite these minor inconveniences, the day ended happily enough. At least we had some signs of shipwrecks. However more and more disquieting aspects of the *Song Saigon* were being revealed. Most of the toilets, prerequisites for the health and happiness of the ship, were already malfunctioning. The cabins were mouldy – they were designed for air-conditioning (non-functioning) and there was no ventilation. Though it was a wooden vessel there was no fire extinguishing system.

Of the five bilge pumps of various kinds, only three were in working order. The anchor winch was also out of order. The main anchor literally weighed a ton. Once it was over the side and on the bottom it seemed it would stay there as a mooring. There was no mechanical way to retrieve it and it was too heavy to raise by hand.

There were no watertight bulkheads. There was one inflatable life raft, but who could tell when it had been last checked or surveyed? Even if it did, by a miracle, inflate, it was not big enough to hold all the people on board in the event of a disaster.

There was a radar which didn't work, a long-range radio which was similarly out of order, and a VHF radio which only operated on line-of-sight in port environs. We were too far from shore to raise anyone with it. The list of broken-down items or omissions went on and on. The masts rolled and swayed from side to side, twanging the slack rusted rigging. How long before something snapped? Would the masts, hardwood sticks which weighed several tons, come tumbling down? Would they go through the deck and hull like javelins?

To add to our woes *both* of the cooks were seasick. Poor little birds of paradise, they lay on the deck, faces the colour of porridge. They made pathetic gestures from time to time indicating that they thought it would be a nice idea to go back to land. Fat chance! Hatcher regarded them stonily. 'Bloody useless,' he muttered. 'Another cock-up!' He stomped angrily below to his cabin.

I remembered the old cure for seasickness – 'Sit under a shady tree' – and sympathised with them. No trees out here in the Gulf of Thailand. Just fishermen, pirates, and us.

Dinner that night was cooked by Olivier the Frenchman. He had a Cambodian wife ashore and aboard he had a crazy laugh and a cheerful disposition. When there were no cooks he was the one who went down into the galley and in due course a large pot of spaghetti had jars of anchovies tossed in and was stirred and served. A sort of poor man's spaghetti marinara.

We slept out on the deck, preferring hard boards to mouldy mattresses and in any event, with the vile stink of the bilge and suspect toilets, the cabins were too hot and smelly to be habitable!

❦

The next day we got to have the long-awaited scuba dive on the reef. Enthusiasm remained high for far more was likely to be revealed breathing air down deep below than by skimming the surface with a snorkel. Indeed on the downward slope there were many signs of shipwrecks. Our anchor count was now up to four, there were several small cannon, and relics ancient and modern. Of most interest were broken shards of blue-and-white pottery and tin ingots. Mike Hatcher thought that the pottery was similar to some of the pieces he had recovered from the unknown junk on Admiral Stellingwerf Reef in 1984. That would have placed them in the right time frame for the loss of Lambton's ship in 1671. The area where the broken blue-and-white pottery lay also yielded cups, copper ingots and other shipwreck evidence. Rahim, with a nose for tin, found a stack of square ingots.

But was this really the last resting place of Ralph Lambton's ship? If so there didn't seem to be enough to constitute a full cargo. Certainly not a salvageable cargo of any value.

'She could easily have hit the reef, stuck to the face a while, then drifted off into deep water with the next change of wind or current,' Hatcher reasoned, ever practical. 'Maybe we should be looking deeper.'

A deep water scuba search revealed a sand plain 120 feet down stretching away into the dim distance. The reef, 20 miles from the nearest land, stood up in the middle of it like a shark's tooth. Down there in the deep were garden eels, far more fish than near the surface, and some extraordinary sea slugs or bêche-de-mer. These were at least a metre long and tessellated at both ends. Scattered across this level sand plain were rags and ribbons of snagged trawl nets and the sand bottom was scarred with the tracks and gouges made by the otter-boards of the trawlers. Clearly a very busy place.

This was not encouraging for us. If there was a wreck on the sand plain it was likely that at least some plates and bowls would have been caught and come up in the trawls. That was the usual way in which fishermen discovered a wrecksite. Scattered pieces of pottery did lie at the base of the reef. Most were broken but we found a few tiny fragile cups still intact.

The big disappointment was that the wreck had not come to light as quickly as we had first hoped. There should also have been other wrecks. Aside from Ralph Lambton's ship, where were the 19th century wrecks *John Wade* and *Condor*?

Mike Hatcher discussed the situation at length over the evening meal. A card table holding the artefacts recovered so far was our only encouragement. There were some intact cups without handles, some broken blue-and-white kraak dishes, some finger-thick copper ingots and some square tin ingots. Clues, but not conclusive evidence. 'Anything on top of the reef would have been broken up in cyclones or bad weather,' Hatcher said. 'Our best chance is for something that has hit and drifted off. It looks as though side-scanning will be the way to go.'

Dinner that night was a variation of the previous spaghetti and anchovies. This time Olivier concocted a mess of rice and anchovies. It was received somewhat less enthusiastically. We all wished the cooks a speedy recovery.

As we were about to turn in there was thunder and lightning on the horizon and the sound of a storm rapidly approaching. Soon enough it hit us with a hissing line squall that turned the water white with spray and bouncing rain drops. Rain swept the decks, the wind howled and Saigon Suzie lurched and leaked in a thousand unexpected places. To go below was like standing under a shower, with the water coming through the deck in rivulets. There was a frantic rush to safeguard precious camera gear, while all the bunks became sopping wet. The storm lasted an hour, then rumbled away to the north east. The wind dropped and the decks dried in rising steam for it was still quite warm.

❁

The next day we awoke to yet another change of weather – 18 knots of wind from the south and a short, angry sea that had the junk dipping and rolling and jerking at the anchor line. *Condor*, tied off astern, was throwing itself about in quite an alarming manner. Mike and the captain consulted on whether to run for shelter behind the mainland islands. Alaine pointed out that it would be a four-hour trip and that the junk would roll diabolically, everything would be thrown about and everyone would be wet. As long as the wind stayed south we did have partial shelter behind the reef. He suggested we ride it out and in retrospect he was probably right.

Hatcher accepted this but, frustrated by all the things that had gone wrong on the expedition, suggested a dive. Was it a crazy idea in terms of the weather?

'At 120 feet you won't notice it,' he said, all fired up and ready to go. 'You never know. *This* may be the day!' He grabbed his mask and fins, his mind made up.

It became a test of courage. The film crew sensibly declined, in any case they would get more action shots staying dry on the surface. The divers had to jump overboard and swim their tanks back to the wildly bucking *Condor* before climbing over the barnacle-covered frame at the stern which protected the jet. Letting the loading ramp down would have resulted in instant flooding.

At the reef the waves were breaking heavily on the pinnacle, threatening to come crashing over the front of *Condor*. Mike was quickly overboard and the rest of us followed him down the slope, glad to get below the maelstrom on the surface.

The trail of broken porcelain led downwards like a paper chase. The bottom levelled out at 17 metres, dropping deeper again in a series of terraces. I found a beautiful and fragile little bowl, pure white (Blanc de Chine) and put it down the front of my wetsuit to protect it. A good start, I thought to myself, but also wondered where the cargo mound was.

The bottom zone was peaceful, sea fans swayed gently, fish looked curiously at us, there were coral trout and groper. A school of trevally surround us briefly, flashing their silver sides like mirrors. But there was still no sign of a major wreck. Our dive computers started to signal that we were dallying too long at depth. It was a salient fact that *Song Saigon* had no decompression chamber and the nearest was in Thailand or Malaysia. Cambodia was no place to get the bends. 'Two minutes to decompression time,' the meter warned with a beep.

So it was back to the surface to find white-water chaos. The sea had risen enormously in the short time we had been below. *Condor* had already broken its wrist-thick anchor line once, Rahim had re-tied it, but there was no chance of dropping the landing craft ramp. We had to again climb over the jet at the stern. This was both difficult and dangerous. Anyone hit by the barnacle-encrusted stern gear could have been seriously hurt. With *Condor* tossing wildly, the jet and the barnacle-studded frame around it went from three feet out of the water to two feet below. SMACK! The diver had to make a swift move forward to grab it at the lower end, hang on for dear life, and eventually scramble over the transom. Everyone managed somehow.

There was no way that *Condor* could come alongside *Song Saigon* on our return to the junk, even with the tyre fenders out. We had to jump into the water again, swim alongside the plunging vessel and grab a loose-swinging tyre when the junk was buried in a wave trough. Neither the junk nor *Condor* had a diving ladder.

'Really hairy!' said Hatcher with a grin, safe on deck wiping his face with a towel. 'That was really pushing it!' He had enjoyed himself and the camera crew had got some excellent film of the derring-do in rough conditions. Hatcher liked to test himself from time to time, to challenge the ocean when it was in a dangerous mood. Getting the adrenaline racing was an antidote to the frustrations and worries that had dogged the expedition.

But what would have happened if someone had been seriously injured when we were so far from shore on a boat with no radio or means of communication? There was no-one aboard with the skill to set a broken bone, to stitch a gash, or to deal with anything worse. I kept those thoughts to myself, there were enough negatives already. Since everyone had survived the dive there seemed no point in looking at hypothetical worst-case scenarios.

The day continued rough and soon the soldiers joined the cooks, helpless in the grip of seasickness. A policeman's lot is sometimes not a happy one. By evening the wind and sea had died down. For those who could stomach it there was spaghetti and anchovies once again.

'What does the barometer read?' I asked Alaine.

'You weel be zurprised to hear,' he said, taking a long, whiskery drag on his cigarette, 'zat zere ees no barometer on ziz boat.'

Surprised? Not I.

'Anyhow,' he said. 'We don' need one.'

Oh yeah!

Mike Hatcher wore a frown. The wreck was proving elusive and the weather wasn't doing us any favours. Quite apart from forcing down spaghetti and anchovies or rice and anchovies for dinner every night.

'Let's go back over the evidence,' he said. 'Maybe we've missed something somewhere.'

Back in England Nigel Pickford had done the research. His information had come from the records of the VOC in the Algemeen Rijksarchief in the Hague, the East India company records in London and from the University Library at Cambridge. 'Ralph Lambton's ship was small,' he said. 'It had a crew of only 20 men. But the value of 150,000 Rix dollars placed on the cargo indicates that there was quality porcelain and other goods aboard. Given the date of 1671, the late Ming period, it seems not improbable that such pieces could fetch from $200 to $2000 each.' There could be, he suggested, as many as 100,000 pieces of porcelain in the cargo.

And the location?

Condor Reef was not named until the 1860s. Dutch accounts

of the time recorded that Lambton's ship had struck a 'blind klip' or submerged rock, that fitted the reef's description. The ship sank so quickly that Lambton and the others were unable to save anything from the wreck. Ten thousand Rix dollars in silver went to the bottom, as well as the letters of credit from the King of Siam. Lambton arrived in Malacca with his crew and servants of the King of Siam in a very distressed state, having been saved by a passing Moorish (Arab) vessel.

The Dutch reported that he did not continue his voyage to Surat. Instead he intended to return to the wrecksite to see what he could salvage from the sunken vessel.

A later VOC account noted the failure of the salvage attempt. 'They got into a storm with thunder and very bad weather, lost their anchors and sails and had to return to Siam.'

Did someone else succeed where Lambton had failed? Or were we in the wrong spot? 'The sinking position would appear to be simple,' Nigel Pickford had said. But I remembered with some disquiet Fergus Hinds' comment in *Riches From Wrecks*. 'One of the most consistent things about shipwrecks is that they are hardly ever where the records say they are,' he said wryly.

Similarly, we had been led to believe that the Cambodians had no diving equipment. But a little boat, barely 24 feet long with only 12 inches freeboard and six men aboard, was putt-putting around the reef with divers going down at regular intervals. They came past asking for cigarettes, the deck of their craft awash with sea slugs and bêche-de-mer. They were diving as deep as the 120-foot sand plain with the most primitive equipment. On deck was a tiny petrol-driven compressor. The diver had a length of the crinkled high-pressure hose of the kind that garages and service stations use for inflating tyres. There was no mouthpiece. The diver, operating with only a mask and without fins, tucked the end of the hose through his belt, gripped it in his teeth and breathed off the bubbles. I wondered what the life expectancy of a Cambodian bêche-de-mer diver might be.

'If there's something down there they may have seen it,' I suggested to Hatcher.

'We'll try them,' he said.

However there was a small communication problem. Hatcher had to ask Olivier the question in English. Olivier asked the soldiers in French. The soldiers spoke Cambodian to the fishermen. They nodded their heads when they were shown the pottery shards. Yes, there was plenty of that on the reef. But questions about an actual wrecksite seemed to puzzle them. I tried drawing the outlines of cannon, anchors and a cargo mound on a piece of paper. But that seemed to confuse them further. Where had we seen these things? They did not know about them. Eventually they went off with a carton of cigarettes, promising to let us know if they came across anything.

'If there was anything valuable on the sea mount,' Hatcher suggested, 'those guys would have had it before now. I think our only chance is that Lambton's ship drifted off and sank down the road somewhere. We'll go back to lawnmowing.'

So *Condor* (if the weather was fine) or the junk (if there was wind) resumed work with the side-scan sonar. The set kept giving trouble because of voltage fluctuations from the hired generator. For those who were not actively involved it was a period of intense boredom. We sat on the high poop of the junk, read books, or gazed out over the water. It was frustrating because we had a period of perfect weather that would have been great for diving, but side-scanning took precedence.

'Two tank dives in 10 days,' I groaned in my diary. 'What *am* I doing here?' Privately I had begun to think that either the wreck was somewhere else or it had been salvaged long before. Perhaps Ralph Lambton had recovered the lost cargo himself without telling the King of Siam.

There were some diversions. Small fishing craft came by and offered us fish. Olivier haggled for a huge and evil looking barracuda – not much of a bargain, in my opinion, in Australia we wouldn't eat barracuda of that size. Too much risk of cigeratura poisoning. However barracuda stew made a change from spaghetti and anchovies, or rice and anchovies. The cooks had now recovered from seasickness but showed no interest in resuming their duties.

'Bloody useless!' fumed Hatcher. 'They'll have to go!'

That would probably have been their dearest wish, but without radio to arrange a speedboat the only way that they could get ashore (unless they swam) would be for *Song Saigon* to go back to port.

Mike Hatcher was still determined to continue. Even in the face of disappointment he still retained his optimism. 'It's got to be here somewhere!' he would say, striking his fist into his palm with a resounding smack. 'It's just gotta be here somewhere!'

The brightest moment for me personally came with the appearance of a whale shark. *Rincondon typus* is the largest of the sharks, growing to more than 12 metres in length, but despite their immense size these creatures are harmless plankton eaters. I had a swim with whale sharks in Australia, at Ningaloo Reef where they appear each March after the coral spawning. Grabbing my mask and fins I leapt over the side, to the horror of the Cambodians who thought that all sharks were man-eaters and I was going to my doom.

The shark, a young female, was beautiful. Like all her species she was brown with dollar-sized white spots forming an intricate pattern on her body. She was shy at first and dived when I followed her. But she was soon back again and if I remained still on the surface she would come so close that I had to actually back away to avoid a collision. She was accompanied by a large trevally and a cobia or black kingfish. Faithful retainers, just like the whale sharks at home. Do the whale sharks have them as pets, like humans, or do the fish just like the company? Whatever the reason, large sharks, especially tiger sharks, often swim with a retinue of smaller fish including cobias. A queen with her courtiers.

Fishing boats came by on a regular basis. Some were huge Thai trawlers, usually painted grey with high-raking bows, while others flew the Cambodian flag. I noticed that the soldiers tended to slide below gunwhale level when the Thai boats came close but when Cambodian boats inspected us they grinned and waved. The Cambodian flag, even in Khmer Rouge days, always featured the temples at Angkor Wat, usually in red with a blue-and-white background. Some of the Cambodian boats were very small but they sailed fearlessly out of sight of land. They fished in a curious way, the fisherman holding the rod and reel separately, one in each hand, and winding in with great dexterity. At the end of the line were half a dozen hooks each with a silver tinsel-cloth lure. The fish they caught were small and silver, about herring size and went into a live well in the bottom of the boat.

Soon we began to run out of bottled water, food was running low, and tempers were shortening. No-one except Hatcher believed we would find the wreck. He maintained a steely resolve, and day after day *Song Saigon* patrolled the reef region, running up and down, up and down, lawnmowing.

Finally a decision was made to go closer to shore in the hope that at least one of the mobile phones might work.

'OK,' said Hatcher. 'Here's what we'll do. We'll go in close tonight, order more stores and have the speedboat come out on Sunday to take the cooks off and drop the stores.'

The marker buoys were brought in from the reef and the junk's mooring line laid along the bottom so that it could be retrieved with a grapple (as the anchor was too heavy to lift). *Song Saigon* turned her bows for land and the point where the bars on Mike's mobile phone would click in. The magic moment when we could talk to the world again. What an absurd situation to be in, I reflected. Relying on climbing the mast with a mobile phone! It seemed to sum up the Gilbert & Sullivan nature of the whole expedition.

As we steamed on into the darkness the wind began to rise,

quickly increased to 15 to 20 knots, and along the horizon lightning began to play. We were in for another storm. The flashes came closer and soon the thunder was rolling and we were hit by line squalls. Rain showers hissed across the water and the sound of the thunder became a deafening cannon roar. Forked lightning struck the water no great distance away, blinding us with its brilliance. We tried not to think about the possibility of a strike ... there were other things to worry about. The junk was pitching and rolling and making little headway. From down below came an ominous slosh of bilge water. Everything was wet.

What *am* I doing here? I asked myself for the umpteenth time.

Finally the showers ceased and John Dyson shinned up the main mast. Eureka! The mobile phone at last made contact with the world.

Why hadn't we been in touch? a voice at the other end asked crossly. 'Everyone's been worried about you!'

The question underlined our vulnerability. It was ridiculous being at sea in a 180-ton vessel with no communication, inadequate life-saving gear and with faulty (or non-existent) pumps and engines. In a chronically-leaking vessel what would happen if all the pumps failed simultaneously? Rahim pointed with his finger downwards and shook his head. We'd go down, he indicated. Down to the bottom of the sea, to Davey Jones' locker.

❋

We slept, as usual, on the deck, the junk rolling heavily in the angry cross sea on the return to the reef. The masts were swaying and groaning in their sockets, the loose rigging flexing and jerking tight. The plan was to drag the grapple in the lee of the reef, but in the angry coffee-coloured sea topped with whitecaps the reef was invisible. We'd removed the buoys and no-one could pinpoint the precise position of the spire of rock. My heart was in my mouth. What if *Song Saigon* were to find the reef in the hardest way possible? By joining the ship of Ralph Lambton, *Condor*, and *John Wade*, as a victim?

'Ees too dangerous!' the captain protested to Hatcher.

'You're right,' he replied, conceding at last. 'Turn her around. We're going in!'

At that moment he had decided that he'd had enough of the junk. 'Junk is the right word!' he said. 'We need a decent boat and decent equipment. This is a bloody waste of time and money!'

The words were music to the ears of everyone on board. We passed back through the islands with their forested slopes, past picturesque Joseph Conrad fishing villages on bamboo stilts, through fleets of fishing boats with wreaths of flowers on their bows. Back to the coconut palm shores of Sihanoukville.

This time the captain spoke respectfully to the harbour master, but memories were long and he was made to wait for hours outside the harbour precinct while the rest of us scooted ashore in the crazy *Condor* and hungrily scoffed down our first good meal in three weeks.

By mid-afternoon the captain was told that he could bring the junk into the harbour and lie alongside a grey-hulled fishing boat.

'But ees too small!' protested Alaine.

'You're not very big yourself,' was the reply.

The captain tried again. 'The water ees too shallow!'

'That is where you were before. Drop an anchor.'

The sadist knew we had no anchors. At length, after many Gallic shrugs and angry puffs on his drooping cigarette, and many 'merdes' muttered between his whiskers, the captain brought the junk in diagonally to the wharf. The bows touched the stonework, but the stern remained stuck on the muddy bottom protruding out into the channel.

The cooks leapt ashore with little cries of joy. No chance that anyone would ever get them on a boat again.

The rest of us, heavy with diving and camera gear, moved

more slowly. I looked back at *Song Saigon* and suddenly felt a surge of affection for her. She had handled the rough conditions with aplomb, and she had been our home in strange and dangerous waters. It was hardly her fault that the men who were her masters had allowed her to fall into such an appalling condition. She still held her tattered dignity, a little like a high-born lady who has fallen on hard times. Forced to clean toilets, but still holding her head high.

Hatcher was the last to leave, looking out to sea one last time. 'It's still out there!' he said. 'Still waiting for us to find it.' Then he turned on his heel. 'Come on,' he said, 'let's go!'

After we left, *Song Saigon* went out once more. This time the foremast did fall down and the pumps failed. Rahim refused to go to sea again until the main mast was checked and John Wade backed him up against French objections. When the mast was lifted up by a crane the base was so rotten that it literally fell apart. If it had fallen down out at sea it could have speared right through the boat or lain alongside like a battering ram pounding the hull. In either event the junk would have joined the legion of lost ships, and we would have been swimming. For a time, at least, until we could swim no more.

We had been luckier than we thought.

❁

Mike Hatcher had no luck in Cambodia. He persevered, finally using *Restless M*, until $US3 million had gone down the drain.

It was not lack of perseverance that eventually defeated him but Cambodia's curse of civil war. Shortly after we left the country, hostilities broke out between the followers of Prince Norodom Ranariddh with his FUNINPEC party and those of his partner in coalition, Second Prime Minister Hun Sen, who led the Cambodian Peoples Party, the CCP. Once again Cambodia was plunged into bloody chaos and westerners were forced to flee the country.

In my last days there (unconsciously running the risk of being caught up in the coup) I did manage to fulfil a promise to myself. I followed in my father's footsteps to the ancient city and temples of Angkor Wat. The base for visiting the temples, Siem Reap, was near the great Lake Tongle Sap, an area 'just down the road' from the Khmer Rouge. They still held a section of territory in the north-east of the country.

In fact the Khmer Rouge tolerated the European tourist traffic to Angkor as a local economic necessity. 'At night they own the countryside in guerilla fashion. Even in daylight they come into town when they feel like it,' one European told me. 'Bold as brass. As if they still run the place. People pretend not to see them. The locals are terrified of them. Businesses make contributions to the Khmer Rouge,' he added. 'Is it extortion? Well let's say, if you don't want your daughter's foot cut off it's better to pay and pay generously.'

Despite the ever-present danger, Angkor Wat was nothing short of spectacular. My father had been right. The main site forms a three-tiered mountain of stone buildings, towers, spires, steps and walk-ways, all set behind a magnificent moat. The highest tower rises 65 metres above ground level. The complex was built in the 12th century and there are thousands of individual carvings, friezes and statues.

I had my fortune told there by a Bhuddist monk in an orange robe. He scattered the traditional sticks and what he said astounded me.

'You will write the book!' he announced. In my own mind I had written off the Hatcher exercise as cursed and doomed to failure. But more than that – how did he know I was a writer at all, when I didn't carry so much as a pad or a ballpoint pen? I still don't have the answer to that.

Like most of the world's great marvels, it is difficult to adequately describe Angkor Wat and the other temples nestled in the jungle north of Siem Reap. Angkor Wat is the world's largest surviving religious building, but it is the quality of the statues and friezes, the symmetry of the towers and escalating levels, which makes it so impressive. The jungle with towering white-trunked trees has its own beauty.

Even here there was the shadow of the immediate past. The Khmer Rouge were active and increasingly daring as the rift widened between the Royalist FUNINPEC party and the CCP. While I was there, in March 1997, the FUNINPEC faction made an ill-starred attempt to win over sections of the Khmer Rouge. Their opponents under Hun Sen had control over the main army, but the Royalists hoped to win men and rifles from the Khmer Rouge ranks to swell their own forces.

They sent in 15 negotiators by helicopter, including a provincial governor, to broker an agreement. The group travelled to Khmer Rouge headquarters in the north east of Cambodia, going in to the heart of enemy territory, confident of their diplomatic status. The Khmer Rouge's answer, when the helicopters landed, was to shoot all but three of the emissaries, including the governor. Twelve died, protesting, in a hail of bullets.

A 37-year-old Englishman by the name of Christopher Howes was working at Angkor with a party of volunteers, risking his life daily clearing landmines from around the temple area. A fortnight after my own visit the group was ambushed by the Khmer Rouge, displeased at the undoing of their handiwork. Howes was taken away by the Khmer Rouge and murdered.

I'd had my own landmine scare at the temples. I was taking a short cut from one group of terrace friezes to another when my driver ran after me, arms waving and shouting 'Stop! Stop!' He motioned me back to the path. 'Never *never* do that again!' he said, and threw his hands up. 'POOF!' He made a noise simulating an explosion. Then he pointed to the path where there were the footprints of many tourists and the hoofprints of cattle.

'Only go where the feet have been,' he said earnestly. 'Cows best. Cows go, you know safe. No feet, no go. You look hard!'

and with that he tapped his eyes with two fingers. He was a good man. I only asked him once about the Khmer Rouge, aware that local people were afraid ever to mention the name and instantly his smile vanished and he looked around to see who might have overheard me, even though we were clattering along the road in his battered Nissan.

'Yes,' he said, almost in a whisper. 'Here, there, everywhere. All around.'

On the way back to Siem Reap the road ran along a pleasant waterway backed by almost impenetrable three-metre high reeds. We came across a road block, a crude barricade consisting of a red-and-white painted tree pole on stands with barbed wire coiling around it. Troops with rifles at the ready and unsmiling faces were in a nearby truck while others were on the road and beside it in strategic positions, automatic rifles across their chests.

On the grassy verge was a brown card table set up with an officer seated behind it and a bevy of soldiers with AK-47s on the hip behind him. There was a cash box on the table. I looked curiously. Road blocks were nothing new in Cambodia. Then I saw the driver's face. He had turned white in sheer terror, and sweat was pouring off him. He had looked once at the man behind the table, then averted his face so quickly I almost expected to hear his neck snap.

I let my camera slide quietly to the floor and kicked it under the seat. Under my sunglasses I snuck a glance sideways, without being observed, and what I saw puzzled me. There was no apparent reason why the driver should be terrified, but I did wonder about the officer. In Cambodia soldiers are very young and it's not uncommon for a general to be just in his 20s. This man was old, even elderly, and he had brown age-spots on his face.

The officer examined us critically for a moment, asked a question of one of his men, and then waved an arm. The barricade was lifted, the car jerked forward and my driver took a hiss of in-drawn breath and shook his head, his hands trembling on the wheel. I sensed that it was not the time to ask him questions, believing that perhaps his licence or his papers were not in order.

❁

When I returned home I watched along with the rest of the world the Cambodian civil war won by Hun Sen's faction and read of the gradual disintegration of the Khmer Rouge, until only a handful of the diehards, including Pol Pot, remained, having retreated to a stronghold on the Thai border. In a final act of savagery in June 1997, some two months after our visit, Pol Pot ordered the execution of one of his lieutenants, Son Sen, whom he suspected of attempting to do a deal with the government. Troops went to the lieutenant's house and dragged Son Sen and his wife Yun Yat, herself an important party figure, and their children outside. There they were all shot. Pol Pot and the other party leaders then drove their cars backwards and forwards over the bodies. Lieutenant Son Sen had operated the notorious Tuol Sleng interrogation centre in Phnom Penh in which a staggering 20,000 'enemies of the state' were tortured and killed. Less than half a dozen people of all who went in there came out alive. There were few tears shed elsewhere for Son Sen, a man with the blood of many on his hands. But killing the children too was indicative of the cold-blooded savagery of the Khmer Rouge.

Finally, in an effort to save themselves and curry favour with the Hun Sen government, the Khmer Rouge put Pol Pot on a show trial and the world's media was invited to see first-hand the man whose face had been kept hidden through the years. Deposed from the leadership, Pol Pot died of natural causes while under technical 'house arrest' in 1999.

Pol Pot had been compared with Adolf Hitler and Joseph Stalin and for the first time his image was circulated widely on international television. I sat fascinated, watching the television back in Australia. Suddenly I froze and a chill came over me. I saw again in my mind the white face of the frightened driver in Cambodia, and that other face of the elderly 'officer'.

I realised then that the reason for the driver's terror was the fact that the troops were Khmer Rouge. The man behind the table, as the reader will have guessed by now, was Pol Pot.

Small world.

I still see that face at times and I wonder whether we were lucky the barricade was lifted that day. And what other unthinkable options there may perhaps have been to that casual wave of the arm.

CHAPTER FIFTEEN

The Great Junk

The great junk *Tek Sing* sailed from Amoy in Fukien, on China's south coast. In December 1821, she gathered way with a furious barrage of firecrackers to bring good luck for the long voyage and a booming of her cannon. Dragon flags and colourful pennants flew from her mastheads. She had been many months in loading and now she was ready for the open sea, her cargo secure below decks. The first cargo, cases and cases of fine porcelain, had been laid down at the bottom of the holds and packed so tight that you could not put a knife blade between the containers. Above the porcelain was a layer of timber planks – saleable items in themselves – and then general cargo intended for the Dutch port of Batavia and beyond.

Aside from the ceramics there were hundreds of trade items, ranging from bales of silk, boxes of needles, crates of parasols and umbrellas, and chests and chests of fine China tea. The all-important human cargo consisted of 1600 passengers – an incredible number – most of whom were emigrant coolies going to labour in the sugarcane fields in Java, though there was a fair representation of the merchant class and relatives of other merchant families already residing overseas.

All of them were going to try their luck in distant lands.

The sheer size of the vessel (nearly 60 metres in length) meant she required a proportionately large crew of 400 skilled and unskilled hands, taking the number aboard to nearly 2000.

In previous years emigration and even foreign trade had been forbidden to the Chinese. The edict of the Emperor far away inland in Beijing was that the nation should remain pure and resist the corrupting influences of Europeans and other tainted Asians beyond the Imperial boundaries. For centuries, in fact, there was a prohibition on Chinese going abroad and those who went and returned risked the death penalty. Despite these restrictions, the southern Chinese of Fukien Province had always turned to the sea for a living – farming lands were poor and utilising the ocean was simply a necessity.

Since the 1500s the Portuguese, then the Dutch and finally the English had dominated the upper echelons of the trade of the Indian Ocean and the South China Sea. Their cargoes of tea and spices and silk were shipped on to Europe, but between China, Thailand, Malacca, the Philippines and the Indonesian Archipelago, there remained a substantial, though lower-level, Chinese junk trade. The Dutch found it cheaper and easier for junks to bring cargoes from China south to Batavia. There they could be trans-shipped to the holds of East Indiamen and carried through the gates of the Sunda Strait and on to the Indian Ocean and Europe via the Cape of Good Hope.

The great junk *Tek Sing* was part of this trading pattern. She helped fill a vacuum. The mighty VOC had been brought to its knees by the Napoleonic Wars of 1795 to 1815 and the vast Dutch shipping trade of the Eastern seas was reduced to a pitiful remnant of its former glory. The VOC was bankrupt and the British were in charge of Batavia and about to set up business at the mouth of the Malacca Straits on Singapore Island under Stamford Raffles. The new Straits settlement would change Asian trading patterns.

As a result there was a wave of Chinese migration, merchants and coolies, to places denied them previously. Especially Indonesia.

Tek Sing translates to 'True' or 'Virtuous Star' but translations can be confusing at times. The name almost certainly refers to Canopus, the second brightest star in the firmament after Sirius. Canopus is in Carina, the southern hemisphere's constellation of the Keel. A fitting star for a ship. Canopus was yellow-white in colour, a particular favourite with the Chinese. One of its characteristics was that it shone brighter the further south a ship sailed toward the equator and the southern seas. Indeed one of the objectives of the century expedition of the famous eunuch Zheng He was to study Canopus as his huge fleets approached the equator.

In December 1821 *Tek Sing* left the sheltered waters of Amoy, gathered the buffeting winds of the northern monsoon under her huge matting sails and steered southward for the equator, for the star Canopus, destination Batavia.

On board the people were crammed into every corner and available space. On the upper deck many had built huts of bamboo and matting to shelter them on the journey and most of them carried their own food and cooking utensils. It was intensely uncomfortable, but those aboard consoled themselves that it would only be for a short time. A month or less, the captain had promised ... provided of course that the winds remained favourable and the gods smiled down on them. There were several miniature temples onboard, and sandalwood joss sticks were burnt on a regular basis to maintain the interest of the Immortals.

The two monsoons – north-east and south-west – were remarkably consistent, with the northerly the more blustery and boisterous of the two. It was the north wind which drove the junk south.

By mid-January *Tek Sing* had completed more than three-quarters of her journey. Sailing in company with a sister junk she was already south of the equator and observing Canopus' brightest gleam. Here she was approaching the Gasper Strait, gateway to the Java Sea with little more than 300 kilometres left to sail. There the winds would be lighter, but she should still be in Batavia Roads in less than a fortnight. How those cramped, choked bodies in the sprawling slum built above her decks looked forward to the day!

It was then that tragedy struck.

A miscalculation by the captain, or perhaps a moment of sheer bad luck, found her bearing down on a small reef in the vicinity of Belvidere Rock, an outcrop north of Gaspar Island. If she had been only a 100 metres to the west she would have missed the reef altogether and sailed on unawares to her destination and a different destiny.

But it was not to be. The monsoon was blowing the white caps off a discoloured sea, with occasional rain squalls hissing past further reducing visibility. On a fine day the reefs show as light green patches between the deeps and a keen-eyed lookout could sight them sufficiently far away to effect a change of course. But under a lowering sky, a sea the colour of coffee, and with spray flying and rain squalls forming dark curtains ahead, there was no warning. No time to take evasive action.

The strike came as a complete surprise, as sudden and devastating as an explosion. *Tek Sing* struck the sloping edge of the reef and slid her keel up the shallowing slope with a fearful grinding noise, so that it looked from a distance as though she had reared up out of the water like a breaching whale. For a few moments she hung precariously balanced on a level keel. Then as she slowed to a shuddering stop, the north wind caught her matting sails and flung her over on her side.

The make-shift cabins and shelters on the upper deck broke their lashings and began to slide towards the sea and bamboo, matting, pots, pans, and human bodies went over the gunwhale in an involuntary landslide, slithering and splashing into the water. How many drowned or were crushed to death in those first appalling minutes will never be known. But it is probable that a large percentage of the 1600 passengers and their belongings were on the upper deck and were unable to prevent themselves from being carried away in that accelerating slide to doom. Those remaining scarcely fared better. It was impossible to move on the steeply sloping deck, and down below many were trapped by shifting cargo.

The captain and officers looked desperately towards the sister junk, hoping for aid in their perilous situation. But the other junk sailed on, leaving *Tek Sing* to the fate from which there was now no escape. For she was pounding heavily and even though she had watertight compartments below, her planking was breached in a number of places and she began to fill. As her ruptured belly filled with sea water she became heavier, the pounding became less and she straightened somewhat.

But now with the wind still bulging her sails, she began to be blown off the reef on a rising tide. With her rudder smashed and decks a shambles she was un-navigable and sinking rapidly. All was confusion with the remaining people either running about in panic or frozen into stillness by the horror of what was happening.

About a kilometre from the reef and after two hours of agony, *Tek Sing* gave a series of lurches like a stricken horse staggering, then, to the final anguished cries of those left on board, she settled and sank below the waves. Going down, down, down, to come to rest on the sandy bottom in 120 feet of water.

Perhaps her passengers and crew would have all died, and *Tek Sing's* story been lost with them, had not an English vessel, *Indiana*, under Captain Pearl, formerly of the Royal Navy, been sailing an opposite northward course from Batavia to India. Captain Pearl was on his quarterdeck, cursing the foul weather, when he suddenly noticed that the sea at the entrance to the Gaspar Strait was full of floating boxes, bundles of umbrellas and bamboo. Also amongst the flotsam were some desperate human faces ... Despite the bad weather, Captain Pearl brought his ship into the wind. The boats were lowered and they plucked from the water those Chinese whom they could reach and who were still alive.

Gaspar Island was strewn with dead bodies, but some had miraculously reached shore alive. Twenty-seven men were rescued from a raft which originally had started out with 47 aboard. Others were rescued from rocks which it was hazardous for the ship's boats to approach.

In this way 150 people were saved from the sea by Captain Pearl's generous and humanitarian action. An action which had placed both his ship and his men in jeopardy. In spite of this, about 1850 people perished, many more than in the infamous *Titanic* disaster in the Atlantic in 1912.

In time the name *Tek Sing* was forgotten, though memories naturally lasted longer in her home port of Amoy. Below the surface of the South China Sea, in her sea grave, her timbers gradually rotted and disintegrated, collapsing inwards and outwards until eventually only the cargo mound remained. Sponges and corals grew on the rims of the bowls and the dishes, softening their sharp sides and turning them into bases for more corals and anemones. Fish and moray eels made homes in the vases and over time *Tek Sing* was transformed into a part of the sea.

❀

A century passed and then another 70 years. The world above changed beyond recognition. There were countless wars and new inventions – piston engines powered by steam or oil and turning propellers replaced the matting sails of the great junks which had sailed from Canton and Amoy. Other hulls, now clad in steel, made the same journey, but under the power of steam or diesel engines it no longer mattered whether it was the south-west or north-east monsoon which was blowing.

❀

In June 1998, the shadow of Michael Hatcher's survey vessel *Restless M* passed over the sleeping remains of *Tek Sing*. Only one vessel in thousands, a vessel equipped specifically to look for wrecks, could have detected those different lines and circles on the bottom.

'There's something there!' said skipper Alastair Feast.

'Reef,' said Rahim, the most experienced diver aboard. 'Only reef.'

As recounted in the opening chapter, the Thai incident and the Cambodian affair had been financially disastrous for Hatcher. Each failure lowered the confidence of his investors. *Restless M* was due to go to Singapore when the south-east monsoon kicked in. Miracles do happen, but the crew had long since ceased to believe in them.

That night they lost their diving tender, the 'rubber duck', Hatcher's favourite toy. He was in Jakarta making one last try to gee up his investors, but running, as he had feared, into a brick wall of negatives. The news of the lost tender coming to him on the satellite phone from *Restless M* was the last straw.

Next morning they decided to check out the seabed anomaly located on the side-scan sonar. The lack of a magnetometer reading seemed to indicate that it was, as Rahim thought, probably a reef. Fish and the two big black stingrays finning on the wreck were surprised to see *Restless M's* big steel anchor come plummeting down to the seabed in a cloud of bubbles.

Shortly afterwards there were more bubbles and the shadowy forms of two scuba divers descending from the silver surface above. They landed on the bottom, like astronauts on the surface of the moon, some distance from their objective. They began searching using a swim-line anchored at their point of descent. The first diver, Rahim, reached the end of his swim-line circle and moved the datum point once more. Then catching the distant shadow of the 'reef' in his eye he began to swim towards it.

As the outlines of fish and sponges grew clearer he saw something else, a very familiar shape. He blinked in astonishment, but the object was still there, reflecting white on the bottom. It was a bowl, blue-and-white like those he had seen on *Geldermalsen* in 1985. Then he saw other objects, dishes, bowls, shards of pottery, vases, pots. Abdul Rahim knew that what he had seen was part of the spill from a cargo and from the size of the artificial reef it had to be a cargo of huge dimensions.

He was joined by the second diver, Yoni, alarmed by the sound of Rahim hooting into his mouthpiece. He thought Rahim may have been attacked by a shark or a sea monster. But when he saw what Rahim had seen he made some sounds of his own. The cargo mound was more than 50 metres long.

The ship that had sailed to a fusillade of firecrackers and cannon fire, and which had sunk to the choking cries of her people, had been discovered after 172 years to the sound of a different kind of triumph.

The calls went out around the world and eventually I too was contacted.

'We've got it,' Hatcher's familiar tones came crisply through the receiver. 'We've got the big one.' There was a pause, then, 'This is really *it*, Hugh. It's sensational. Better get your gear and get up here.'

There had been a false alarm some months before when *Restless M* had found a Portuguese bronze cannon off Ternate in the Moluccas, the legendary Spice Islands. Hatcher had called me then too.

'You fly in through Ambon,' he'd said.

The next day in the newspaper there were horrific pictures of Christians and Muslims massacring each other in Ambon, of burning mosques and churches and of Europeans fleeing in the face of civil war.

'No way,' I said, and just as well, because the wreck proved to be a dud.

Now Hatcher was calling from the South China Sea …

'You fly in through Bangka. Sumatra. We're out on the Belvidere Shoals.'

Bangka, I wondered. Where the hell was Bangka? And who would be shooting at whom in that particular neck of the south-east Asian woods?

'We'll be seeing you, then?' His question regained my attention. I could think of perhaps a hundred reasons why I should decline his offer with thanks. They were logical reasons, sound reasons.

'OK,' I said. 'I'll be there.'

'Good,' he said, and hung up.

Not long after, I was in Bangka, which I had learnt was a large island famous for tin mining, in the southern region of Sumatra. I had met Hatcher in Singapore, proceeding through Jakarta where I was lucky enough to be able to visit the site of the old Batavia fort and warehouses at the old port of the VOC years.

In the ensuing 35 years since we had found the wreck of the 1629 treasure ship *Batavia* on the Western Australian coast, I had dreamt of visiting the historic site. It was a magic day. The warehouses, now into their fourth century, were built with huge internal timbers, like ships upside down. They may well last another 1000 years.

Later I saw the dock where the Suluwesi schooners were lined up with their raking bows and bowsprits extending far over the wharf. Some of the world's last working sailing ships. Another beautiful sight.

Shortly after my visit came the massacres in East Timor, the Australian intervention and the series of riots against Australians in Jakarta. It would have been impossible then to go to the old port. There was no animosity as we passed through Bangka. The news of the troubles in East Timor had yet to reach the world.

We journeyed to the sea in *Restless M* down a picturesque, coconut palm-lined river, and then out through dozens of fishing platforms on bamboo stilts. Above the spot where *Tek Sing* had spent her final moments afloat, a huge salvage barge was anchored, with an ocean-going tug in attendance.

Swissco Marie II was 180 feet long and 45 feet in the beam. At the stern were three storeys of crew facilities, accommodation and a conference room. Forty-two men, divers and crew lived and worked aboard her. At the utility end was a large A-frame, a decompression chamber and a diving equipment maintenance cabin. In between were compressors, a 50-ton crane, boats, machinery and sea containers. There was hardly a square metre that was not occupied by machinery, diving equipment or boats, ropes and floats.

Divers were working continual shifts, two at a time, from dawn to dusk. Rahim was in charge of operations as well as diving himself and he proudly showed me drawings he had made of the junk hull underwater.

'Let's have a look first hand,' said Hatcher, selecting a twin-tank scuba unit. 'The depth is 100 feet, plus a bit, so make sure your Mickey Mouse is turned on.' The Mickey Mouse was the dive computer, every diver's friend. It took over the complicated task of working out how much bottom time was available before there was risk of the bends. It also calculated how much decompression time was needed under the barge if the bottom time was exceeded.

The professional divers were using Kirby suits with full helmets, surface communication and camera connection. Their air was surface-supplied through yellow hoses and they spent 90 minutes working on the bottom and 40 minutes in the 'pot' – the decompression chamber – when they surfaced, breathing oxygen to purge the nitrogen in their systems.

With the scuba gear we would have about 20 minutes bottom time on the wreck and would have to clear the nitrogen from our systems for 5 minutes at 20 feet and 5 minutes at 10 feet, to be on the safe side. It was a little more complicated than the ordinary scuba dive because visibility was greatly reduced by the debris from the airlift, and because large mesh baskets were going up and down. We had to be careful to keep clear of the working divers.

'Watch out for baskets coming down,' warned Hatch. 'It could spoil your morning if one landed on your head.' I needed no reminder that the baskets weighed 200 kilos and had sharp edges.

We went down in unaccustomed luxury. The divers had a lift, and once a shift had gone below Hatcher and I were able to use the lift cage for the descent. It was a novel way of going to the bottom and certainly saved time and effort.

'Don't get any fancy ideas about the return trip,' said Hatcher. 'We swim back.'

On the bottom we stepped out of the lift – on the end of its cable it was exactly like a miners' cage – and into a dark fog of sediment. For the moment we could see neither up nor down, nor anything in front of us. Unfazed, Hatcher picked up the divers' lines and followed them along – logically they would lead to the action. I followed close on his tail, anxious not to be left behind in the dark.

Quite abruptly we came upon clearer water and found the other divers. The airlift was sucking muddy sediment away from rows and rows of dishes. They showed us one. It had an intricate fishnet pattern and looked as though it had come off the kiln shelf that very morning. The dishes, handled carefully, were going into big plastic buckets. Another container was saved for the more unusual objects – statuettes, Chinese ink pads, candlesticks, some brass sections of a telescope and coins.

Among the debris was a human skeleton. It was respectfully moved out of the way to the rear of the compartment under excavation, the spoil from the airlift re-burying it within a few minutes. The divers had agreed that human bones would remain on the wreck. Most of the crew were Asian, Indonesian, Singaporean, Malaysian and Chinese, and they believed that bad luck would follow disturbing the dead. *Han tu*. I saw a human thigh bone trapped beneath a beam, and I shivered. It told its own story of the shipwreck.

The excavation had revealed that the timbers, some of them almost a metre thick, were perfect up to the level of the waterline where the junk had settled. The sand and weight of cargo protected them from rot and marine borers. Everything above had rotted or been consumed through the years.

We passed down the wreck observing a pile of iron cannon and wondered whether it was part of the cargo or had been thrown together during the sinking.

Hatcher pointed to a series of huge iron rings lying out to starboard in an orderly progression. They were the rings which had bound the junk's main mast and those nearest the hull were about a metre across. Since the main mast was reported as breaking the surface by 10 feet it must have been nearly 100 feet tall.

A little further on we came to a section where the cargo was still covered with colourful corals and sponges. I took a series of pictures of Hatcher with blue-and-white bowls, and jumped when one of the big black stingrays and I accidentally collided. Too soon I heard a beep from my dive computer and checking the time I was surprised to find how long we had been below. Hatcher was tapping his watch and pointing upwards. It was time to go.

Back on deck after the decompression stops, we inspected the artefacts that had come up in the baskets that day. Trevor McInery from Sydney was in charge of sorting, packing, and photographing the items after they had been scrubbed and cleaned. Dishes, bowls and plates, which fitted snugly into each other, were packed in cartons in plastic beads and then placed in sea containers. Trevor had a special table by his workplace for unusual artefacts and for the photographic records. The table was covered with fascinating items, some in perfect condition, others encrusted with coral and barely recognisable. Among them were Spanish pillar dollars. Two were dated 1797 and 1804, and they had been over-stamped with Chinese or Japanese 'chops'. Pillar dollars, exceptionally pure silver, were much in demand by the Chinese and have been found on wrecks around the world. The American ship, *Rapid*, was carrying 350,000 of them when she was wrecked on the Western Australian coast on her way to China in 1811. These coins carried the long-dead face of Charles III of Spain and the castles and lions of Leon and Castille on one side, while the other depicted the 'pillars of Hercules', symbolic of the Straits of Gibraltar. I wondered where those coins had been in their wanderings from the mint in Potosi in South America through Asia, before they sank to the bottom of the South China Sea.

Among the relics was a European sextant and the brass sections and lenses of a telescope. There were also European wine glasses and wine and port bottles, which might have meant that there were Europeans aboard. Although the fact that there were none of the characteristic Dutch 'square-face' gin bottles meant that it was unlikely that any of the passengers aboard *Tek Sing* were from the Netherlands.

Items that fascinated me were Chinese ink pads used by the merchants. The 'ink' was red ferrous (iron) oxide and when mixed with water on a pad it made a crimson paste. When a stamp was dipped in the ink it transferred a 'chop', the signature of the merchant, to a document or cargo list, in Chinese characters. Some of the pads and chops were in perfect condition.

There were brass padlocks in an unusual style, boxes of needles, the handles of umbrellas, elaborate candlesticks, statues of domestic gods and rows of figures of little boys with perfect sexual apparatus. There were miniature charcoal stoves (probably from the unfortunate coolies who had been deck cargo), hair pins, fans, a huge range of teapots from tiny fragile pieces to 15-litre monsters. A curiosity was a box of human hair – the pig-tail of a deceased kept out of loving memory perhaps. There was also a small quantity of fine gold and some opium.

Some of the big 'five-gallon' teapots had magnificent dragons on their sides. Among the ceramics were thousands and thousands of spoons exactly like those used in Chinese restaurants everywhere today. Among the thousands of bowls and dishes there was a variety of quality and design. Some were obviously rough, domestic pieces, probably intended for Asian use, but others were exquisite, with delicate designs of birds, trees, flowers and insects. Even when bowls and dishes carried the same design, each one was fractionally different, indicating that each item had been individually hand-painted.

While we were watching the cargo items coming up, dripping, in the baskets from below, there was naturally a good deal of speculation about the name and nature of the vessel, information which Nigel Pickford would provide at a later date. The only clues we had at that time were the dates on the Spanish coins, 1797 and 1804, and the types of ceramics. Dating the pottery was more difficult because it was from the late Qing period. At the time Europeans like Joseph Wedgewood in England had discovered the art of making fine porcelain in competition with Chinese imports. In fact it was thought that the flow of Chinese porcelain had largely ceased in this period, though America continued to take large quantities.

Back in England Nigel was already searching the records. There was a concern that, like Mike Hatcher's 1984 un-named junk on the Admiral Stellingwerf Reef, this latest discovery might remain unidentified. The successful *Geldermalsen* auction had underlined the importance of a name and a story to go with the artefacts if the public were to be inspired. As it turned out, Pickford was happily able to collect a substantial amount of information about the junk, her tragic end and the rescue by Captain Pearl.

'Pearl must have been a pretty good guy,' Hatcher reflected later. 'That's a very dangerous piece of water. He put his own vessel, *Indiana*, and his crew in danger to save those distressed people from another nation. Many European skippers of that time would have sailed on, just like the other junk did, and left them all to their fate.' Captain Pearl did more than that. Having rescued them he had the extra problem of feeding and sleeping an additional 150 people with no belongings on his own vessel. Some with no clothes. He did a very generous thing. Pearl diverted from his own voyage and sailed across to Pontianak in Borneo [Kalimantan] where there was a big Chinese gold mining community who would look after the poor beggars.

'He complained later that the rescue cost him a lot of money in lost time and stores. But I reckon that in later years, when he thought about it, it probably gave him a pretty good feeling. Somewhere in Indonesia today there are probably descendants of those 150 survivors who have cause to bless Captain Pearl for what he did.'

Rahim, who had an archaeological interest in the ships he dived on which went far beyond salvage, did some splendid drawings of the junk timbers underwater. He pointed out to us the huge size of the main bearers, the watertight compartments and the thickness of the planking.

Tek Sing was described in the records as a 'Canton junk', which could mean either that she was built at Canton, or was one of a particular class and style of ocean-going cargo carrier. European sailors tended to look down on junks, hence the other use of the name for 'junk' meaning 'rubbish'. But in fact the Chinese were making major ocean voyages long before Christopher Columbus reached the Americas in 1492, or Vasco da Gama sailed to India in 1498. The Chinese had the ability to sail to Europe, or indeed anywhere in the world, centuries before Europeans. They simply did not have the inclination. Though they did thoroughly explore the waters of their own region and the Indian Ocean.

The most famous voyages were those of the eunuch Zheng He who sailed from the mouth of the Yangtze River in 1402 with 60 vessels which were described as being 134 metres in length, 54 metres in the beam, and displacing more than 3000 tons. Their sails were said to be made of pure silk and on those figures any European vessel of the time would have been a cockle-shell in comparison. He took with him (according to Eric Rolls in his book *Sojourners, The Relationship of the Chinese with Australia*) 27,000 soldiers, sailors and seamen. The cavalry took their horses on board, and there were even vegetable gardens with herbs and ginger – no scurvy for the Chinese.

They had excellent navigation through the stars and compasses. Rolls says that they knew the South China Sea so well that they could tell from the taste and texture of the mud on their sounding leads where they were.

Zheng He made six major voyages over 19 years and Rolls records that each one took approximately 18 months to prepare and 18 months to complete. The fleets ranged far afield, going to India, Sri Lanka, the Persian Gulf, Africa and Madagascar, as well as the Indonesian archipelago east as far as New Guinea. It is not unlikely that they sighted the north coast of Australia which was probably already known to the Bhughi sea people as the 'Fire Land' because bushfire smoke in northern Australia sometimes drifted on the wind as far as the Indonesian islands. Zheng He sent one of his ships south as far as it could go to offer sacrifices to Canopus, our already familiar star, representing the god of longevity.

Among the curiosities which the junks brought back to China were African zebras, ostriches, antelopes and a giraffe to be paraded in a manner reminiscent of the triumphs of the old Roman emperors. There is still a strong belief in China that 'hopping creatures' – kangaroos – were also brought back at that time.

Were Zheng He's vessels as big as legends claim? Perhaps not. Zheng He himself was said to be an improbable nine feet tall with a girth of 90 inches! Nonetheless there is no doubt that the Chinese built some very large vessels, and there is no question about the authenticity of the voyages.

The Mongols, a land-people who conquered China, eventually put the kybosh on Chinese sea power. Invaders themselves, they were paranoid about being invaded by other barbarian tribes from the west and north. Their expenditure went into fortifications such as the Great Wall and military rather than naval strength. However sea traditions continued on the south coast where remnants of the Ming emperors' support groups had fled. The southern Chinese continued to go to sea despite official prohibitions, and by the time of *Tek Sing* some very large sea-going junks were being built and were sailing to overseas destinations.

❈

Tek Sing's cargo covered 54 metres in length and a width of more than 10 metres. We know very little of Chinese ships and navigation during the 19th century. This is not because ships weren't built, nor because they didn't sail. They were built, and they did sail. But because it was technically illegal it was prudent not to keep records. Most things about *Tek Sing* were illegal it seems. She shouldn't have been built, she should not have been sailing, nor should she have been carrying export human freight in the form of coolies. However, though we don't know as much as we would like about her, there were other comparable ships of the same period.

One of the most famous was *Keying*, a very large 100-year-old junk which sailed from Canton to New York and then to London from 1847 to 1849. Her dimensions appear to have been similar to those of *Tek Sing*. According to an article by HH Brindley in the *Mariner's Mirror*, October 1922, researched by Nick Burningham of the Western Australian Duyfken Foundation, *Keying* was 160 feet in length and had a beam of 33 feet. She was built of teak and had 15 compartments, 'several of which were watertight'. Her foremast was 75 feet high and 1 foot 6 inches in diameter. *Keying's* main mast was 90 feet tall and 3.3 feet (a metre) in diameter, and the mizzen mast was 50 feet. The main mast was hooped like that of *Tek Sing*, and the main yard of the main sail was 67 feet in length.

The rudder was perforated with lines of holes, presumably to make it easier to put hard over, and it weighed eight tons and drew 24 feet. In heavy weather it was worked by 15 to 20 men using a luff tackle (a tackle with a double block at the top and a single one at the bottom), but in fine weather two men could steer her. Her anchor shanks were 30 feet long and her hull below the waterline was caulked and coated with a lime cement of burnt oyster shells mixed with wood oil. The mixture not only prevented leaks, it also made the hull impervious to teredo worm.

Keying was eventually bought as a novelty by a consortium of young Englishmen in Canton in 1848. She was a huge vessel by any standards. A photograph of a similar junk by John Thompson shows her dwarfing sampans alongside her in harbour. She was then already 100 years old.

The Chinese authorities officially forbade such junks to go overseas. Eric Rolls in *Sojourners* noted that 'It required many petitions covering fat bribes before the "grand chop", the final approval, was issued. Thirty Chinese and 12 Englishmen manned it.' He Sing, a mandarin of the 5th Class, was in charge of the Chinese. 'The rattan mainsail weighed nine tonnes and took the whole crew two hours to hoist up a mast a metre thick at the base.'

The rudder was raised and lowered by two windlasses, and 'the wide saloon was roofed over with oyster shells so thin that they were transparent' to let the light in. The owners had to pretend that they were only sailing locally to get out of the confines of Cantonese waters.

Brindley records that the 'moving spirit and commander' was Captain Charles A Kellett. His associates were G Burton, mate; S Revett, second mate; and TA Lane. Brindley gives a different Chinese captain, So Yin Sang Hsi. Or perhaps it was just a different spelling of the name of the same man? When *Keying* made her 'escape' the Englishmen dressed in Chinese clothes as a disguise.

The enterprising Captain Kellett took her south through the Gaspar and Sunda Straits on the same course as the ill-fated *Tek Sing*. She even left Canton in the same month as *Tek Sing* to catch the north-eastern monsoon to blow her down through the South China Sea. Because of lack of wind it took her six weeks to get through the Java Sea and Sunda Strait. She weathered what may have been a cyclone off Mauritius and rounded the Cape of Good Hope – perhaps the first Chinese junk ever to do so – in March. By mid-April she was well north in the Atlantic and experiencing headwinds.

The Chinese in the crew had had never undertaken such a long voyage and were in a state of mutiny. So it was decided to make for New York, and they arrived there early in July, 1847. The junk was put on exhibition in New York and Boston for several months, before sailing for England on February 17, 1848. 'She now met with bad weather the whole way,' Brindley recorded. It was, after all, the northern hemisphere winter and in a strong gale, 'Two boats were washed away and the foresail split. One rudder rope parted on the 25th of March and the other on the 5th of April, when the rudder took charge. Repairs were effected after about six hours. At some time, probably then, Revett the second mate was drowned while over the side seeing to the rudder. Under these trying conditions the junk gave excellent proof of her seaworthy qualities, and it was said she "Never shipped a drop of water".'

Keying made a fast passage, arriving off Jersey on March 15, 1849 and reached Gravesend on March 28, 16 months after leaving Canton. She had made the longest ever recorded voyage by a Chinese junk. She was exhibited in various British ports, including Liverpool, and was the only junk to be visited by a European crowned head. The young Queen Victoria stepped aboard while *Keying* was moored in the Thames.

Eventually (and sadly) she was sold to the ship breakers Redhead, Harland, & Brown on the Mersey and scrapped. 'Her teak planking was used to build two ferry boats, work boxes, and other small souvenirs,' Brindley records.

Keying's voyage did prove the sea-going qualities of the junk design and its ability to make long voyages in rough conditions. Her story is of interest because of her almost identical size and other similarities with *Tek Sing*.

The main deck was described as 'arched' or rounded and while this would help quickly disperse a wave coming 'green' on deck it would also have accentuated the problems for passengers when *Tek Sing* was laid hard over on the reef. *Keying* had a raised quarter deck rising again to two poops, 'The first containing cabins. The main saloon was 30 by 25 feet and 12 feet high'. At the bow she had a raised for'castle, 'With a high verandah above that again'. She had quarter galleries at the stern.

'It wasn't an accident that we found her,' Mike Hatcher said. 'I knew she was there. I found the reference to her in my copy of James Horsburgh's *Directions For Sailing To The East Indies* while I was catching up on my reading at Bardool Station.'

In 1827 Horsburgh described the area of *Tek Sing's* sad end. 'The south-westernmost end of the Belvidere Shoals is in latitude 2 degrees 15 minutes south and bears from Gaspar Island peak North 27 degrees west, distant about 12 or 13 miles. They extend from thence to the north-eastward about 4 miles, being composed of several patches with from 6 to 10 feet of water on them and a rock above water at the north eastern extremity. The sea breaks on the Belvidere Shoals when there is much swell and they may be easily avoided in daylight with a good lookout.'

That was a fair description of what we could see from the top deck of the salvage barge *Swissco Marie II* while the divers worked below in the bows of *Tek Sing*. Horsburgh continued, '. . . a large Chinese junk was wrecked there. Part of her people floated to Gaspar Island, and some were found floating about on pieces of timber and other fragments of the wreck, who were saved by the laudable exertions of a country ship belonging to Calcutta that fell in with them at the time.'

Bravo Captain Pearl.

❊

As Australia celebrated the arrival of the new millennium, *Tek Sing's* precious cargo had been lifted from the bottom of the South China Sea and had travelled to South Australia via Singapore. As experts looked awestruck at the quantity, quality, and variety of the porcelain in a port warehouse shed outside Adelaide, Hatcher mused about the future.

'We have a licence from the Indonesian Government to explore further,' he said. 'And of course they're sharing in this cargo with us.'

While his associates planned the marketing and auction of the enormous quantity of porcelain from *Tek Sing*, Mike Hatcher was already making plans for further wreck searches.

'At 360,000 pieces of porcelain *Tek Sing* will be the largest ceramics salvage ever carried out,' he said. 'The biggest in the world and certainly the most valuable. She'll be hard to beat!'

And quite a challenge to sell!

Most of the *Tek Sing* cargo was porcelain from Dehua, made in the 18th and early 19th centuries for export to south-east Asia, but there were also pieces dating back to the 15th century. A large number of items of different shapes and sizes carried the same design, so that there was the unique opportunity to put together an entire dining service. As the merchandise was intended for the Asian market it is purely and genuinely 'Asian', not trimmed to European taste or needs. Besides the porcelain, a host of other extremely interesting objects were recovered, such as personal belongings of the passengers and equipment of the ship, nautical instruments and cannon.

Nagel Auktionen from Stuttgart, Germany, a leader in 'asiatica' in continental Europe, got the order to stage the auction in November 2000, and a website has been set up at www.teksing.com for virtual visits and continuous information on the project.

Back in Adelaide, Mike Hatcher's eyes wandered, his mind momentarily drifting on the vast expanses of the South China Sea. After a lifetime of salvage and on the cusp of reaping the significant monetary rewards of his greatest discovery, he was already thinking of other things, chafing at the bit, anxious to be back in the field of action again.

He gave me a cheerful grin. 'Now you go off and write the book. And save some ink in your pen for the next one!'

I have, and I am.

APPENDIX

Following the massive salvage operation, the cargo of *Tek Sing* was transported to Adelaide, Australia, where it was washed, restored, sorted and catalogued. Experts from the South Australian Art Gallery and the auction houses Christies, Sotheby's and Nagel viewed, authenticated and valued the cargo for insurance purposes. After much discussion and investigation all of the blue-and-white porcelain, ceramics and unique pieces were consigned to Nagel Auction House of Stuttgart, Germany, for auction. It will be the largest of its type in the world and is scheduled to commence on 18 November 2000 running through to the 29 November 2000, with over 8000 lots on offer.

The auction will commence with an exhibition of artefacts to be presented in a three-storey representation of *Tek Sing* being built in the Stuttgart Railway Station. 'The Glory of the *Tek Sing*' will be viewed by over 250,000 people who travel through the railway station each day.

The story of *Tek Sing* and its amazing cargo will be told at presentations to be held in 13 major capital cities around the world prior to the auction. Mike Hatcher and Nigel Pickford will be special guests at each of these presentations. The story has also been captured on film to ensure that this significant find and part of the world history remains alive and with us for all time.